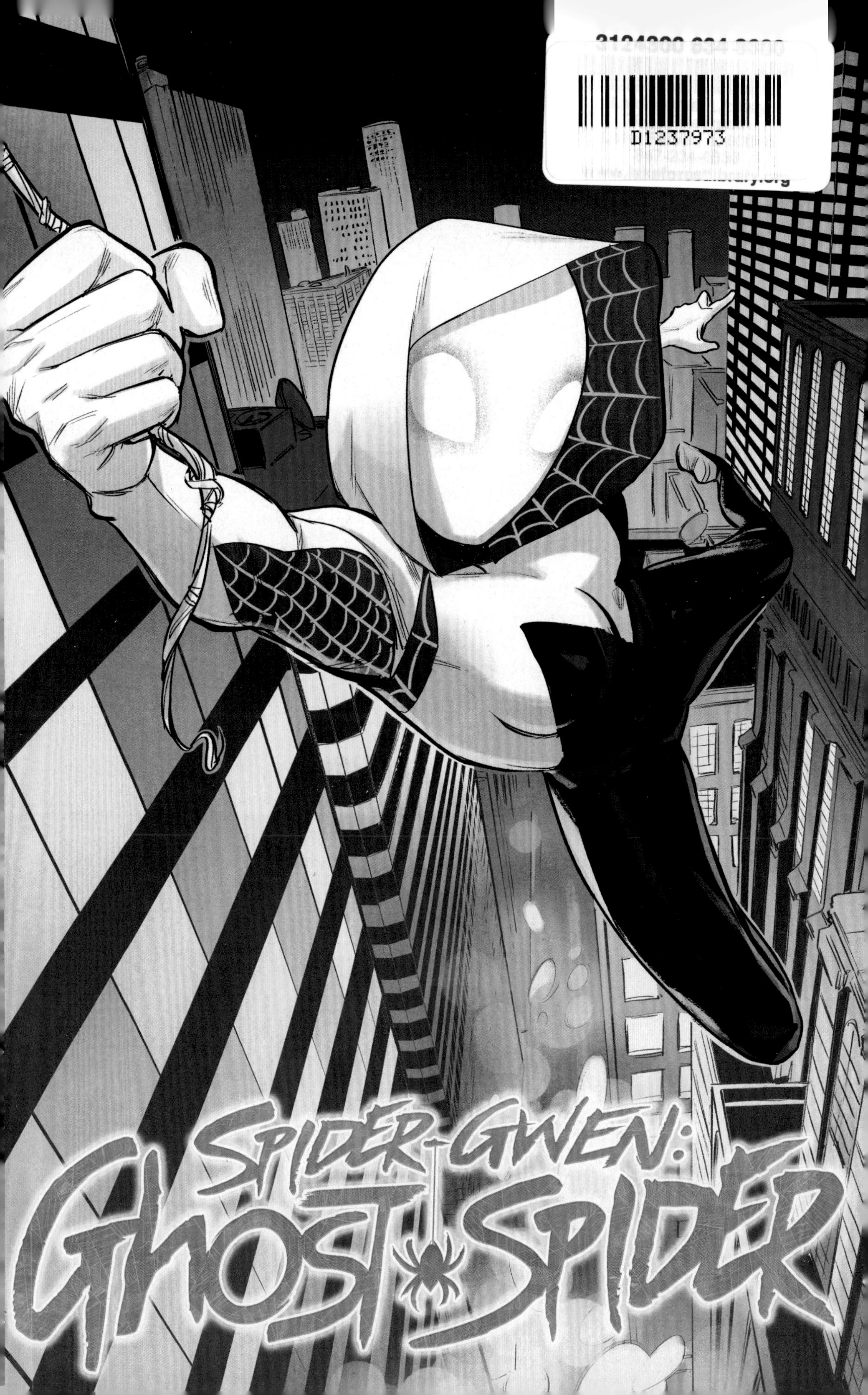
SPIDER-GWEN:
GHOST-SPIDER

PREVIOUSLY

AS A TEENAGER, GWEN STACY WAS BITTEN BY A MUTATED SPIDER AND TRANSFORMED!
THE BITE GRANTED HER AMAZING POWERS: A PRECOGNITIVE AWARENESS OF DANGER,
ADHESIVE FINGERTIPS AND TOES AND THE PROPORTIONAL SPEED AND STRENGTH OF A SPIDER.

SHE'S HAD RUN-INS WITH SUPERSPYS, NINJAS AND MAD SCIENTISTS. SHE'S FOUGHT
GOVERNMENT AGENTS, TRAVERSED DIMENSIONS AND EVEN SERVED SOME TIME BEHIND BARS.

[IT'S BEEN A COMPLICATED COUPLE YEARS.]

BUT NO MATTER THE UPS OR DOWNS, WHENEVER DANGER CALLS, GWEN STACY
ANSWERS AS SPIDER-GWEN.

GWEN STACY CREATED BY
STAN LEE & STEVE DITKO

JENNIFER GRÜNWALD
COLLECTION EDITOR

CAITLIN O'CONNELL
ASSISTANT EDITOR

KATERI WOODY
ASSOCIATE MANAGING EDITOR

MARK D. BEAZLEY
EDITOR, SPECIAL PROJECTS

JEFF YOUNGQUIST
VP PRODUCTION
& SPECIAL PROJECTS

DAVID GABRIEL
SVP PRINT, SALES
& MARKETING

STACIE ZUCKER
BOOK DESIGNER

C.B. CEBULSKI
EDITOR IN CHIEF

JOE QUESADA
CHIEF CREATIVE OFFICER

DAN BUCKLEY
PRESIDENT

ALAN FINE
EXECUTIVE PRODUCER

SPIDER-GWEN: GHOST-SPIDER VOL. 1 — SPIDER-GEDDON. Contains material originally published in magazine form as SPIDER-GWEN: GHOST SPIDER #1-4. First printing 2019. ISBN 978-1-302-91476-9. Published by MARVEL WORLDWIDE, INC., a subsidiary of MARVEL ENTERTAINMENT, LLC. OFFICE OF PUBLICATION: 135 West 50th Street, New York, NY 10020. © 2019 MARVEL No similarity between any of the names, characters, persons, and/or institutions in this magazine with those of any living or dead person or institution is intended, and any such similarity which may exist is purely coincidental. **Printed in Canada.** DAN BUCKLEY, President, Marvel Entertainment; JOHN NEE, Publisher; JOE QUESADA, Chief Creative Officer; TOM BREVOORT, SVP of Publishing; DAVID BOGART, Associate Publisher & SVP of Talent Affairs; DAVID GABRIEL, SVP of Sales & Marketing, Publishing; JEFF YOUNGQUIST, VP of Production & Special Projects; DAN CARR, Executive Director of Publishing Technology; ALEX MORALES, Director of Publishing Operations; DAN EDINGTON, Managing Editor; SUSAN CRESPI, Production Manager; STAN LEE, Chairman Emeritus. For information regarding advertising in Marvel Comics or on Marvel.com, please contact Vit DeBellis, Custom Solutions & Integrated Advertising Manager, at vdebellis@marvel.com. For Marvel subscription inquiries, please call 888-511-5480. **Manufactured between 3/15/2019 and 4/16/2019 by SOLISCO PRINTERS, SCOTT, QC, CANADA.**

10 9 8 7 6 5 4 3 2 1

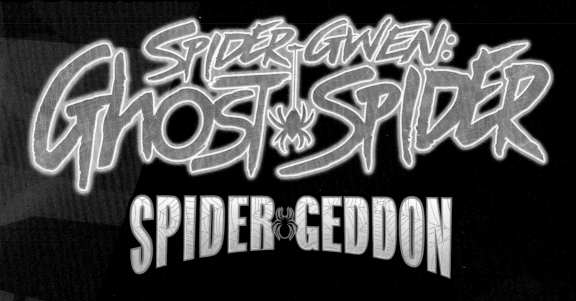

SPIDER-GWEN: GHOST-SPIDER

SPIDER-GEDDON

SEANAN McGUIRE
WRITER

ROSI KÄMPE
WITH **TAKESHI MIYAZAWA** (#4)
ARTISTS

IAN HERRING
COLOR ARTIST

VC'S CLAYTON COWLES
LETTERER

BENGAL
COVER ART

KATHLEEN WISNESKI & LAUREN AMARO
ASSISTANT EDITORS

DEVIN LEWIS
EDITOR

NICK LOWE
EXECUTIVE EDITOR

SPIDER-GEDDON:
SPIDER-GWEN — GHOST-SPIDER VIDEO COMIC

SEANAN McGUIRE
WRITER

ALTI FIRMANSYAH
ARTIST

ANDRES MOSSA
COLOR ARTIST

JEFF ECKLEBERRY
LETTERER

PACO DIAZ
COVER ART

ANNIE CHENG
PRODUCTION

TIM SMITH 3
PRODUCTION MANAGER

TIM ELDRED
LAYOUTS

LINDSEY COHICK, MARK BASSO & JAKE THOMAS
EDITORS

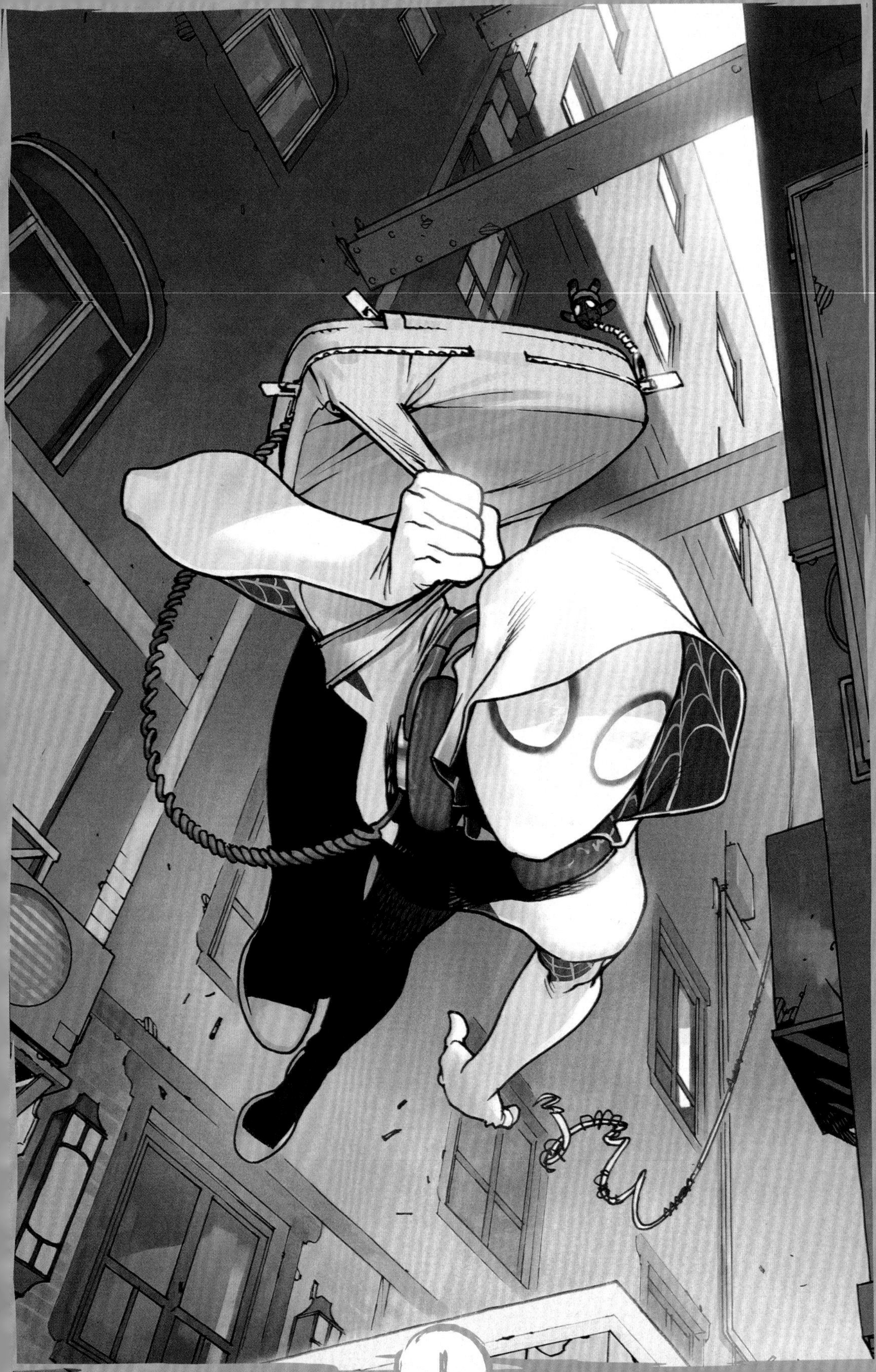

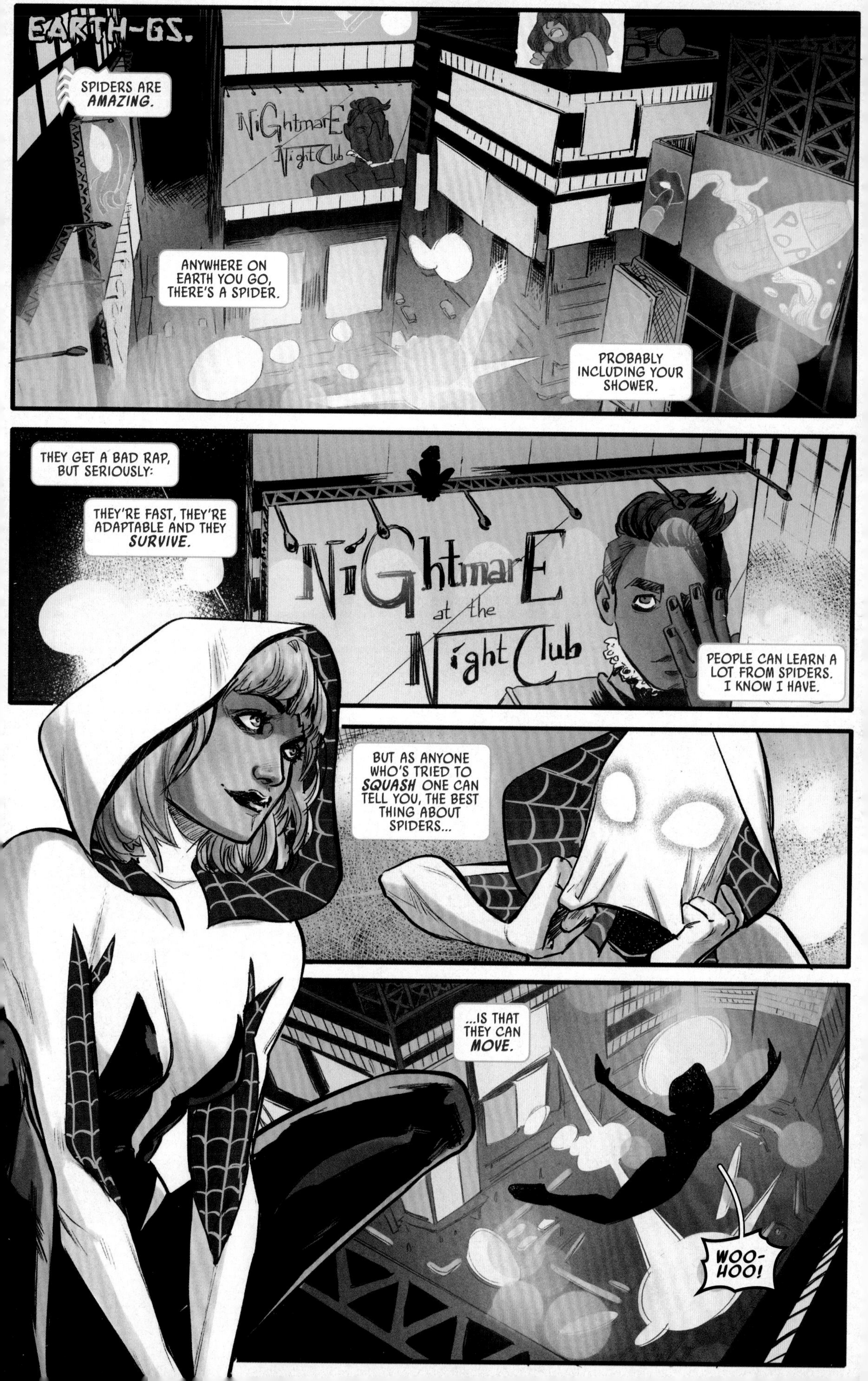
EARTH-GS.
SPIDERS ARE AMAZING.
ANYWHERE ON EARTH YOU GO, THERE'S A SPIDER.
PROBABLY INCLUDING YOUR SHOWER.
NiGhtmarE Night Club
THEY GET A BAD RAP, BUT SERIOUSLY:
THEY'RE FAST, THEY'RE ADAPTABLE AND THEY SURVIVE.
NiGhtmarE at the Night Club
PEOPLE CAN LEARN A LOT FROM SPIDERS. I KNOW I HAVE.
BUT AS ANYONE WHO'S TRIED TO SQUASH ONE CAN TELL YOU, THE BEST THING ABOUT SPIDERS...
...IS THAT THEY CAN MOVE.
WOO-HOO!

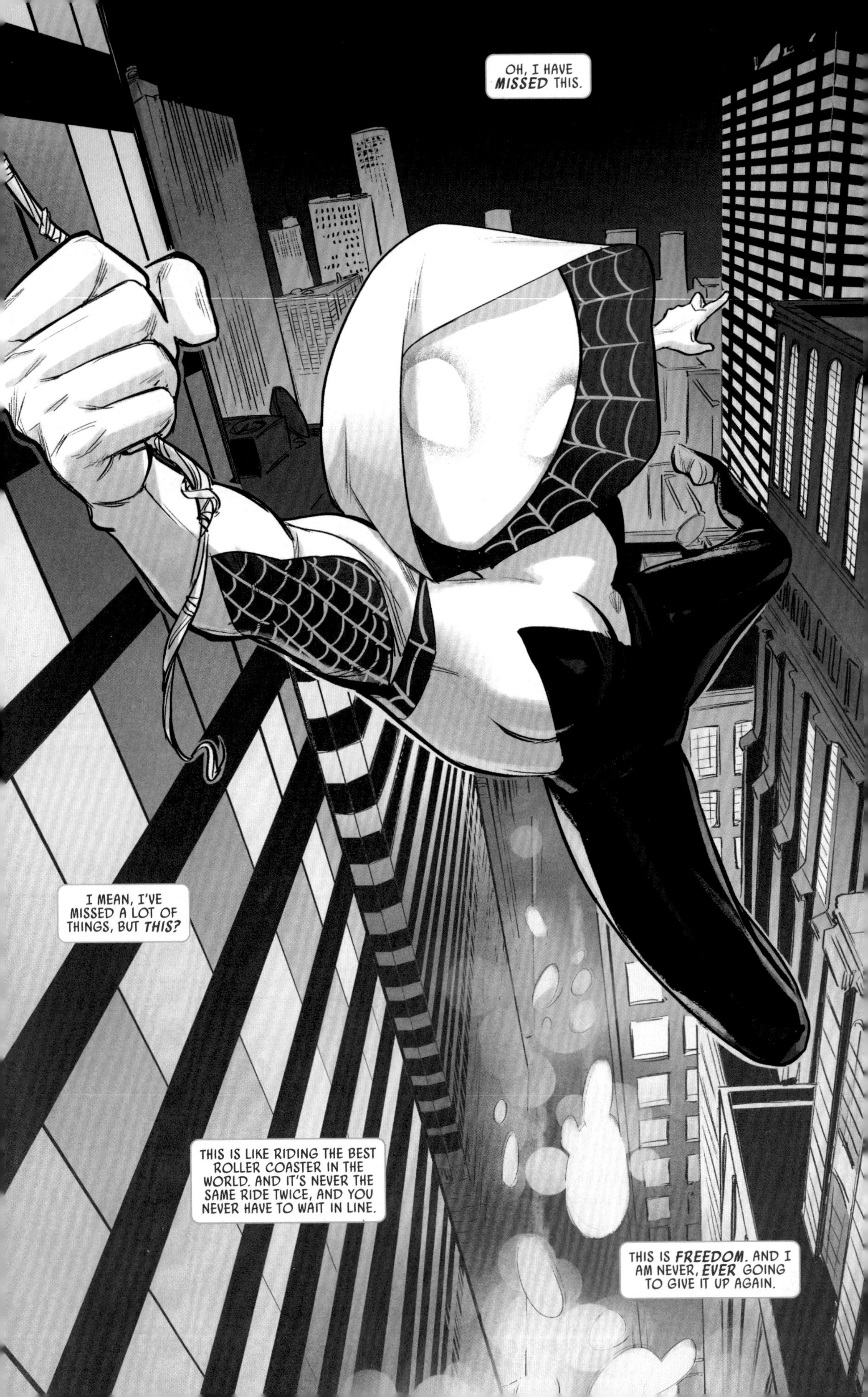
OH, I HAVE **MISSED** THIS.
I MEAN, I'VE MISSED A LOT OF THINGS, BUT **THIS?**
THIS IS LIKE RIDING THE BEST ROLLER COASTER IN THE WORLD. AND IT'S NEVER THE SAME RIDE TWICE, AND YOU NEVER HAVE TO WAIT IN LINE.
THIS IS **FREEDOM.** AND I AM NEVER, **EVER** GOING TO GIVE IT UP AGAIN.

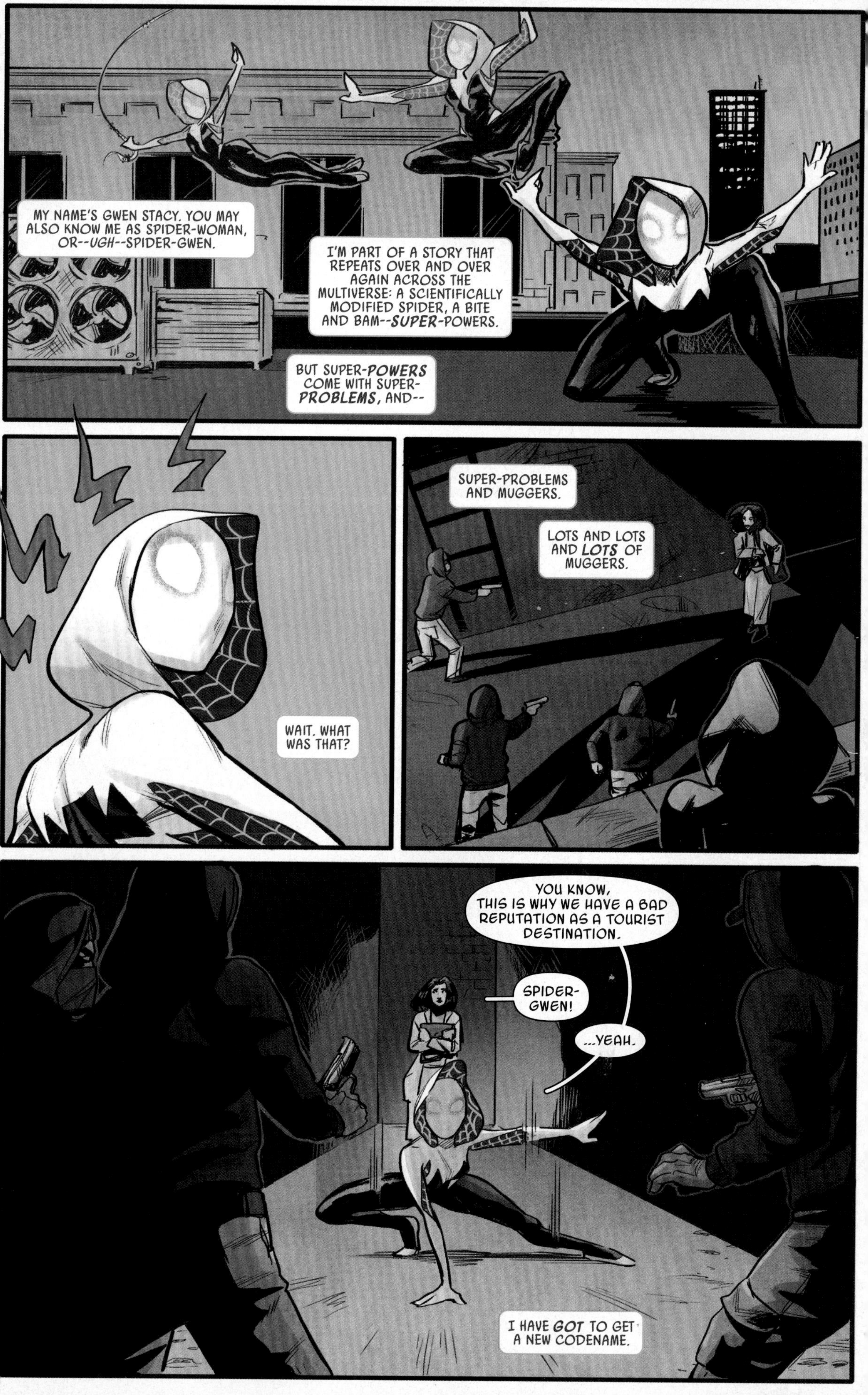
MY NAME'S GWEN STACY. YOU MAY ALSO KNOW ME AS SPIDER-WOMAN, OR--UGH--SPIDER-GWEN.
I'M PART OF A STORY THAT REPEATS OVER AND OVER AGAIN ACROSS THE MULTIVERSE: A SCIENTIFICALLY MODIFIED SPIDER, A BITE AND BAM--SUPER-POWERS.
BUT SUPER-POWERS COME WITH SUPER-PROBLEMS, AND--
WAIT. WHAT WAS THAT?
SUPER-PROBLEMS AND MUGGERS.
LOTS AND LOTS AND LOTS OF MUGGERS.
YOU KNOW, THIS IS WHY WE HAVE A BAD REPUTATION AS A TOURIST DESTINATION.
SPIDER-GWEN!
...YEAH.
I HAVE GOT TO GET A NEW CODENAME.

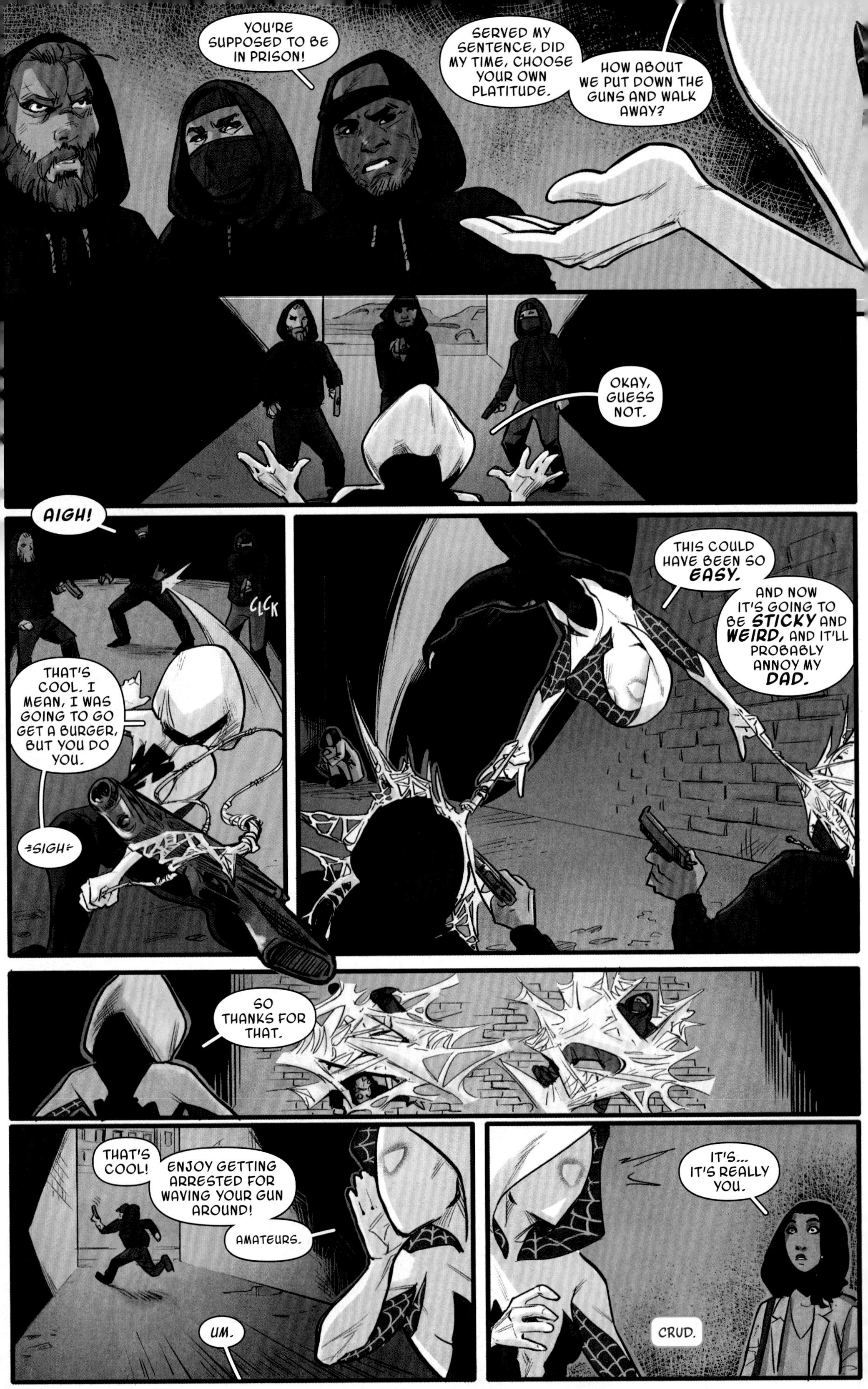
YOU'RE SUPPOSED TO BE IN PRISON!
SERVED MY SENTENCE, DID MY TIME, CHOOSE YOUR OWN PLATITUDE.
HOW ABOUT WE PUT DOWN THE GUNS AND WALK AWAY?
OKAY, GUESS NOT.
AIGH!
CLCK
THAT'S COOL. I MEAN, I WAS GOING TO GO GET A BURGER, BUT YOU DO YOU.
=SIGH=
THIS COULD HAVE BEEN SO EASY.
AND NOW IT'S GOING TO BE STICKY AND WEIRD, AND IT'LL PROBABLY ANNOY MY DAD.
SO THANKS FOR THAT.
THAT'S COOL!
ENJOY GETTING ARRESTED FOR WAVING YOUR GUN AROUND!
AMATEURS.
UM.
IT'S... IT'S REALLY YOU.
CRUD.

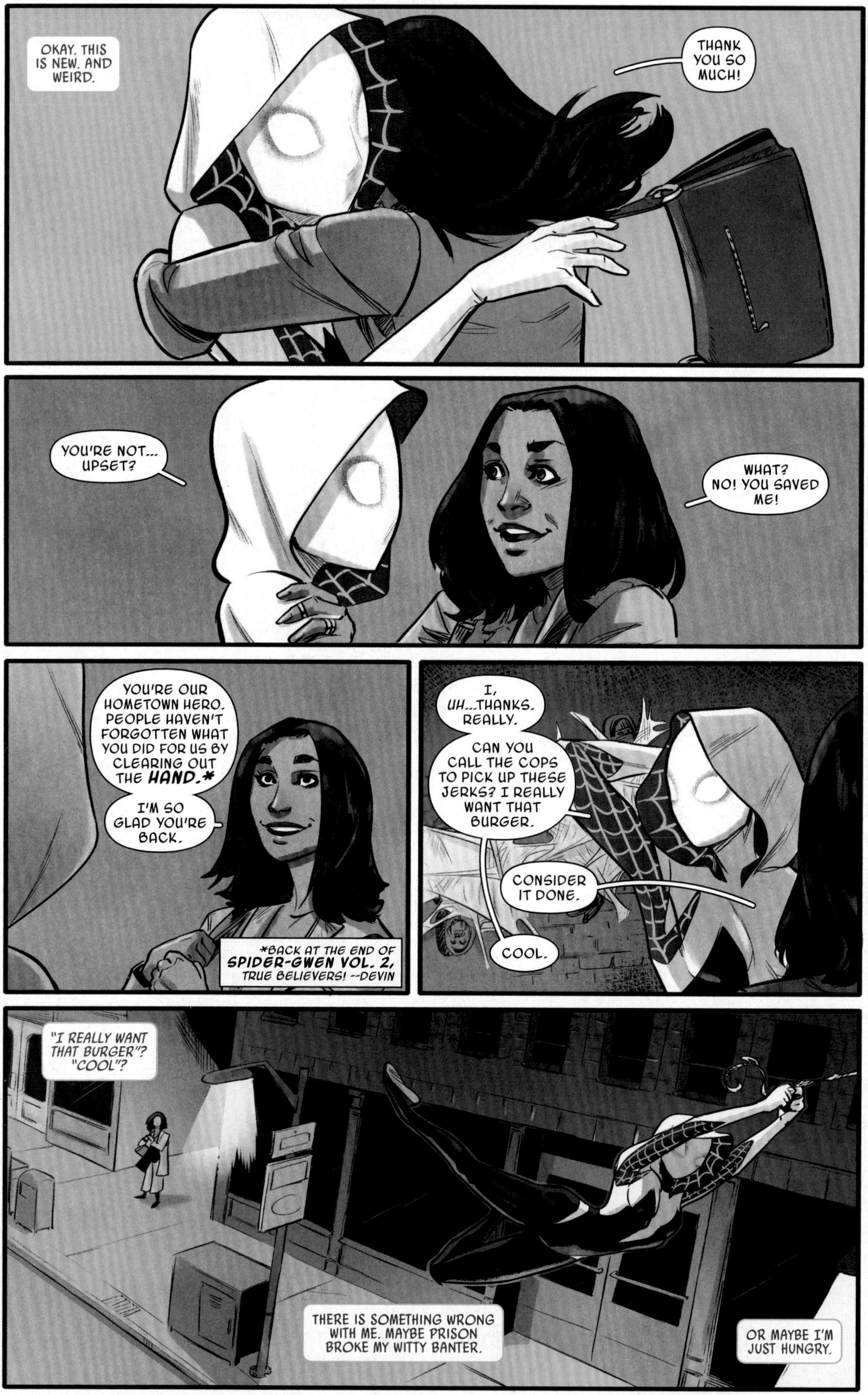
OKAY. THIS IS NEW. AND WEIRD.
THANK YOU SO MUCH!
YOU'RE NOT... UPSET?
WHAT? NO! YOU SAVED ME!
YOU'RE OUR HOMETOWN HERO. PEOPLE HAVEN'T FORGOTTEN WHAT YOU DID FOR US BY CLEARING OUT THE HAND.*
I'M SO GLAD YOU'RE BACK.
*BACK AT THE END OF SPIDER-GWEN VOL. 2, TRUE BELIEVERS! --DEVIN
I, UH...THANKS. REALLY.
CAN YOU CALL THE COPS TO PICK UP THESE JERKS? I REALLY WANT THAT BURGER.
CONSIDER IT DONE.
COOL.
"I REALLY WANT THAT BURGER"? "COOL"?
THERE IS SOMETHING WRONG WITH ME. MAYBE PRISON BROKE MY WITTY BANTER.
OR MAYBE I'M JUST HUNGRY.

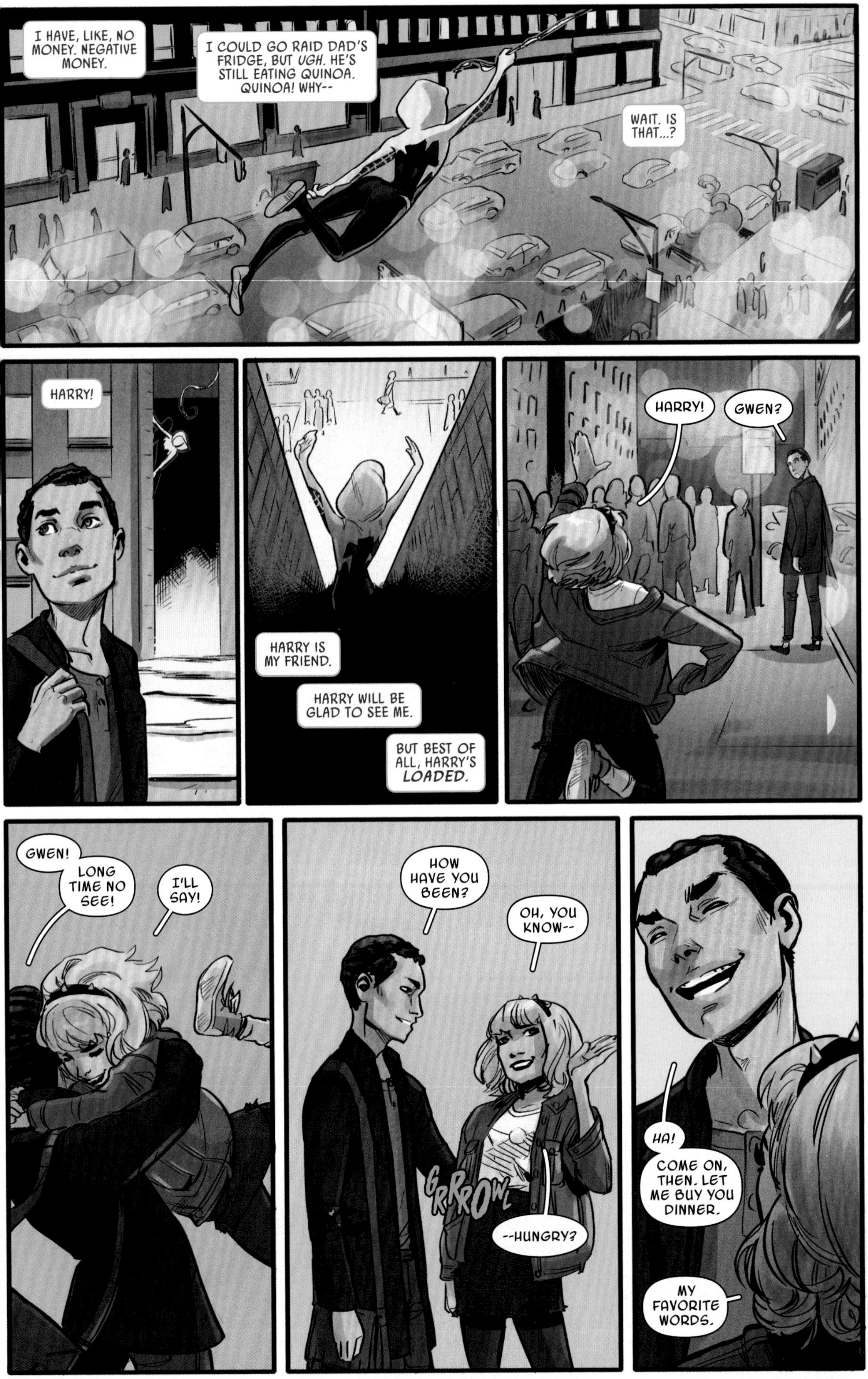

I HAVE, LIKE, NO MONEY. NEGATIVE MONEY.
I COULD GO RAID DAD'S FRIDGE, BUT UGH. HE'S STILL EATING QUINOA. QUINOA! WHY--
WAIT. IS THAT...?
HARRY!
HARRY IS MY FRIEND.
HARRY WILL BE GLAD TO SEE ME.
BUT BEST OF ALL, HARRY'S LOADED.
HARRY!
GWEN?
GWEN!
LONG TIME NO SEE!
I'LL SAY!
HOW HAVE YOU BEEN?
OH, YOU KNOW--
GRRROWL
--HUNGRY?
HA!
COME ON, THEN. LET ME BUY YOU DINNER.
MY FAVORITE WORDS.

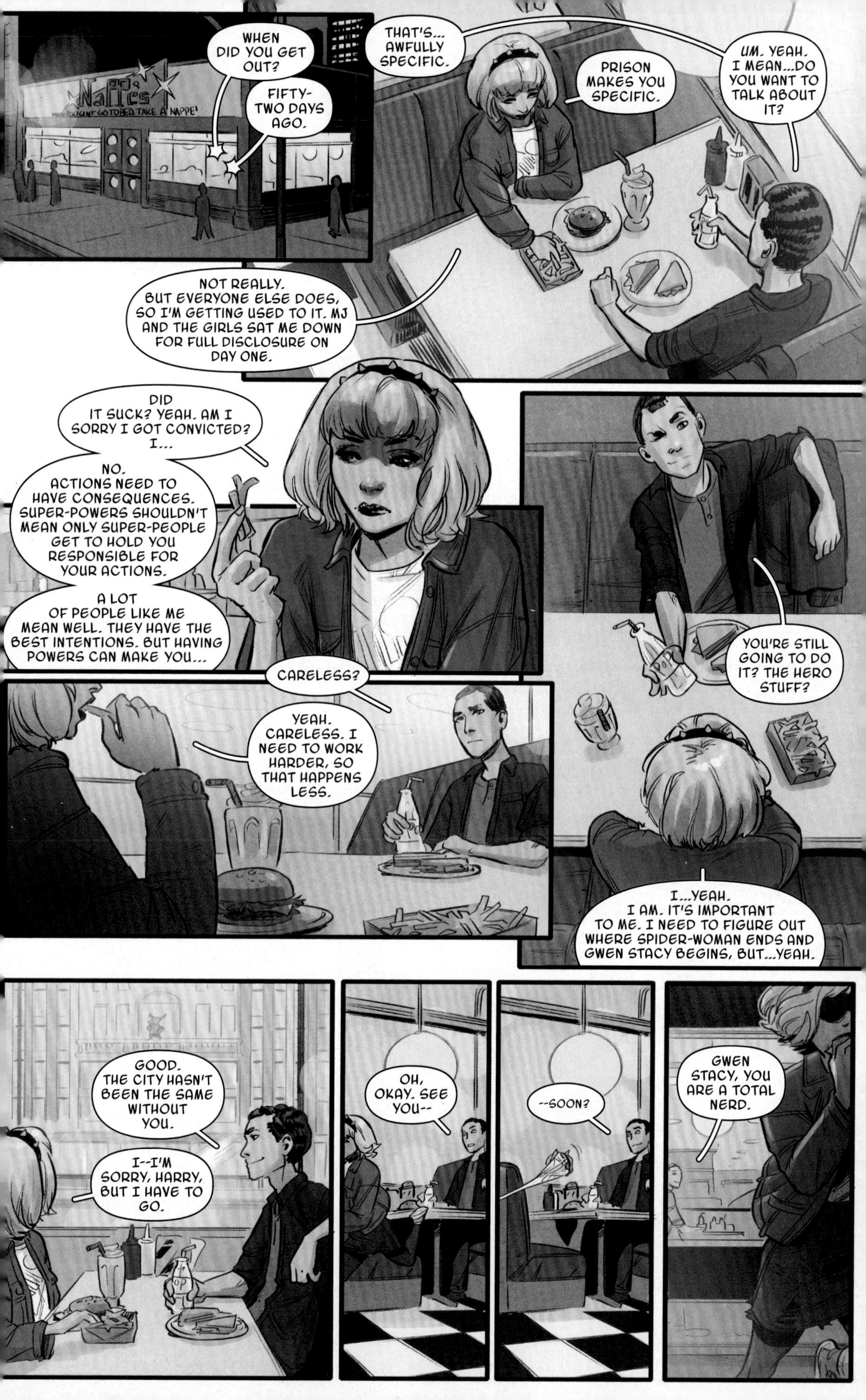
WHEN DID YOU GET OUT?
FIFTY-TWO DAYS AGO.
THAT'S... AWFULLY SPECIFIC.
PRISON MAKES YOU SPECIFIC.
UM. YEAH. I MEAN...DO YOU WANT TO TALK ABOUT IT?
NOT REALLY. BUT EVERYONE ELSE DOES, SO I'M GETTING USED TO IT. MJ AND THE GIRLS SAT ME DOWN FOR FULL DISCLOSURE ON DAY ONE.
DID IT SUCK? YEAH. AM I SORRY I GOT CONVICTED? I...
NO. ACTIONS NEED TO HAVE CONSEQUENCES. SUPER-POWERS SHOULDN'T MEAN ONLY SUPER-PEOPLE GET TO HOLD YOU RESPONSIBLE FOR YOUR ACTIONS.
A LOT OF PEOPLE LIKE ME MEAN WELL. THEY HAVE THE BEST INTENTIONS. BUT HAVING POWERS CAN MAKE YOU...
CARELESS?
YEAH. CARELESS. I NEED TO WORK HARDER, SO THAT HAPPENS LESS.
YOU'RE STILL GOING TO DO IT? THE HERO STUFF?
I...YEAH. I AM. IT'S IMPORTANT TO ME. I NEED TO FIGURE OUT WHERE SPIDER-WOMAN ENDS AND GWEN STACY BEGINS, BUT...YEAH.
GOOD. THE CITY HASN'T BEEN THE SAME WITHOUT YOU.
I--I'M SORRY, HARRY, BUT I HAVE TO GO.
OH, OKAY. SEE YOU--
--SOON?
GWEN STACY, YOU ARE A TOTAL NERD.

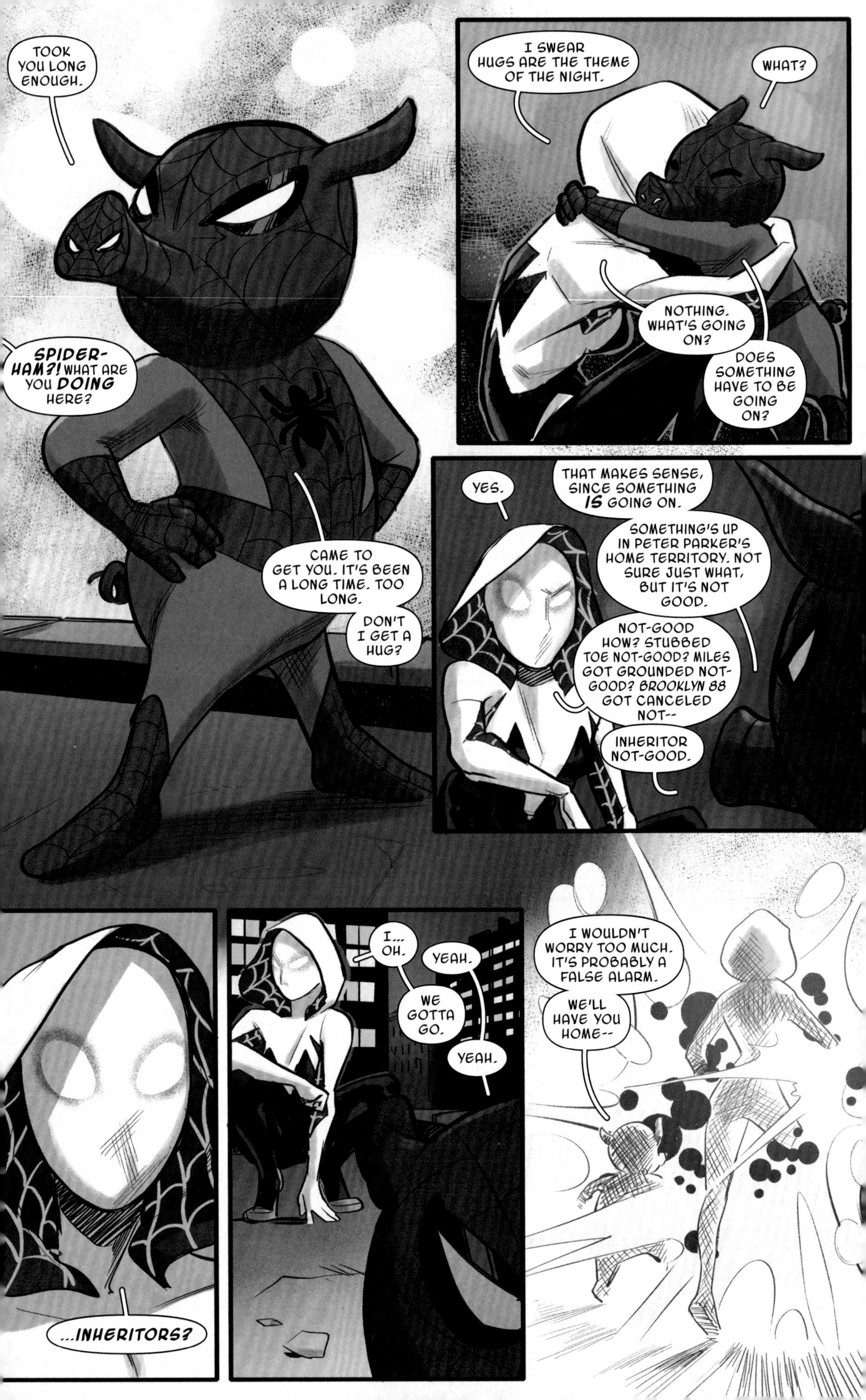
TOOK YOU LONG ENOUGH.
SPIDER-HAM?! WHAT ARE YOU DOING HERE?
CAME TO GET YOU. IT'S BEEN A LONG TIME. TOO LONG.
DON'T I GET A HUG?
I SWEAR HUGS ARE THE THEME OF THE NIGHT.
WHAT?
NOTHING. WHAT'S GOING ON?
DOES SOMETHING HAVE TO BE GOING ON?
YES.
THAT MAKES SENSE, SINCE SOMETHING IS GOING ON.
SOMETHING'S UP IN PETER PARKER'S HOME TERRITORY. NOT SURE JUST WHAT, BUT IT'S NOT GOOD.
NOT-GOOD HOW? STUBBED TOE NOT-GOOD? MILES GOT GROUNDED NOT-GOOD? BROOKLYN 88 GOT CANCELED NOT--
INHERITOR NOT-GOOD.
...INHERITORS?
I... OH.
YEAH.
WE GOTTA GO.
YEAH.
I WOULDN'T WORRY TOO MUCH. IT'S PROBABLY A FALSE ALARM.
WE'LL HAVE YOU HOME--

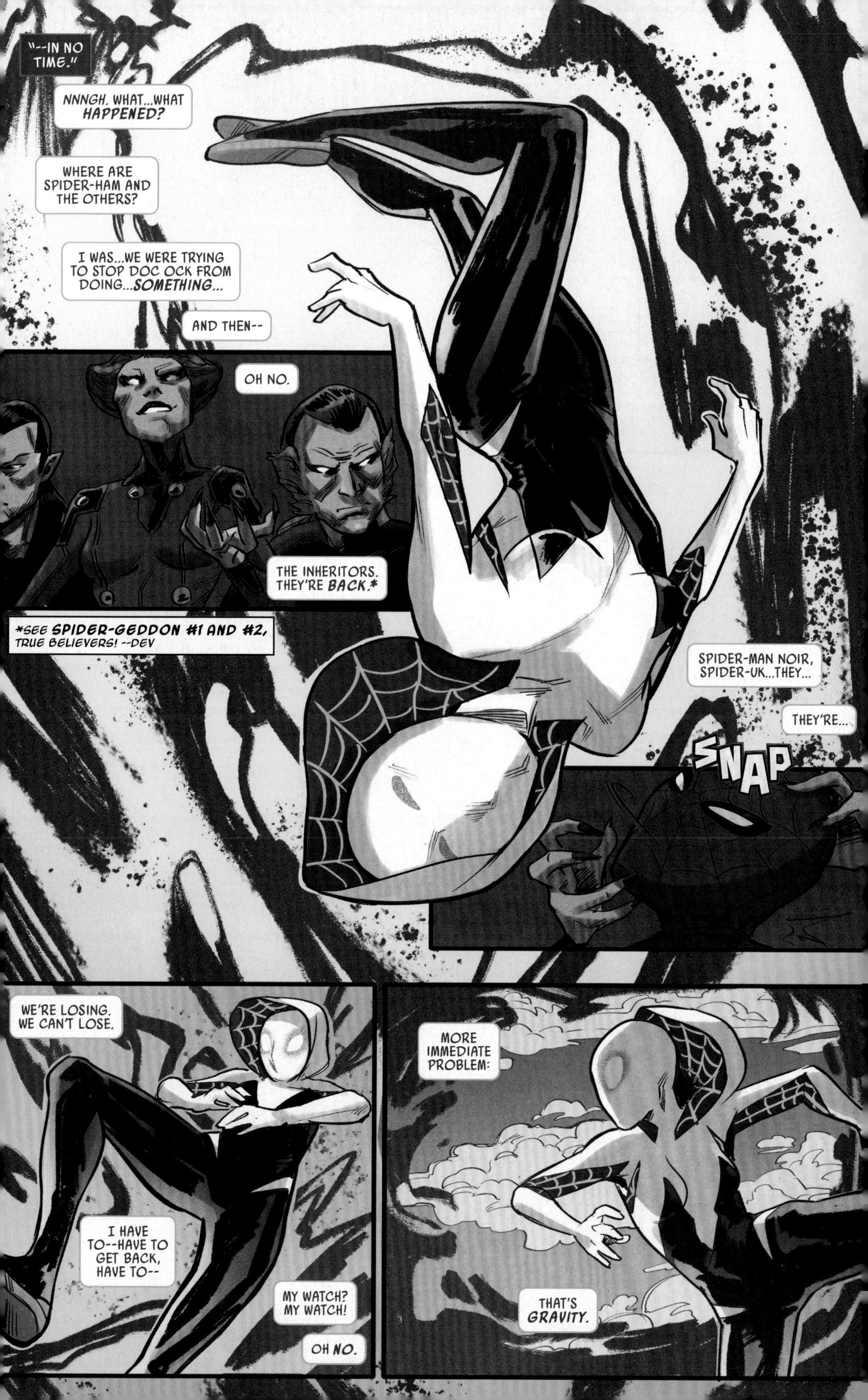
"--IN NO TIME."
NNNGH. WHAT...WHAT HAPPENED?
WHERE ARE SPIDER-HAM AND THE OTHERS?
I WAS...WE WERE TRYING TO STOP DOC OCK FROM DOING...SOMETHING...
AND THEN--
OH NO.
THE INHERITORS. THEY'RE BACK.*
*SEE SPIDER-GEDDON #1 AND #2, TRUE BELIEVERS! --DEV
SPIDER-MAN NOIR, SPIDER-UK...THEY...
THEY'RE...
SNAP
WE'RE LOSING. WE CAN'T LOSE.
I HAVE TO--HAVE TO GET BACK, HAVE TO--
MY WATCH? MY WATCH!
OH NO.
MORE IMMEDIATE PROBLEM:
THAT'S GRAVITY.

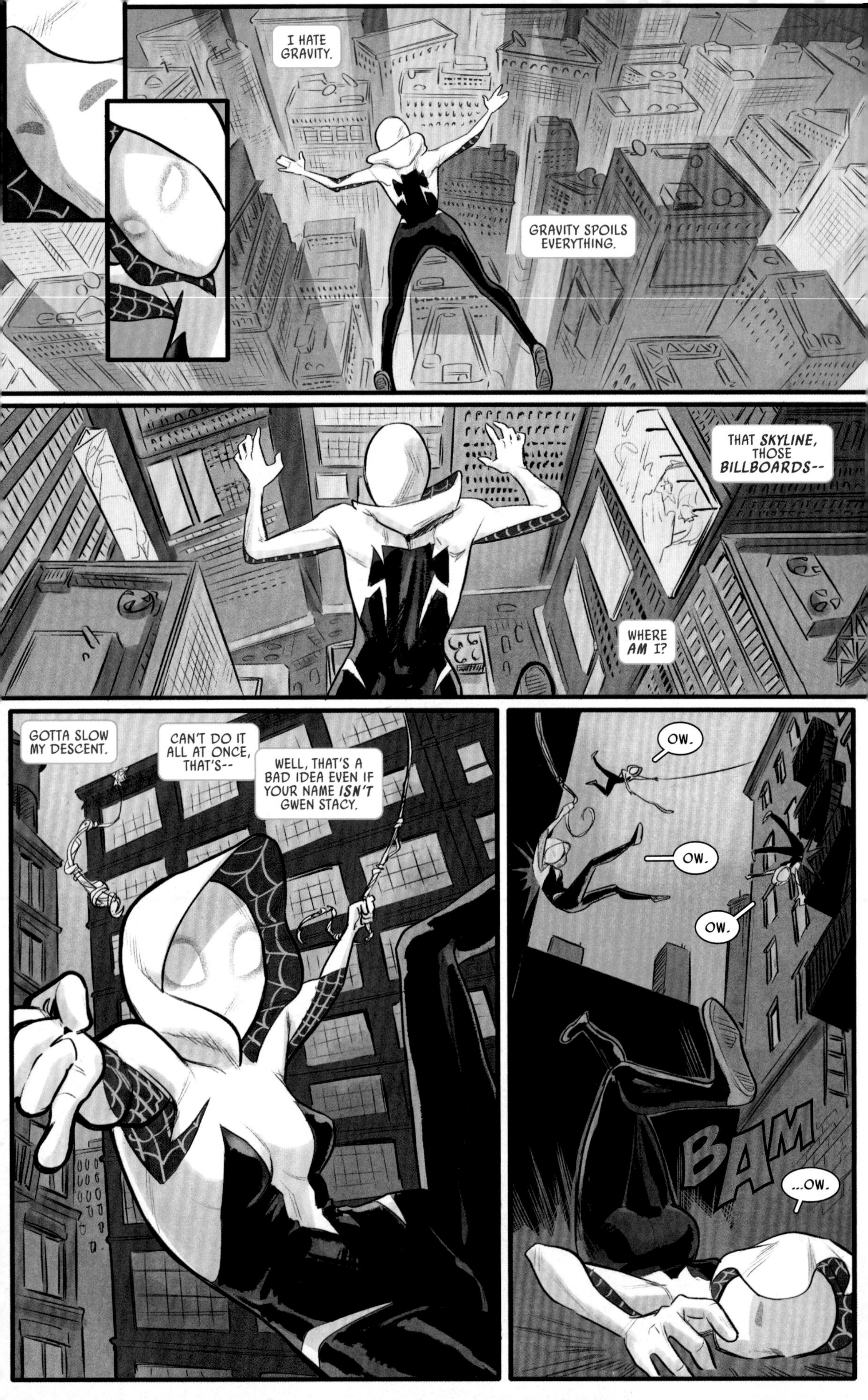
I HATE GRAVITY.
GRAVITY SPOILS EVERYTHING.
THAT SKYLINE, THOSE BILLBOARDS--
WHERE AM I?
GOTTA SLOW MY DESCENT.
CAN'T DO IT ALL AT ONCE, THAT'S--
WELL, THAT'S A BAD IDEA EVEN IF YOUR NAME ISN'T GWEN STACY.
OW.
OW.
OW.
BAM
...OW.

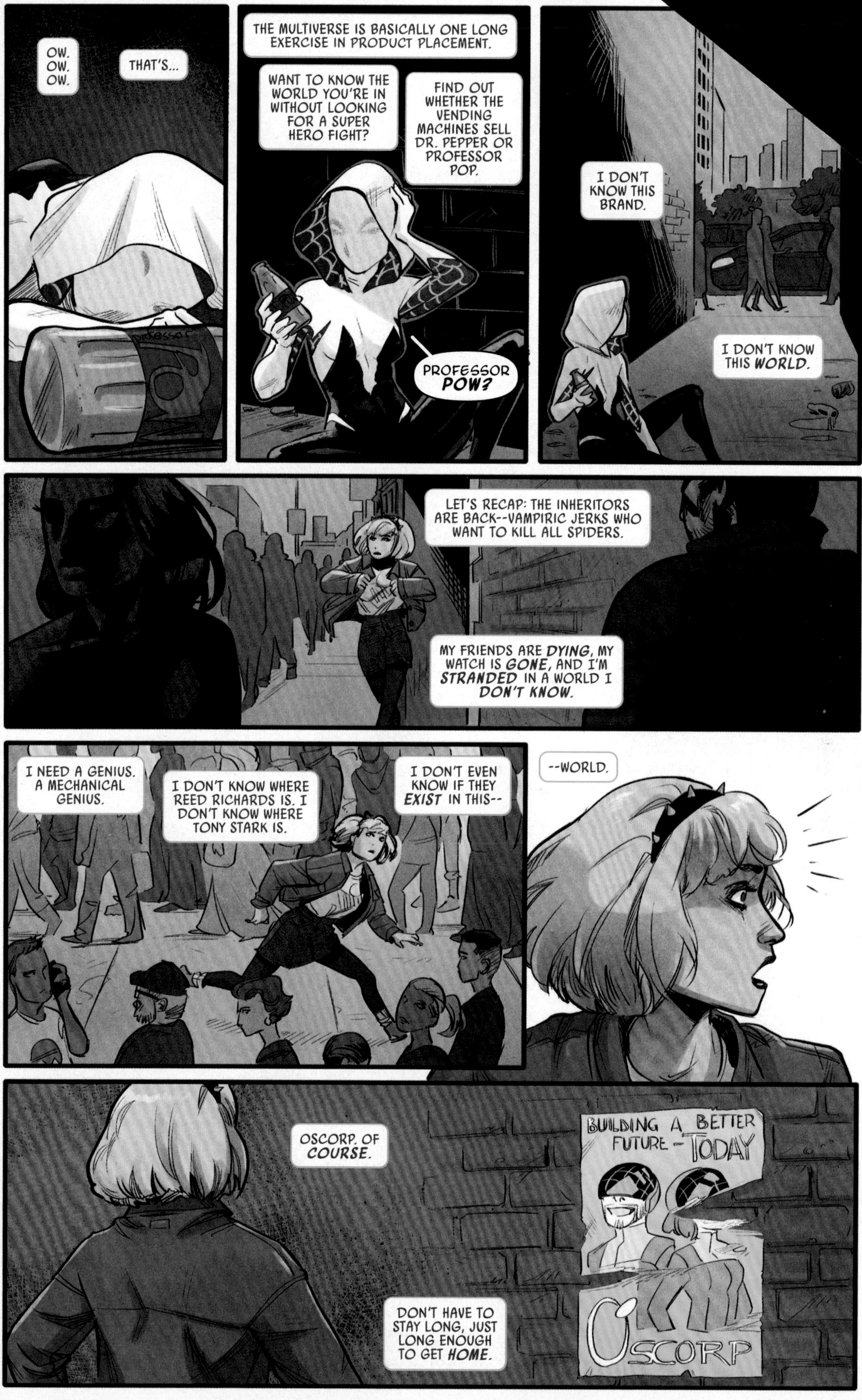
OW.
OW.
OW.
THAT'S...
THE MULTIVERSE IS BASICALLY ONE LONG EXERCISE IN PRODUCT PLACEMENT.
WANT TO KNOW THE WORLD YOU'RE IN WITHOUT LOOKING FOR A SUPER HERO FIGHT?
FIND OUT WHETHER THE VENDING MACHINES SELL DR. PEPPER OR PROFESSOR POP.
PROFESSOR POW?
I DON'T KNOW THIS BRAND.
I DON'T KNOW THIS WORLD.
LET'S RECAP: THE INHERITORS ARE BACK--VAMPIRIC JERKS WHO WANT TO KILL ALL SPIDERS.
MY FRIENDS ARE DYING, MY WATCH IS GONE, AND I'M STRANDED IN A WORLD I DON'T KNOW.
I NEED A GENIUS. A MECHANICAL GENIUS.
I DON'T KNOW WHERE REED RICHARDS IS. I DON'T KNOW WHERE TONY STARK IS.
I DON'T EVEN KNOW IF THEY EXIST IN THIS--
--WORLD.
OSCORP. OF COURSE.
BUILDING A BETTER FUTURE - TODAY
OSCORP
DON'T HAVE TO STAY LONG, JUST LONG ENOUGH TO GET HOME.

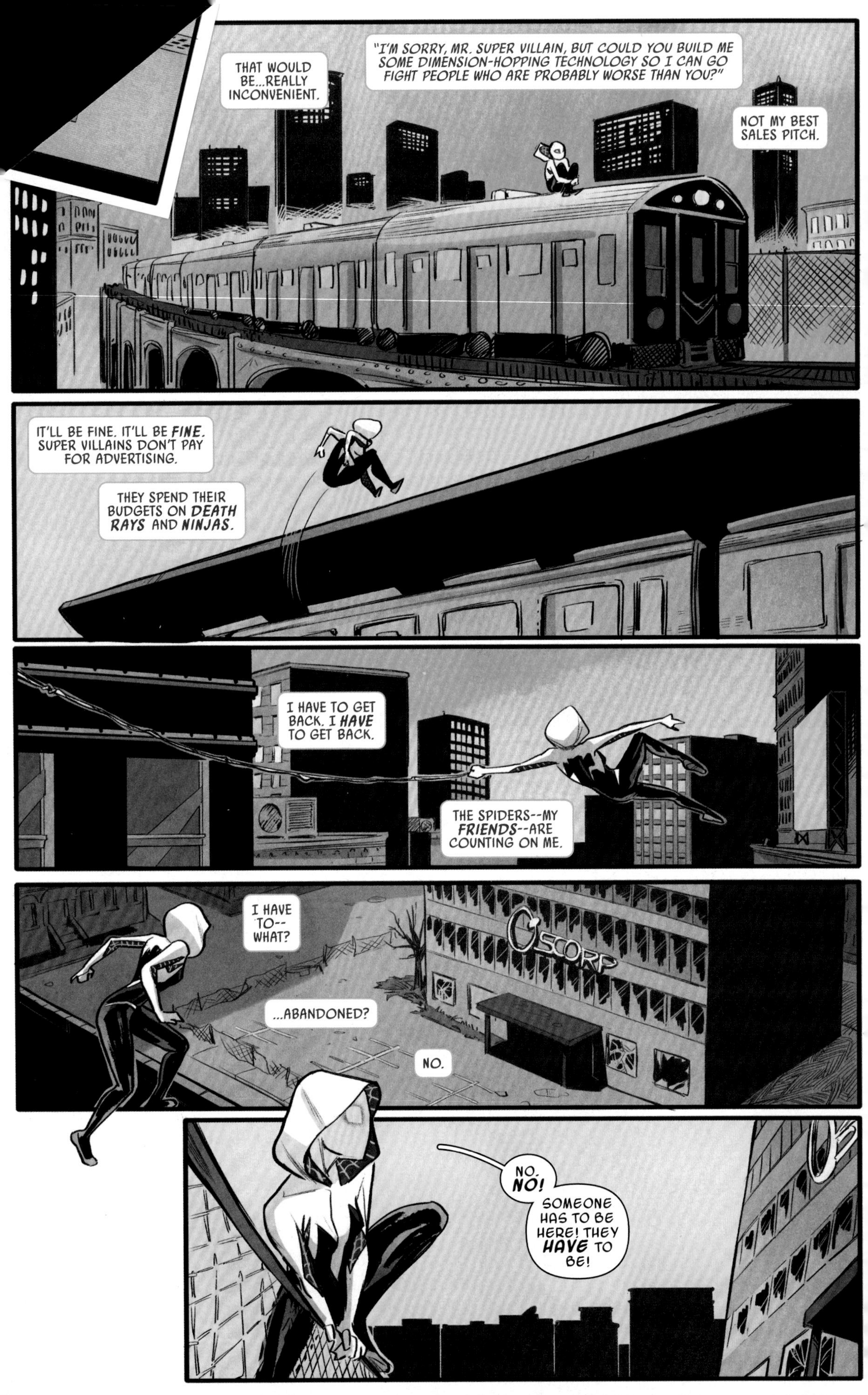

THAT WOULD BE...REALLY INCONVENIENT.
"I'M SORRY, MR. SUPER VILLAIN, BUT COULD YOU BUILD ME SOME DIMENSION-HOPPING TECHNOLOGY SO I CAN GO FIGHT PEOPLE WHO ARE PROBABLY WORSE THAN YOU?"
NOT MY BEST SALES PITCH.
IT'LL BE FINE. IT'LL BE FINE. SUPER VILLAINS DON'T PAY FOR ADVERTISING.
THEY SPEND THEIR BUDGETS ON DEATH RAYS AND NINJAS.
I HAVE TO GET BACK. I HAVE TO GET BACK.
THE SPIDERS--MY FRIENDS--ARE COUNTING ON ME.
I HAVE TO--WHAT?
OSCORP
...ABANDONED?
NO.
NO. NO!
SOMEONE HAS TO BE HERE! THEY HAVE TO BE!

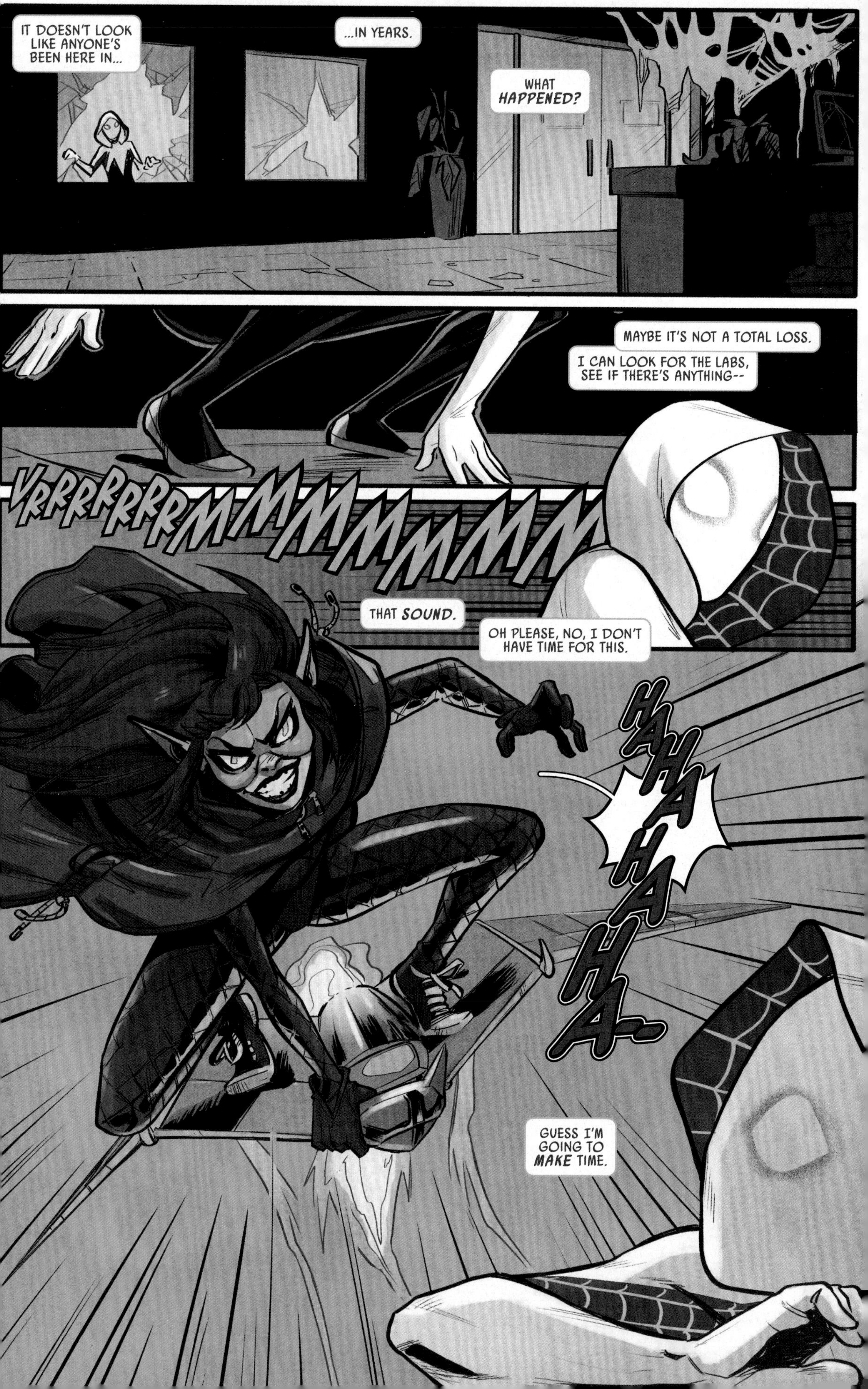
IT DOESN'T LOOK LIKE ANYONE'S BEEN HERE IN...
...IN YEARS.
WHAT HAPPENED?
MAYBE IT'S NOT A TOTAL LOSS.
I CAN LOOK FOR THE LABS, SEE IF THERE'S ANYTHING--
VRRRRRRRMMMMMMMMMM
THAT SOUND.
OH PLEASE, NO, I DON'T HAVE TIME FOR THIS.
HAHAHAHAHAHA--
GUESS I'M GOING TO MAKE TIME.

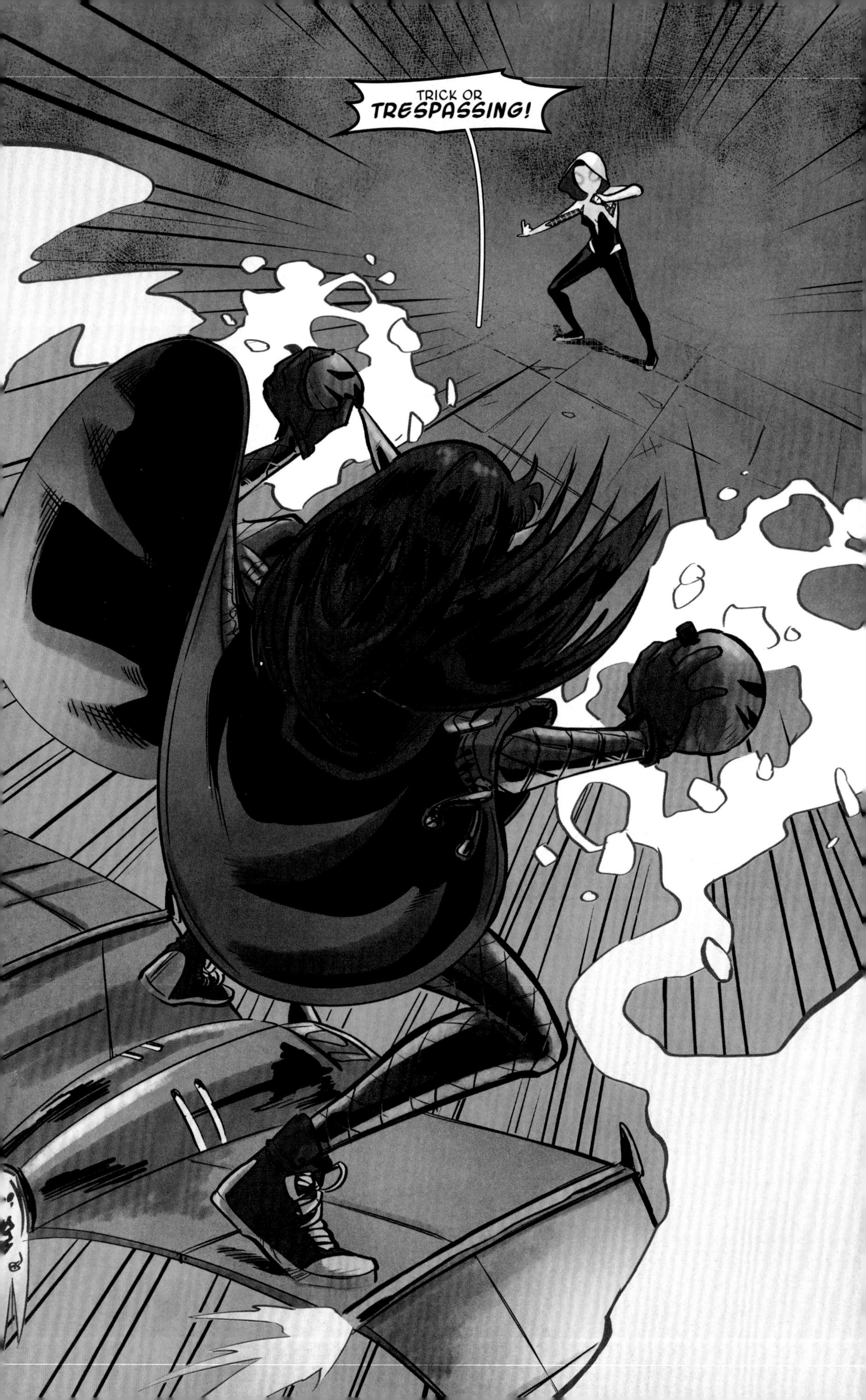
TRICK OR TRESPASSING!

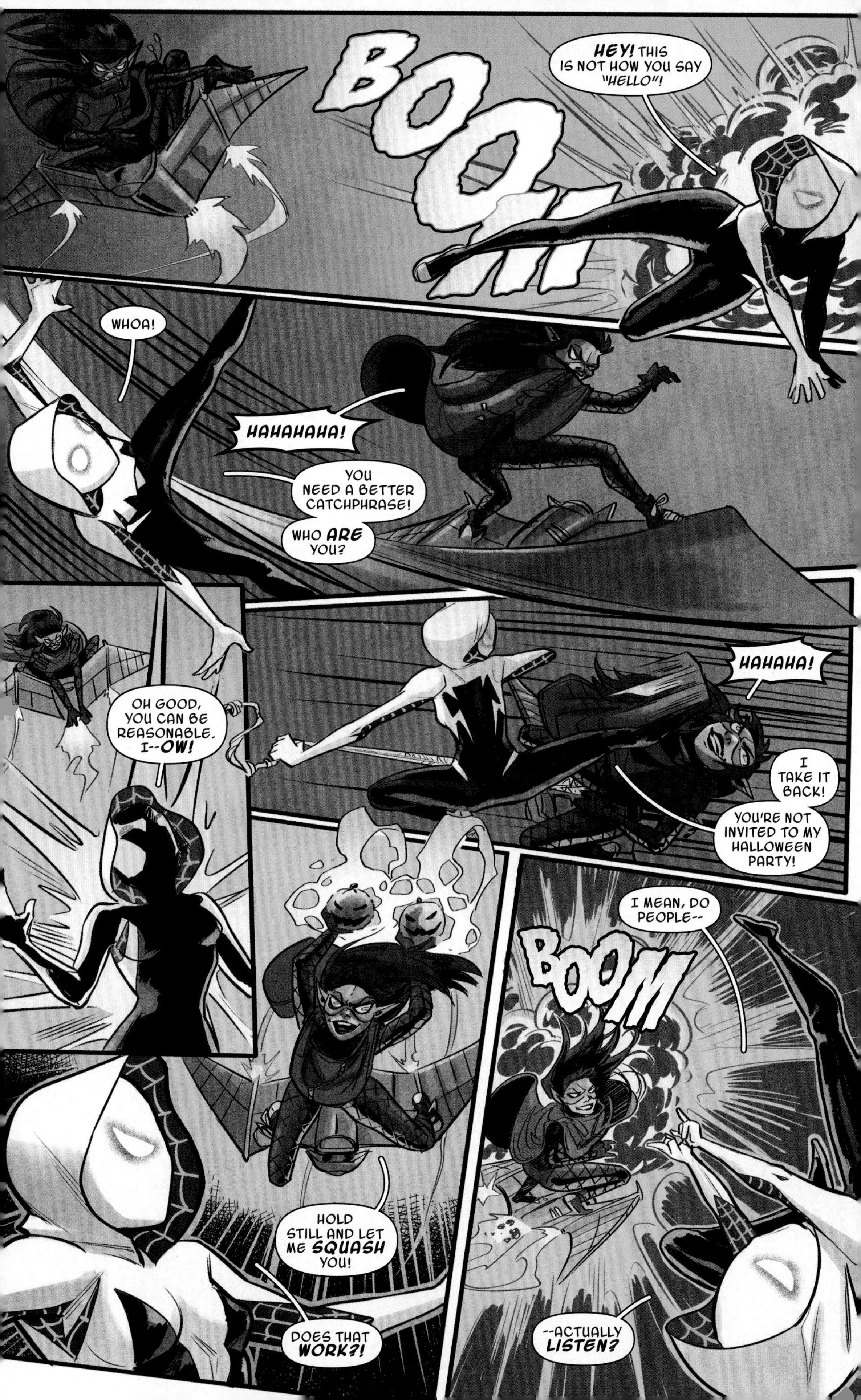
BOOM!
HEY! THIS IS NOT HOW YOU SAY "HELLO"!
WHOA!
HAHAHAHA!
YOU NEED A BETTER CATCHPHRASE!
WHO ARE YOU?
OH GOOD, YOU CAN BE REASONABLE. I--OW!
HAHAHA!
I TAKE IT BACK!
YOU'RE NOT INVITED TO MY HALLOWEEN PARTY!
HOLD STILL AND LET ME SQUASH YOU!
DOES THAT WORK?!
I MEAN, DO PEOPLE--
BOOM
--ACTUALLY LISTEN?

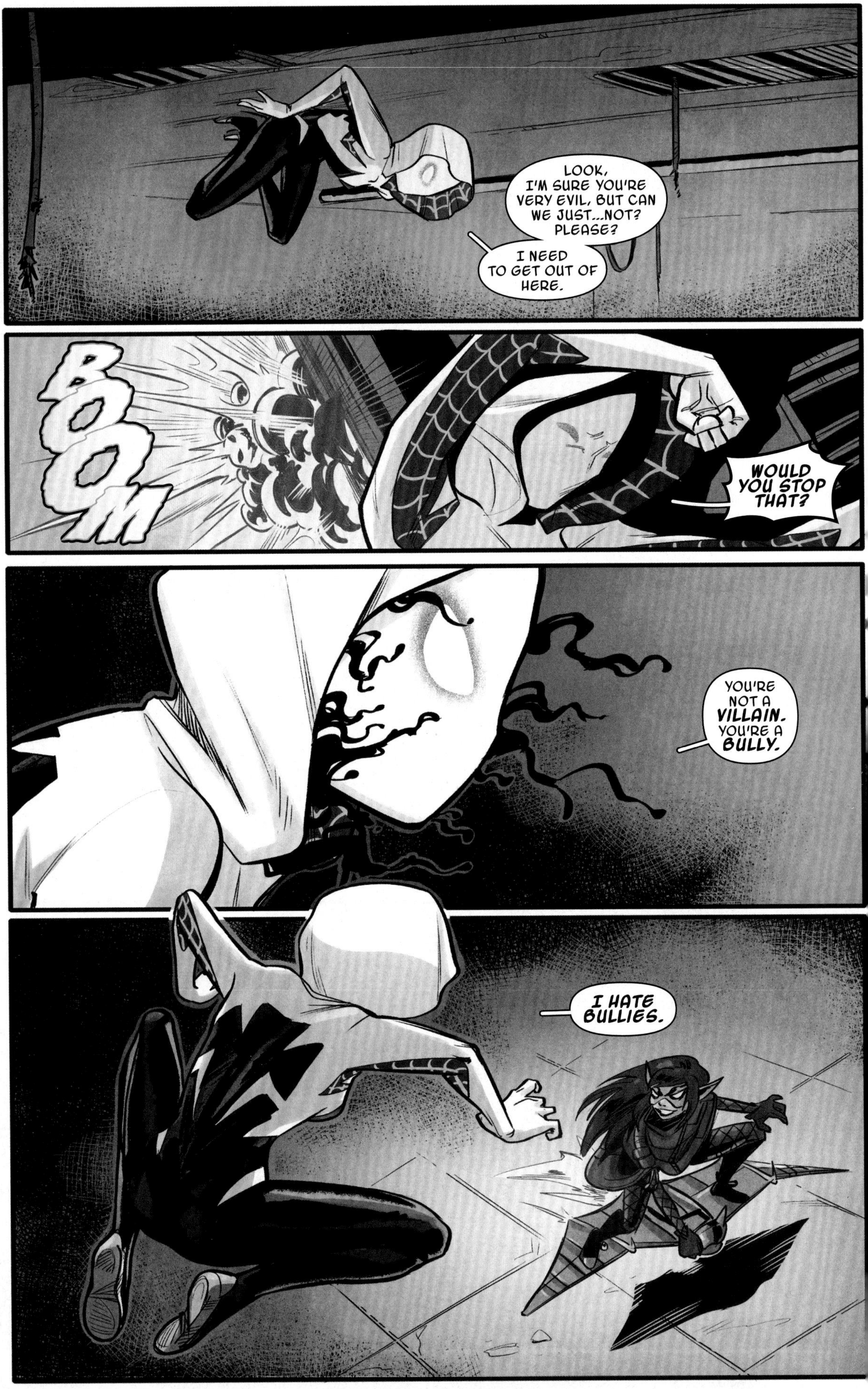
LOOK, I'M SURE YOU'RE VERY EVIL, BUT CAN WE JUST...NOT? PLEASE?
I NEED TO GET OUT OF HERE.
BOOM
WOULD YOU STOP THAT?
YOU'RE NOT A VILLAIN. YOU'RE A BULLY.
I HATE BULLIES.

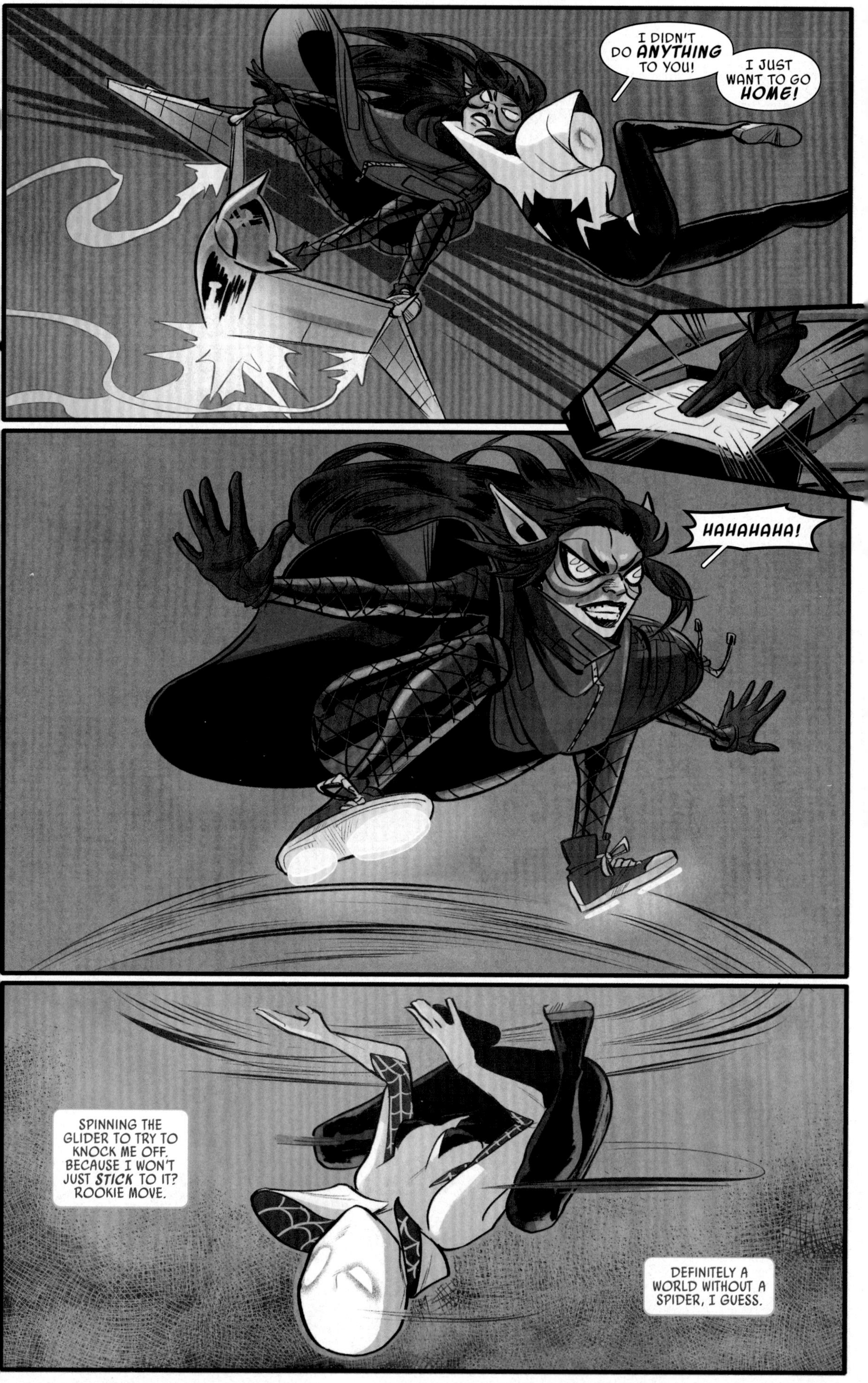
I DIDN'T DO **ANYTHING** TO YOU!
I JUST WANT TO GO ***HOME!***
HAHAHAHA!
SPINNING THE GLIDER TO TRY TO KNOCK ME OFF. BECAUSE I WON'T JUST ***STICK*** TO IT? ROOKIE MOVE.
DEFINITELY A WORLD WITHOUT A SPIDER, I GUESS.

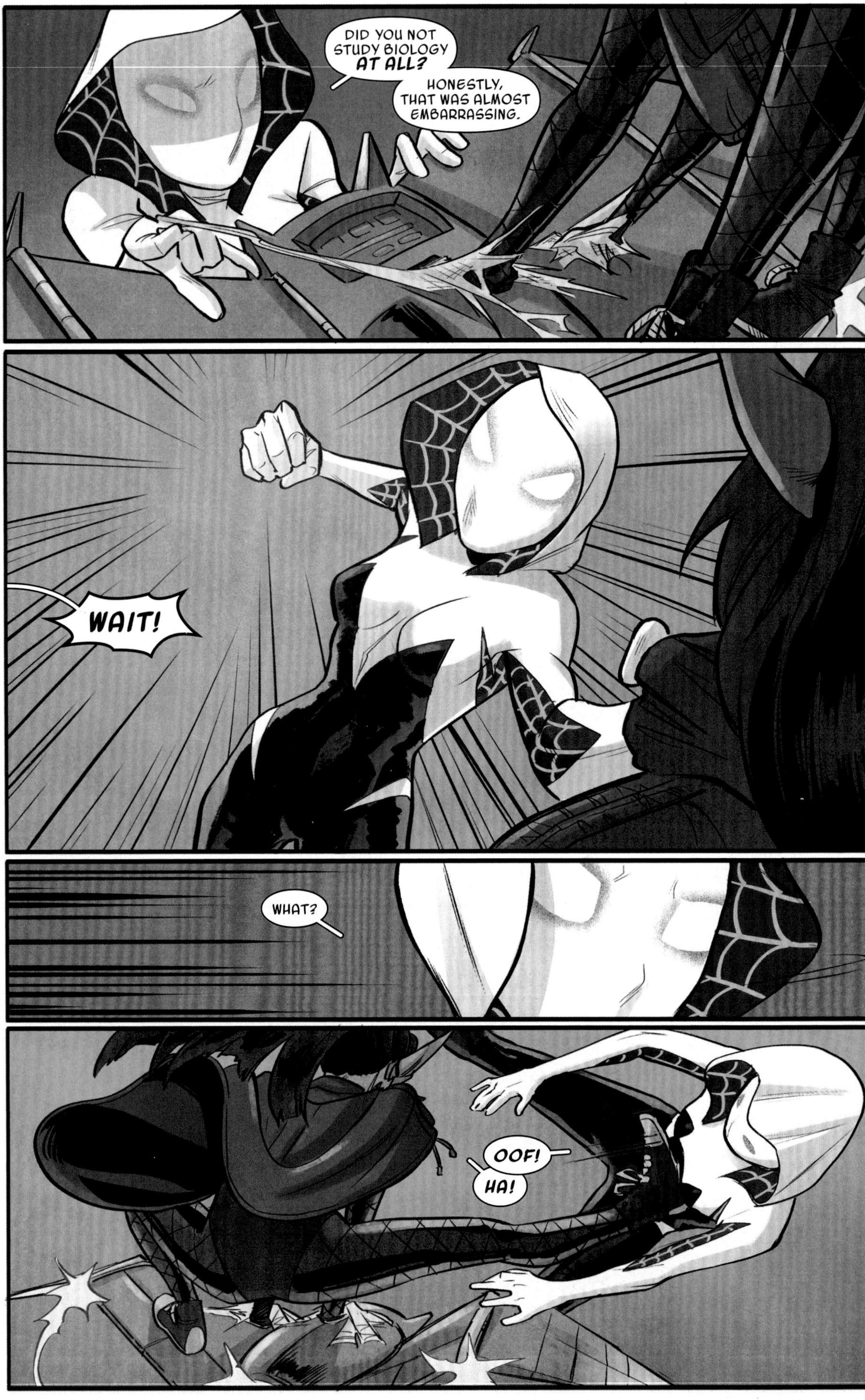
DID YOU NOT STUDY BIOLOGY AT ALL?
HONESTLY, THAT WAS ALMOST EMBARRASSING.
WAIT!
WHAT?
OOF!
HA!

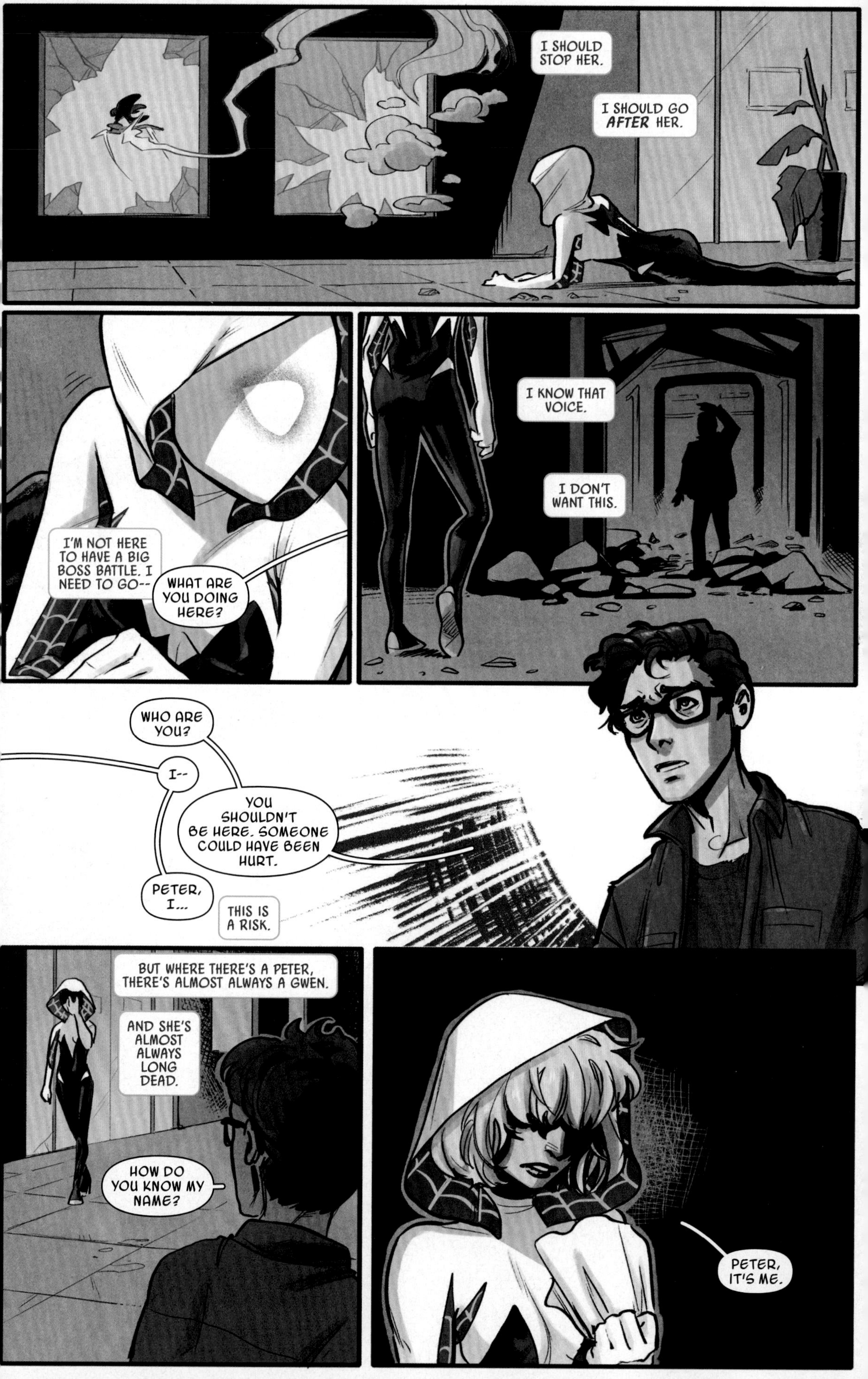
I SHOULD STOP HER.
I SHOULD GO AFTER HER.
I'M NOT HERE TO HAVE A BIG BOSS BATTLE. I NEED TO GO--
WHAT ARE YOU DOING HERE?
I KNOW THAT VOICE.
I DON'T WANT THIS.
WHO ARE YOU?
I--
YOU SHOULDN'T BE HERE. SOMEONE COULD HAVE BEEN HURT.
PETER, I...
THIS IS A RISK.
BUT WHERE THERE'S A PETER, THERE'S ALMOST ALWAYS A GWEN.
AND SHE'S ALMOST ALWAYS LONG DEAD.
HOW DO YOU KNOW MY NAME?
PETER, IT'S ME.

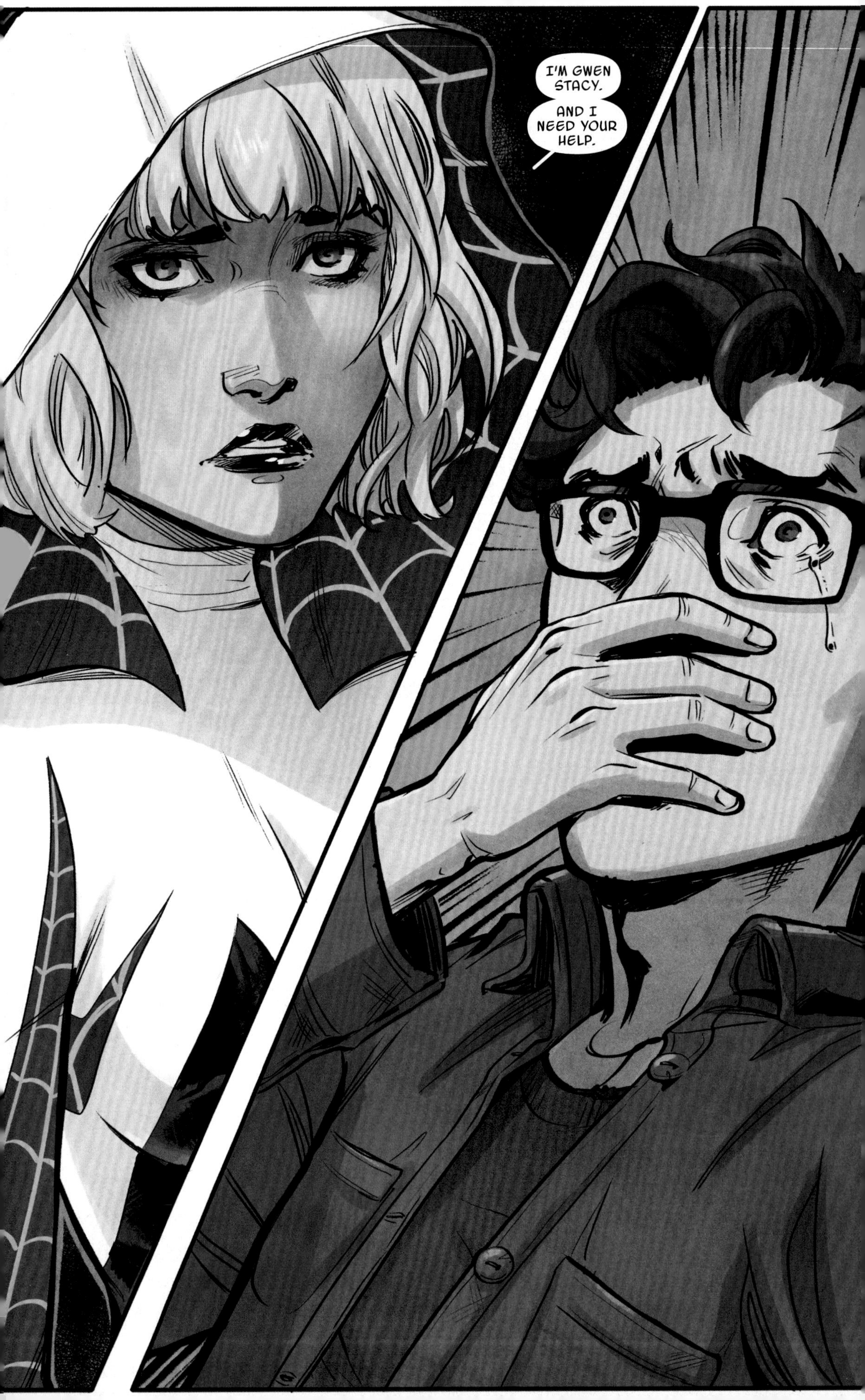
I'M GWEN STACY.
AND I NEED YOUR HELP.

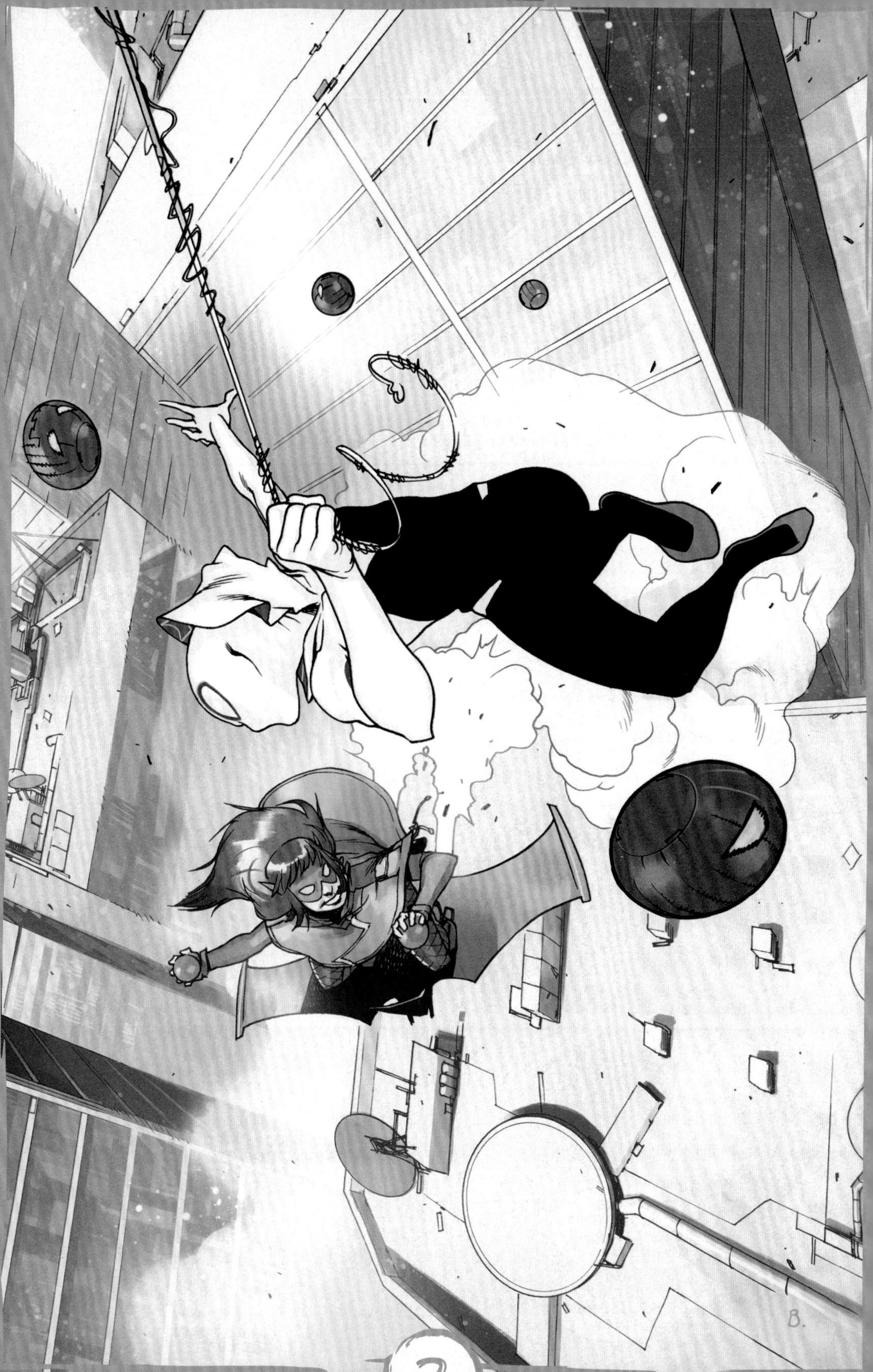

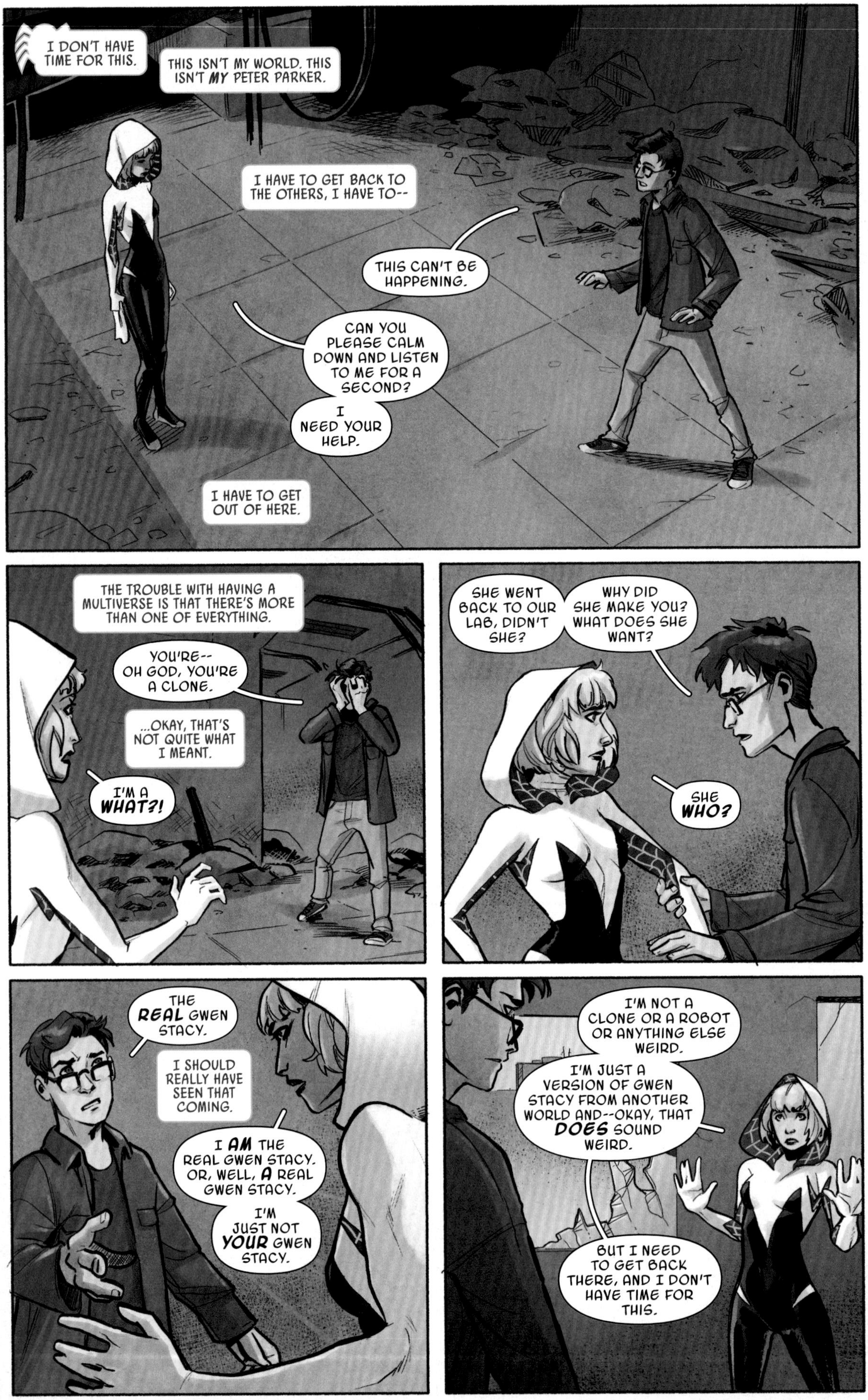
I DON'T HAVE TIME FOR THIS.
THIS ISN'T MY WORLD. THIS ISN'T MY PETER PARKER.
I HAVE TO GET BACK TO THE OTHERS, I HAVE TO--
THIS CAN'T BE HAPPENING.
CAN YOU PLEASE CALM DOWN AND LISTEN TO ME FOR A SECOND?
I NEED YOUR HELP.
I HAVE TO GET OUT OF HERE.
THE TROUBLE WITH HAVING A MULTIVERSE IS THAT THERE'S MORE THAN ONE OF EVERYTHING.
YOU'RE-- OH GOD, YOU'RE A CLONE.
...OKAY, THAT'S NOT QUITE WHAT I MEANT.
I'M A WHAT?!
SHE WENT BACK TO OUR LAB, DIDN'T SHE?
WHY DID SHE MAKE YOU? WHAT DOES SHE WANT?
SHE WHO?
THE REAL GWEN STACY.
I SHOULD REALLY HAVE SEEN THAT COMING.
I AM THE REAL GWEN STACY. OR, WELL, A REAL GWEN STACY.
I'M JUST NOT YOUR GWEN STACY.
I'M NOT A CLONE OR A ROBOT OR ANYTHING ELSE WEIRD.
I'M JUST A VERSION OF GWEN STACY FROM ANOTHER WORLD AND--OKAY, THAT DOES SOUND WEIRD.
BUT I NEED TO GET BACK THERE, AND I DON'T HAVE TIME FOR THIS.

TCK

I KNOW THIS IS A LOT TO TAKE IN, BUT, PLEASE, I NEED YOUR HELP.

I NEED TO FIND SOMEONE WHO UNDERSTANDS THE BASICS OF DIMENSIONAL TRAVEL.

I DON'T SUPPOSE YOU KNOW *REED RICHARDS,* DO YOU?

TCK

HAHAHAHA--

WELL, *THAT'S* NOT GREAT.

PETER? UH...ARE YOU OKAY?

I AM REALLY STARTING TO *HATE* THIS *GOBLIN.*

LOOK OUT!

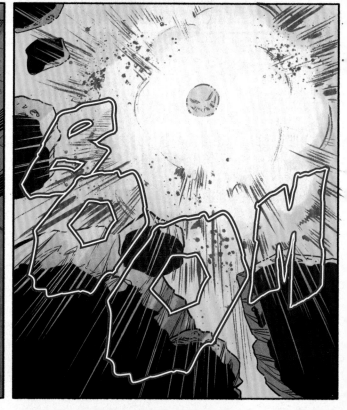

BOOM

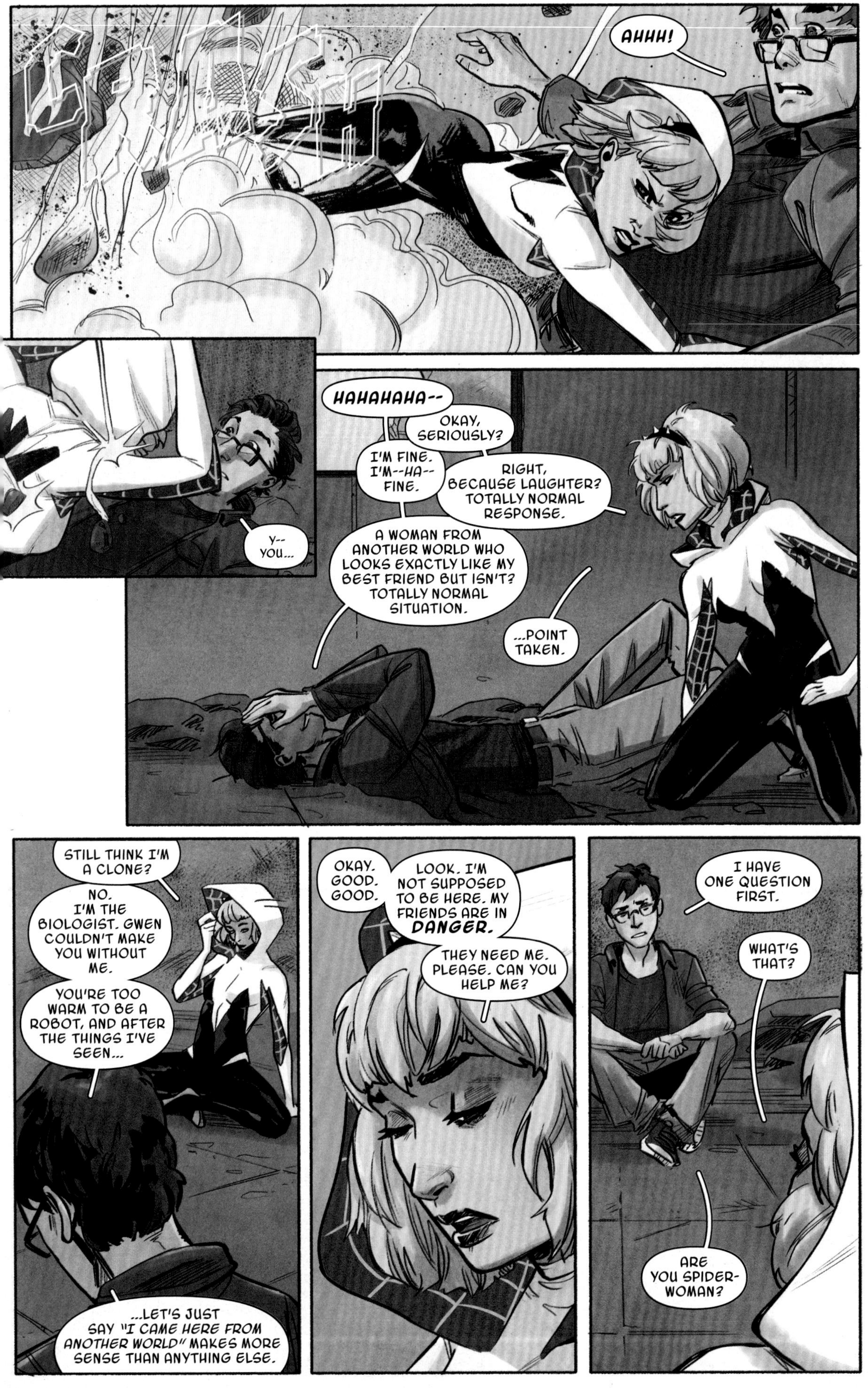
AHHH!
Y--
YOU...
HAHAHAHA--
OKAY, SERIOUSLY?
I'M FINE. I'M--HA--FINE.
RIGHT, BECAUSE LAUGHTER? TOTALLY NORMAL RESPONSE.
A WOMAN FROM ANOTHER WORLD WHO LOOKS EXACTLY LIKE MY BEST FRIEND BUT ISN'T? TOTALLY NORMAL SITUATION.
...POINT TAKEN.
STILL THINK I'M A CLONE?
NO. I'M THE BIOLOGIST. GWEN COULDN'T MAKE YOU WITHOUT ME.
YOU'RE TOO WARM TO BE A ROBOT, AND AFTER THE THINGS I'VE SEEN...
...LET'S JUST SAY "I CAME HERE FROM ANOTHER WORLD" MAKES MORE SENSE THAN ANYTHING ELSE.
OKAY. GOOD. GOOD.
LOOK. I'M NOT SUPPOSED TO BE HERE. MY FRIENDS ARE IN DANGER.
THEY NEED ME. PLEASE. CAN YOU HELP ME?
I HAVE ONE QUESTION FIRST.
WHAT'S THAT?
ARE YOU SPIDER-WOMAN?

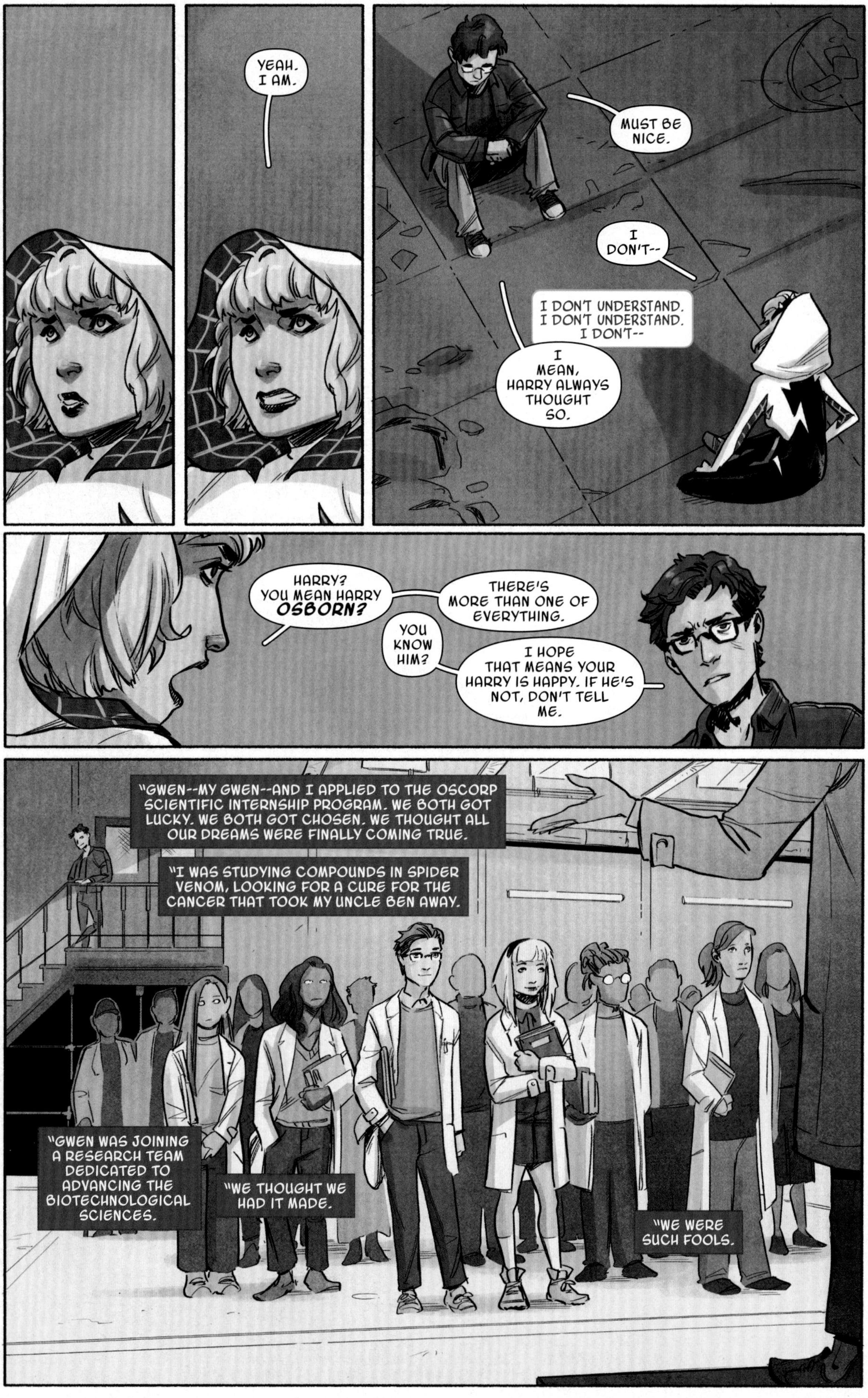
YEAH. I AM.
MUST BE NICE.
I DON'T--
I DON'T UNDERSTAND. I DON'T UNDERSTAND. I DON'T--
I MEAN, HARRY ALWAYS THOUGHT SO.
HARRY? YOU MEAN HARRY OSBORN?
THERE'S MORE THAN ONE OF EVERYTHING.
YOU KNOW HIM?
I HOPE THAT MEANS YOUR HARRY IS HAPPY. IF HE'S NOT, DON'T TELL ME.
"GWEN--MY GWEN--AND I APPLIED TO THE OSCORP SCIENTIFIC INTERNSHIP PROGRAM. WE BOTH GOT LUCKY. WE BOTH GOT CHOSEN. WE THOUGHT ALL OUR DREAMS WERE FINALLY COMING TRUE.
"I WAS STUDYING COMPOUNDS IN SPIDER VENOM, LOOKING FOR A CURE FOR THE CANCER THAT TOOK MY UNCLE BEN AWAY.
"GWEN WAS JOINING A RESEARCH TEAM DEDICATED TO ADVANCING THE BIOTECHNOLOGICAL SCIENCES.
"WE THOUGHT WE HAD IT MADE.
"WE WERE SUCH FOOLS.

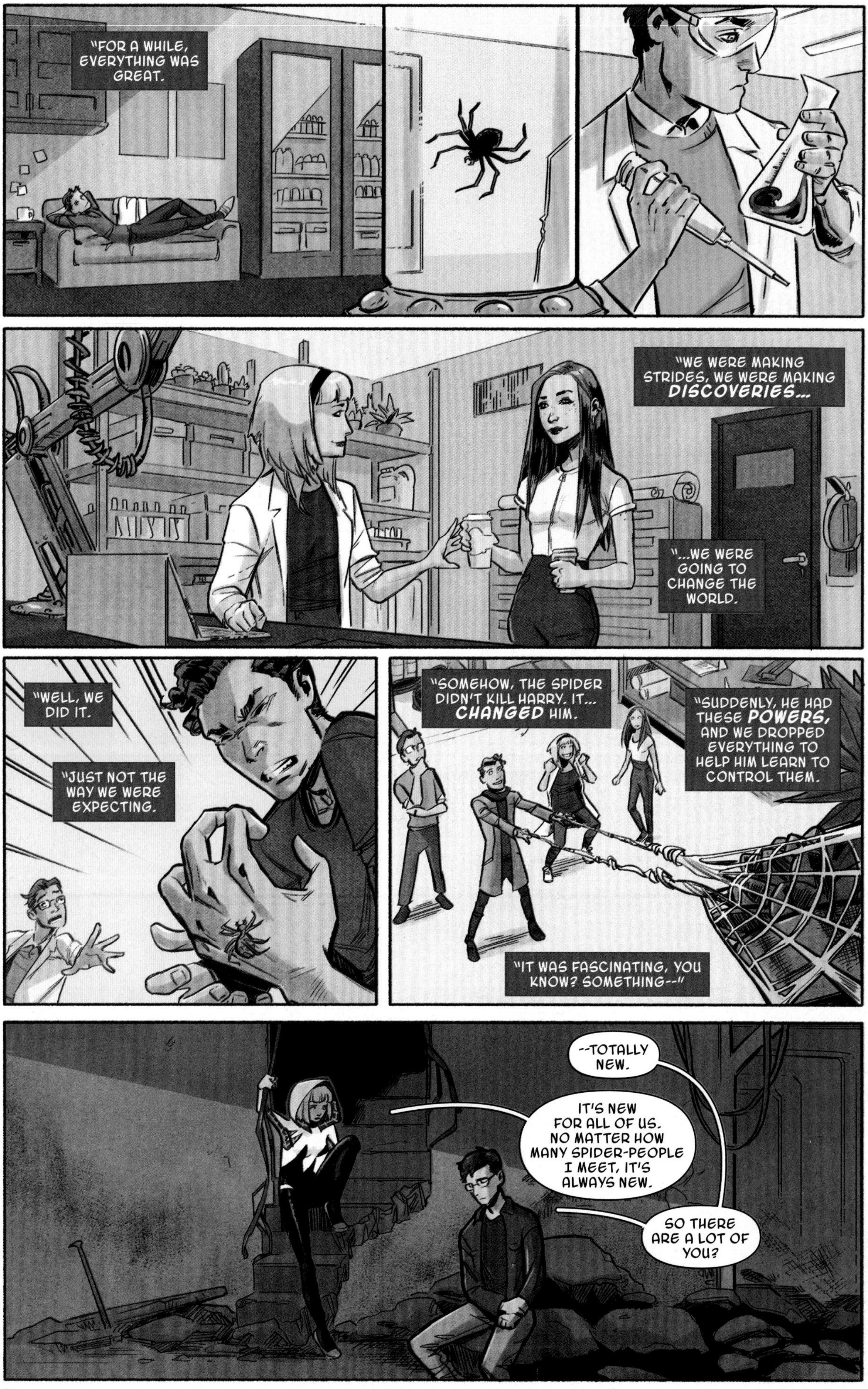
"FOR A WHILE, EVERYTHING WAS GREAT.
"WE WERE MAKING STRIDES, WE WERE MAKING DISCOVERIES...
"...WE WERE GOING TO CHANGE THE WORLD.
"WELL, WE DID IT.
"JUST NOT THE WAY WE WERE EXPECTING.
"SOMEHOW, THE SPIDER DIDN'T KILL HARRY. IT... CHANGED HIM.
"SUDDENLY, HE HAD THESE POWERS, AND WE DROPPED EVERYTHING TO HELP HIM LEARN TO CONTROL THEM.
"IT WAS FASCINATING, YOU KNOW? SOMETHING--"
--TOTALLY NEW.
IT'S NEW FOR ALL OF US. NO MATTER HOW MANY SPIDER-PEOPLE I MEET, IT'S ALWAYS NEW.
SO THERE ARE A LOT OF YOU?

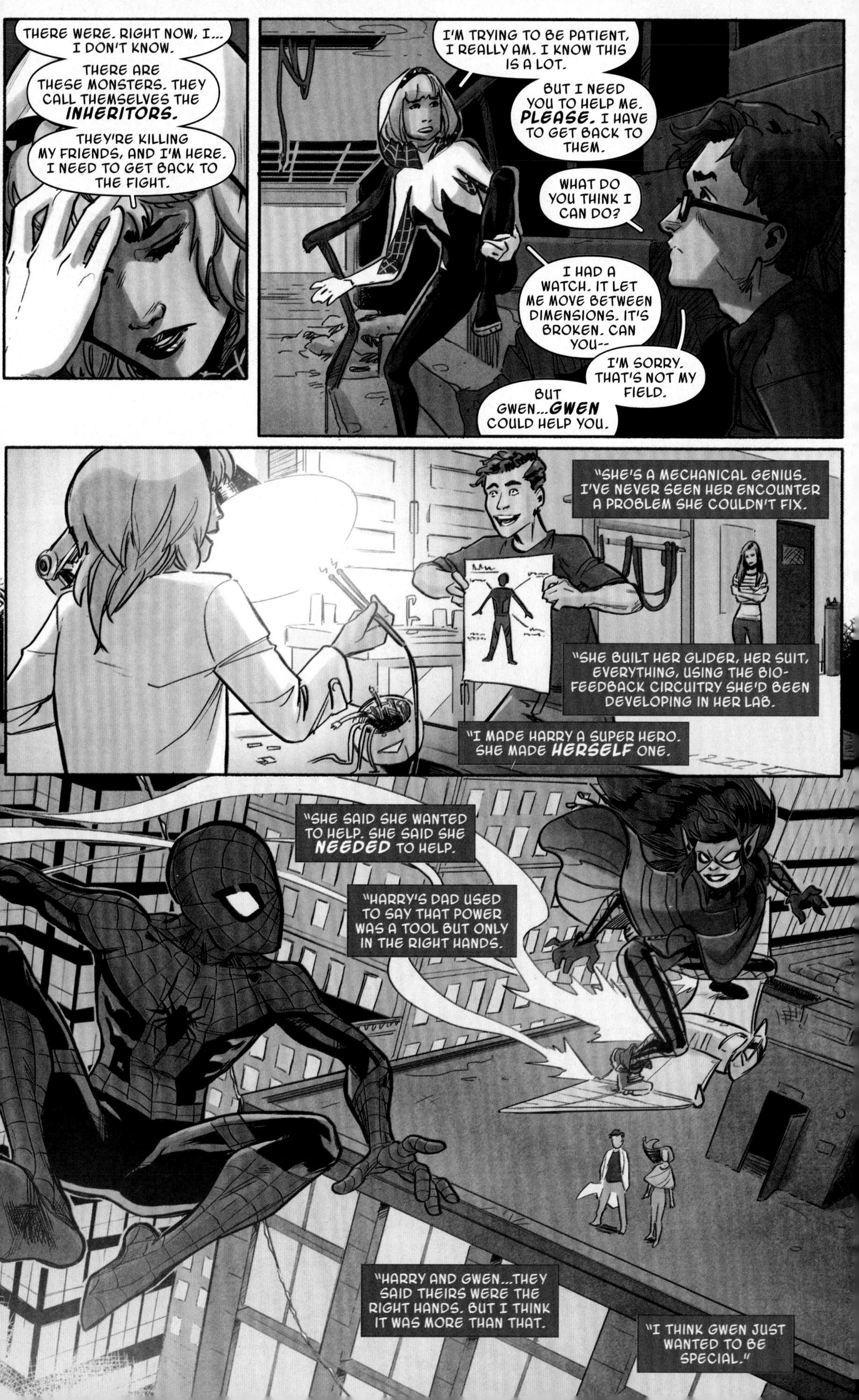
THERE WERE. RIGHT NOW, I... I DON'T KNOW.
THERE ARE THESE MONSTERS. THEY CALL THEMSELVES THE **INHERITORS.**
THEY'RE KILLING MY FRIENDS, AND I'M HERE. I NEED TO GET BACK TO THE FIGHT.
I'M TRYING TO BE PATIENT, I REALLY AM. I KNOW THIS IS A LOT.
BUT I NEED YOU TO HELP ME. **PLEASE.** I HAVE TO GET BACK TO THEM.
WHAT DO YOU THINK I CAN DO?
I HAD A WATCH. IT LET ME MOVE BETWEEN DIMENSIONS. IT'S BROKEN. CAN YOU--
I'M SORRY. THAT'S NOT MY FIELD.
BUT GWEN...**GWEN** COULD HELP YOU.
"SHE'S A MECHANICAL GENIUS. I'VE NEVER SEEN HER ENCOUNTER A PROBLEM SHE COULDN'T FIX.
"SHE BUILT HER GLIDER, HER SUIT, EVERYTHING, USING THE BIO-FEEDBACK CIRCUITRY SHE'D BEEN DEVELOPING IN HER LAB.
"I MADE HARRY A SUPER HERO. SHE MADE **HERSELF** ONE.
"SHE SAID SHE WANTED TO HELP. SHE SAID SHE **NEEDED** TO HELP.
"HARRY'S DAD USED TO SAY THAT POWER WAS A TOOL BUT ONLY IN THE RIGHT HANDS.
"HARRY AND GWEN...THEY SAID THEIRS WERE THE RIGHT HANDS. BUT I THINK IT WAS MORE THAN THAT.
"I THINK GWEN JUST WANTED TO BE SPECIAL."

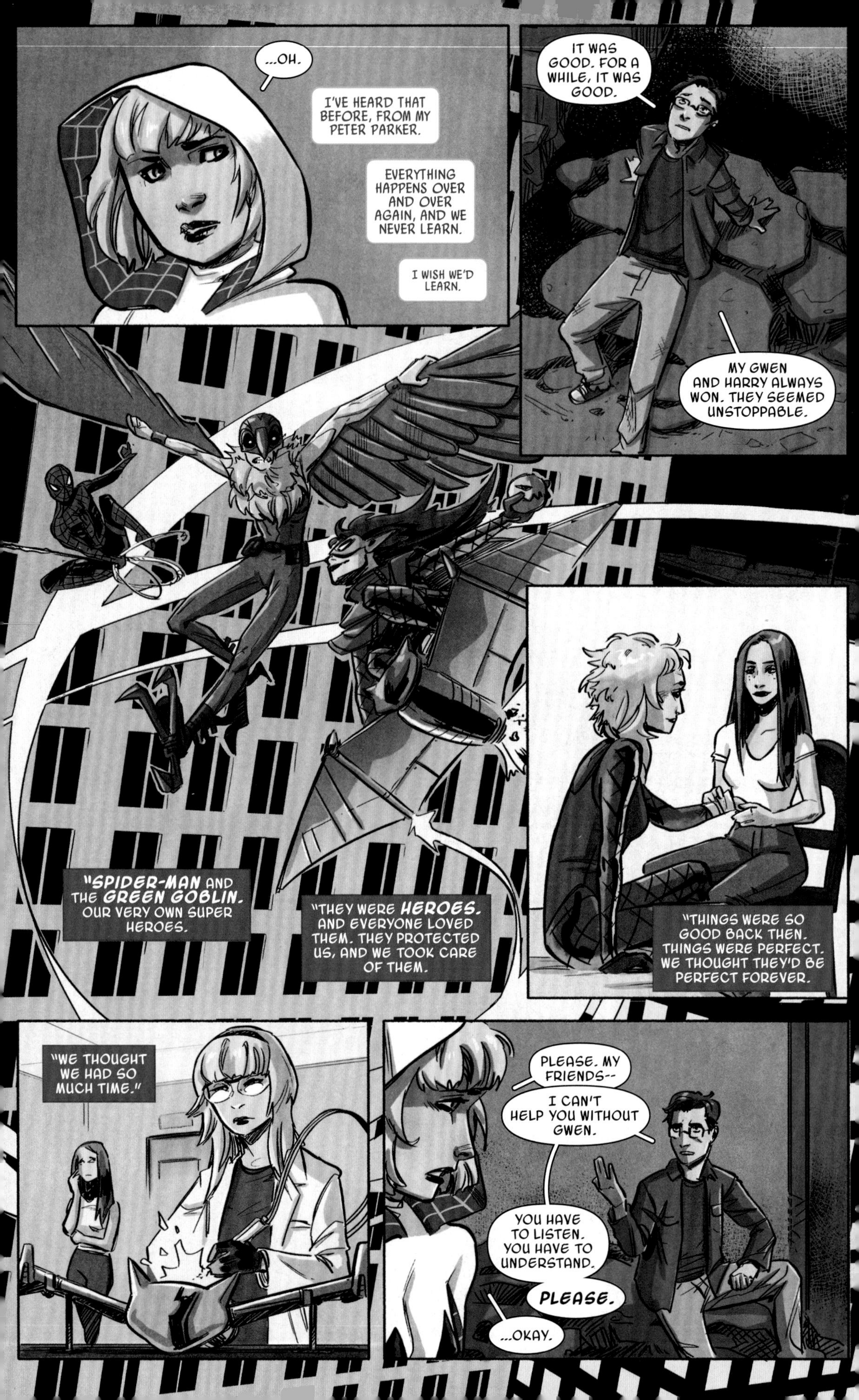
...OH.
I'VE HEARD THAT BEFORE, FROM MY PETER PARKER.
EVERYTHING HAPPENS OVER AND OVER AGAIN, AND WE NEVER LEARN.
I WISH WE'D LEARN.
IT WAS GOOD. FOR A WHILE, IT WAS GOOD.
MY GWEN AND HARRY ALWAYS WON. THEY SEEMED UNSTOPPABLE.
"SPIDER-MAN AND THE GREEN GOBLIN. OUR VERY OWN SUPER HEROES.
"THEY WERE HEROES. AND EVERYONE LOVED THEM. THEY PROTECTED US, AND WE TOOK CARE OF THEM.
"THINGS WERE SO GOOD BACK THEN. THINGS WERE PERFECT. WE THOUGHT THEY'D BE PERFECT FOREVER.
"WE THOUGHT WE HAD SO MUCH TIME."
PLEASE. MY FRIENDS--
I CAN'T HELP YOU WITHOUT GWEN.
YOU HAVE TO LISTEN. YOU HAVE TO UNDERSTAND.
PLEASE.
...OKAY.

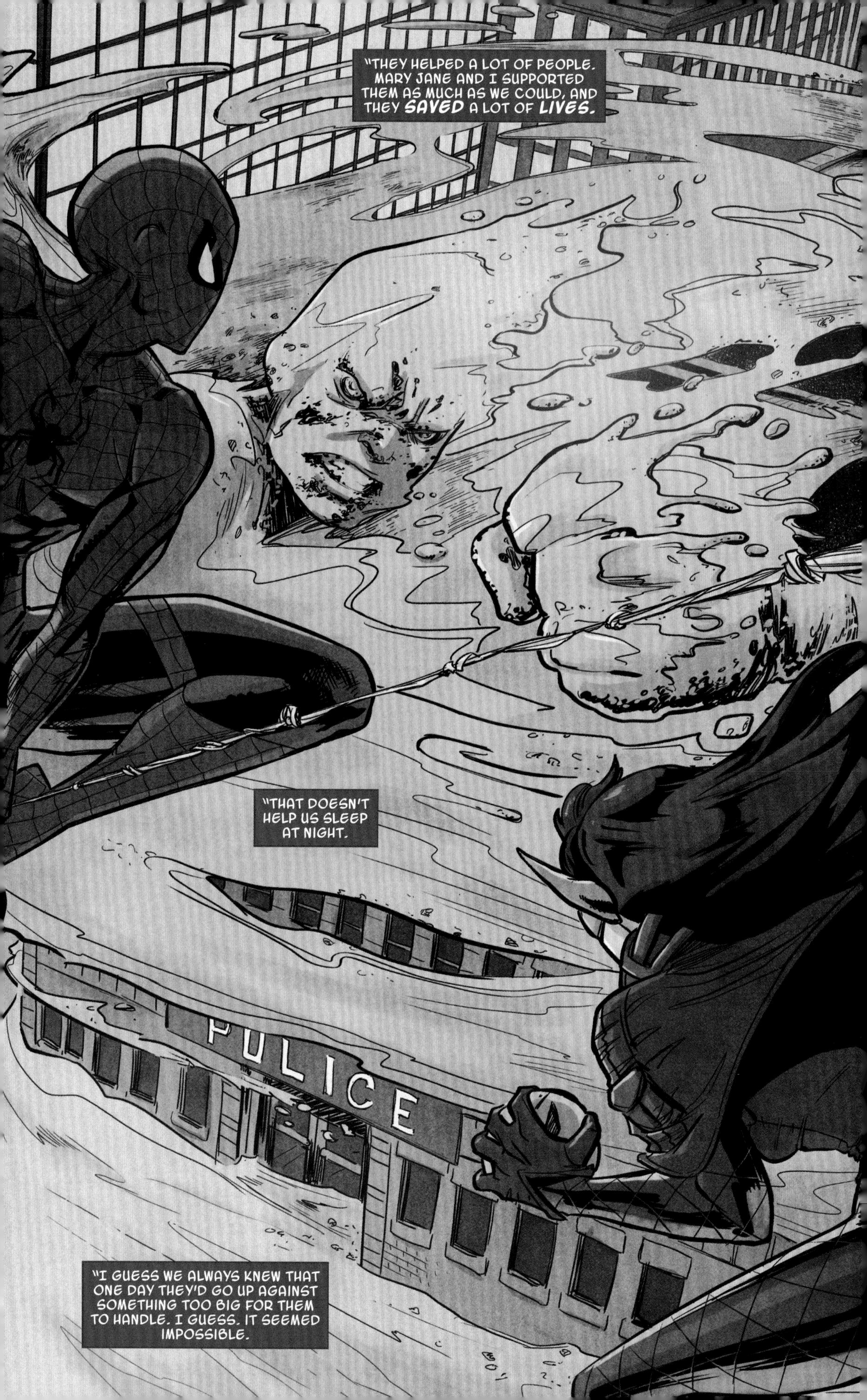
"THEY HELPED A LOT OF PEOPLE. MARY JANE AND I SUPPORTED THEM AS MUCH AS WE COULD, AND THEY SAVED A LOT OF LIVES.
"THAT DOESN'T HELP US SLEEP AT NIGHT.
POLICE
"I GUESS WE ALWAYS KNEW THAT ONE DAY THEY'D GO UP AGAINST SOMETHING TOO BIG FOR THEM TO HANDLE. I GUESS. IT SEEMED IMPOSSIBLE.

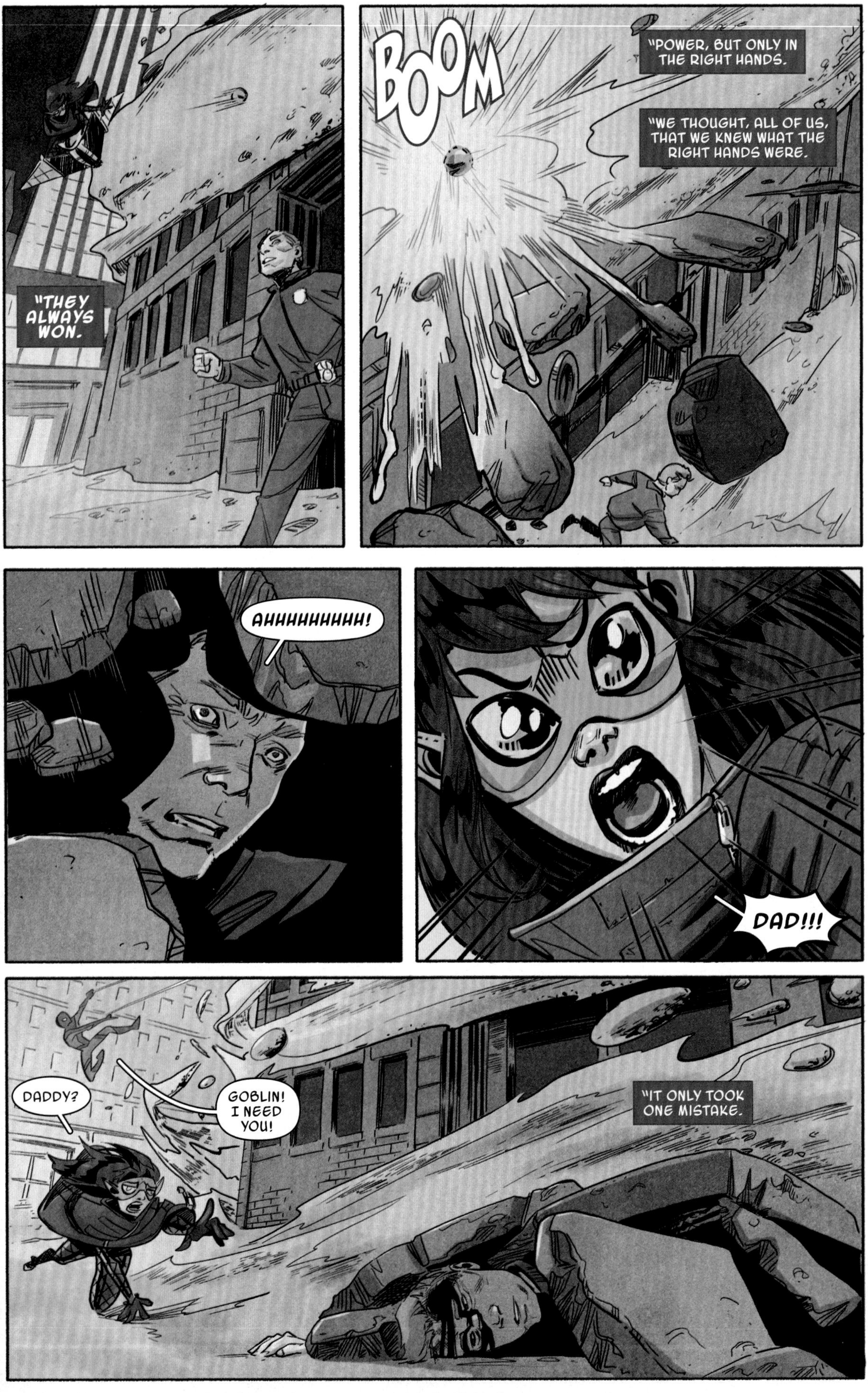
"THEY ALWAYS WON.
BOOM
"POWER, BUT ONLY IN THE RIGHT HANDS.
"WE THOUGHT, ALL OF US, THAT WE KNEW WHAT THE RIGHT HANDS WERE.
AHHHHHHHHH!
DAD!!!
DADDY?
GOBLIN! I NEED YOU!
"IT ONLY TOOK ONE MISTAKE.

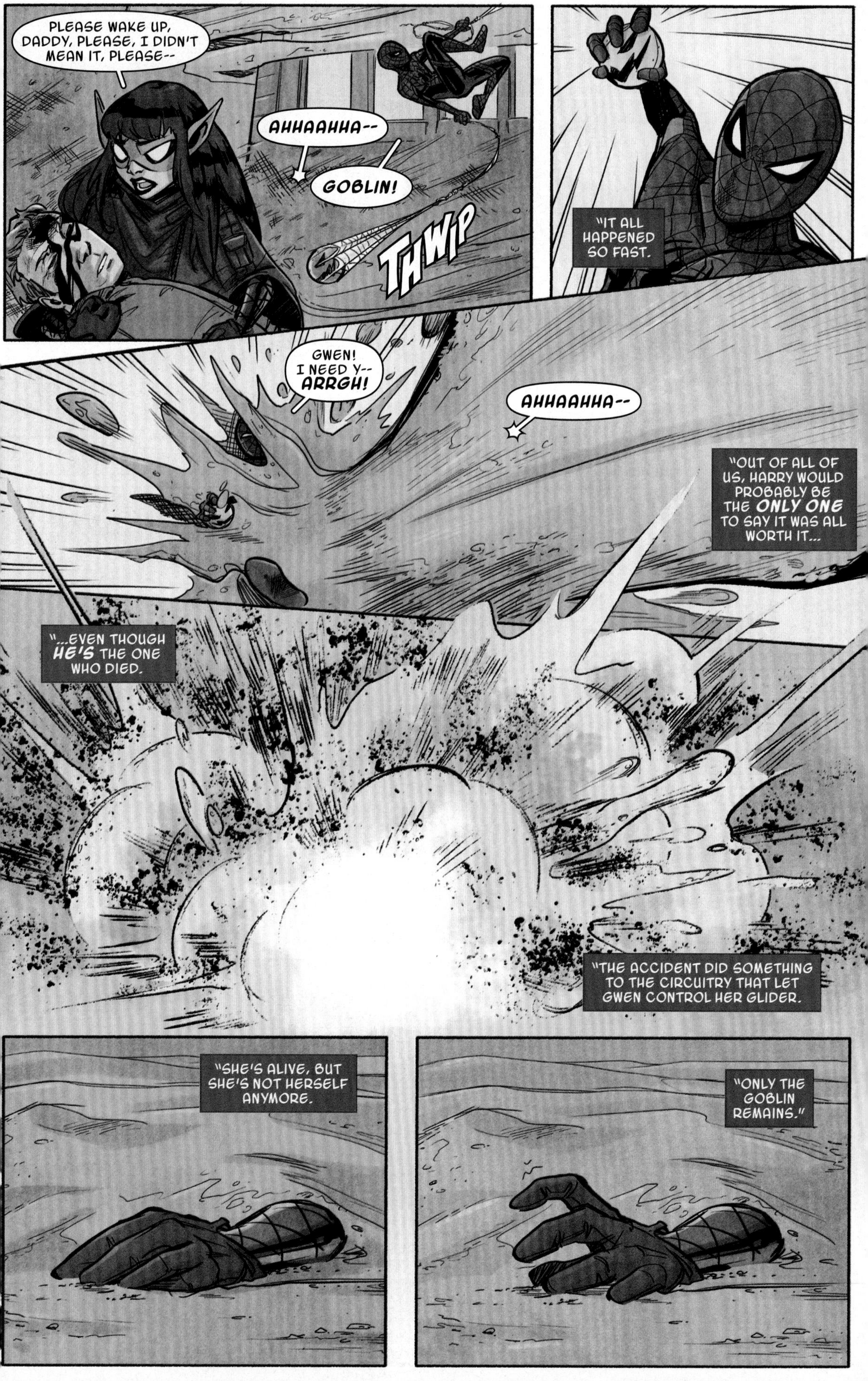
PLEASE WAKE UP, DADDY, PLEASE, I DIDN'T MEAN IT, PLEASE--
AHHAAHHA--
GOBLIN!
THWIP
"IT ALL HAPPENED SO FAST.
GWEN! I NEED Y-- ARRGH!
AHHAAHHA--
"OUT OF ALL OF US, HARRY WOULD PROBABLY BE THE ONLY ONE TO SAY IT WAS ALL WORTH IT...
"...EVEN THOUGH HE'S THE ONE WHO DIED.
"THE ACCIDENT DID SOMETHING TO THE CIRCUITRY THAT LET GWEN CONTROL HER GLIDER.
"SHE'S ALIVE, BUT SHE'S NOT HERSELF ANYMORE.
"ONLY THE GOBLIN REMAINS."

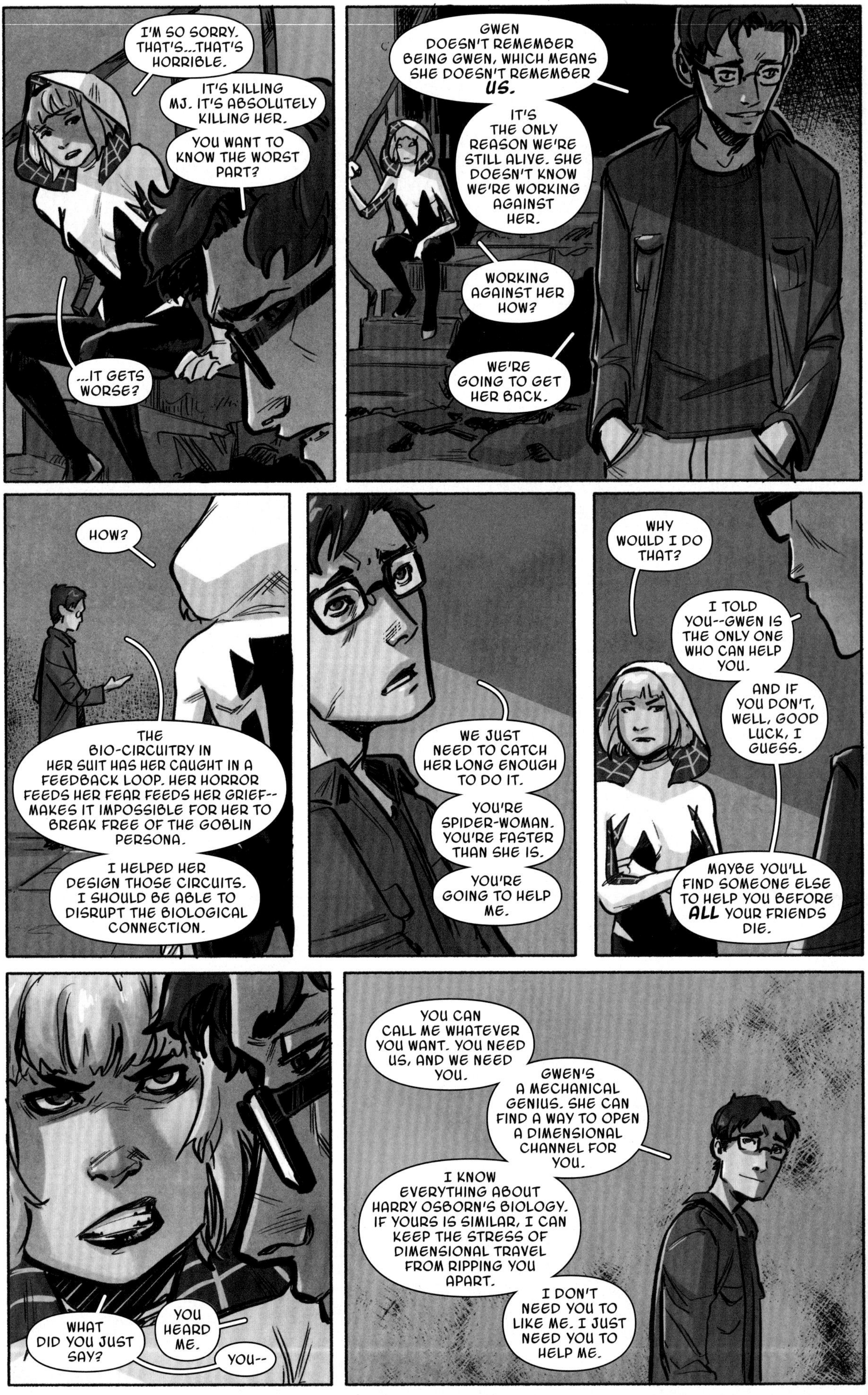
I'M SO SORRY. THAT'S...THAT'S HORRIBLE.
IT'S KILLING MJ. IT'S ABSOLUTELY KILLING HER.
YOU WANT TO KNOW THE WORST PART?
...IT GETS WORSE?
GWEN DOESN'T REMEMBER BEING GWEN, WHICH MEANS SHE DOESN'T REMEMBER US.
IT'S THE ONLY REASON WE'RE STILL ALIVE. SHE DOESN'T KNOW WE'RE WORKING AGAINST HER.
WORKING AGAINST HER HOW?
WE'RE GOING TO GET HER BACK.
HOW?
THE BIO-CIRCUITRY IN HER SUIT HAS HER CAUGHT IN A FEEDBACK LOOP. HER HORROR FEEDS HER FEAR FEEDS HER GRIEF--MAKES IT IMPOSSIBLE FOR HER TO BREAK FREE OF THE GOBLIN PERSONA.
I HELPED HER DESIGN THOSE CIRCUITS. I SHOULD BE ABLE TO DISRUPT THE BIOLOGICAL CONNECTION.
WE JUST NEED TO CATCH HER LONG ENOUGH TO DO IT.
YOU'RE SPIDER-WOMAN. YOU'RE FASTER THAN SHE IS.
YOU'RE GOING TO HELP ME.
WHY WOULD I DO THAT?
I TOLD YOU--GWEN IS THE ONLY ONE WHO CAN HELP YOU.
AND IF YOU DON'T, WELL, GOOD LUCK, I GUESS.
MAYBE YOU'LL FIND SOMEONE ELSE TO HELP YOU BEFORE ALL YOUR FRIENDS DIE.
WHAT DID YOU JUST SAY?
YOU HEARD ME.
YOU--
YOU CAN CALL ME WHATEVER YOU WANT. YOU NEED US, AND WE NEED YOU.
GWEN'S A MECHANICAL GENIUS. SHE CAN FIND A WAY TO OPEN A DIMENSIONAL CHANNEL FOR YOU.
I KNOW EVERYTHING ABOUT HARRY OSBORN'S BIOLOGY. IF YOURS IS SIMILAR, I CAN KEEP THE STRESS OF DIMENSIONAL TRAVEL FROM RIPPING YOU APART.
I DON'T NEED YOU TO LIKE ME. I JUST NEED YOU TO HELP ME.

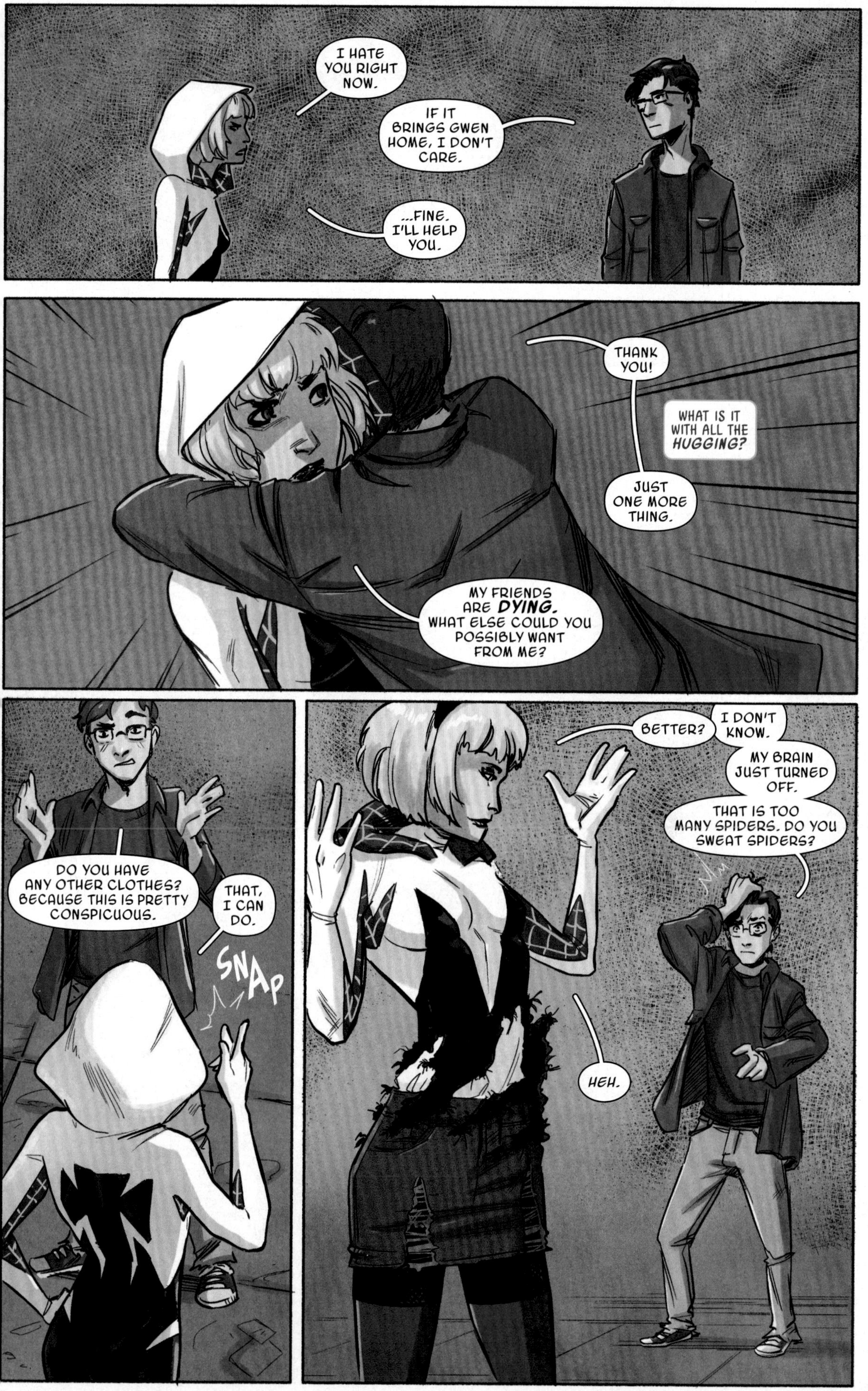
I HATE YOU RIGHT NOW.
IF IT BRINGS GWEN HOME, I DON'T CARE.
...FINE. I'LL HELP YOU.
THANK YOU!
WHAT IS IT WITH ALL THE HUGGING?
JUST ONE MORE THING.
MY FRIENDS ARE DYING. WHAT ELSE COULD YOU POSSIBLY WANT FROM ME?
DO YOU HAVE ANY OTHER CLOTHES? BECAUSE THIS IS PRETTY CONSPICUOUS.
THAT, I CAN DO.
SNAP
BETTER?
I DON'T KNOW.
MY BRAIN JUST TURNED OFF.
THAT IS TOO MANY SPIDERS. DO YOU SWEAT SPIDERS?
HEH.

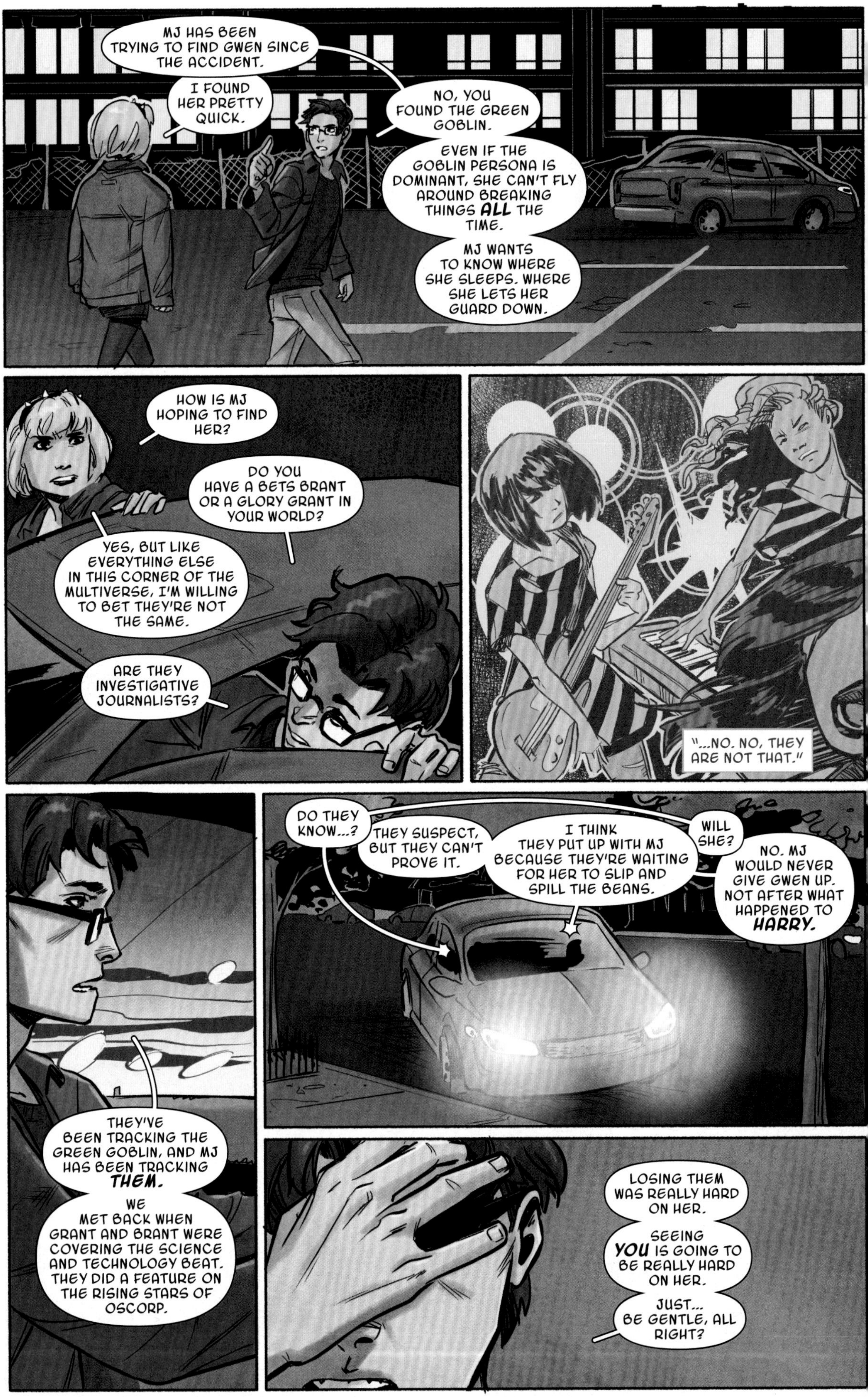
MJ HAS BEEN TRYING TO FIND GWEN SINCE THE ACCIDENT.
I FOUND HER PRETTY QUICK.
NO, YOU FOUND THE GREEN GOBLIN.
EVEN IF THE GOBLIN PERSONA IS DOMINANT, SHE CAN'T FLY AROUND BREAKING THINGS ALL THE TIME.
MJ WANTS TO KNOW WHERE SHE SLEEPS. WHERE SHE LETS HER GUARD DOWN.
HOW IS MJ HOPING TO FIND HER?
DO YOU HAVE A BETS BRANT OR A GLORY GRANT IN YOUR WORLD?
YES, BUT LIKE EVERYTHING ELSE IN THIS CORNER OF THE MULTIVERSE, I'M WILLING TO BET THEY'RE NOT THE SAME.
ARE THEY INVESTIGATIVE JOURNALISTS?
"...NO. NO, THEY ARE NOT THAT."
THEY'VE BEEN TRACKING THE GREEN GOBLIN, AND MJ HAS BEEN TRACKING THEM.
WE MET BACK WHEN GRANT AND BRANT WERE COVERING THE SCIENCE AND TECHNOLOGY BEAT. THEY DID A FEATURE ON THE RISING STARS OF OSCORP.
DO THEY KNOW...?
THEY SUSPECT, BUT THEY CAN'T PROVE IT.
I THINK THEY PUT UP WITH MJ BECAUSE THEY'RE WAITING FOR HER TO SLIP AND SPILL THE BEANS.
WILL SHE?
NO. MJ WOULD NEVER GIVE GWEN UP. NOT AFTER WHAT HAPPENED TO HARRY.
LOSING THEM WAS REALLY HARD ON HER.
SEEING YOU IS GOING TO BE REALLY HARD ON HER.
JUST... BE GENTLE, ALL RIGHT?

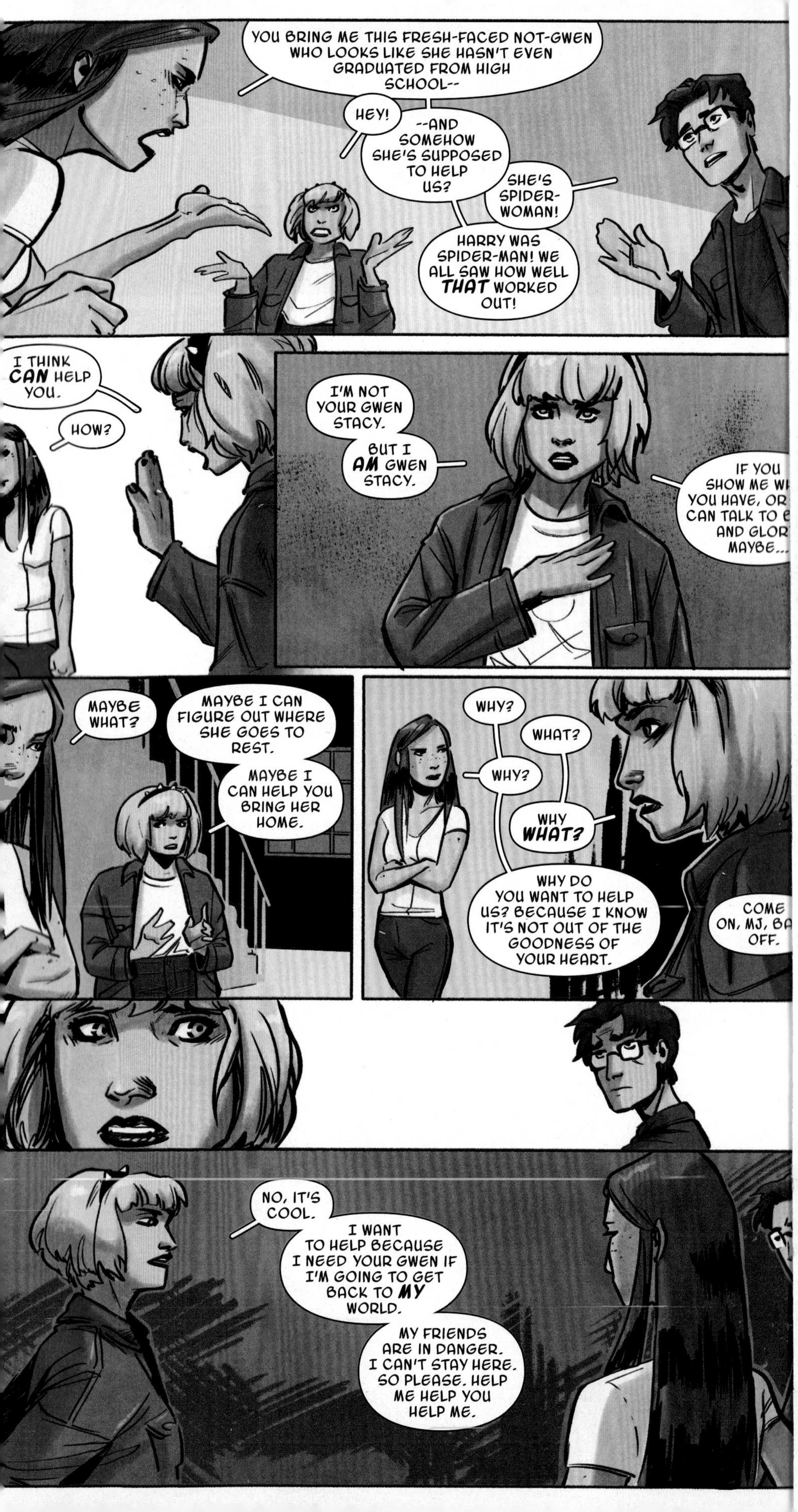
YOU BRING ME THIS FRESH-FACED NOT-GWEN WHO LOOKS LIKE SHE HASN'T EVEN GRADUATED FROM HIGH SCHOOL--
HEY!
--AND SOMEHOW SHE'S SUPPOSED TO HELP US?
SHE'S SPIDER-WOMAN!
HARRY WAS SPIDER-MAN! WE ALL SAW HOW WELL THAT WORKED OUT!
I THINK CAN HELP YOU.
HOW?
I'M NOT YOUR GWEN STACY.
BUT I AM GWEN STACY.
MAYBE WHAT?
MAYBE I CAN FIGURE OUT WHERE SHE GOES TO REST.
MAYBE I CAN HELP YOU BRING HER HOME.
WHY?
WHAT?
WHY?
WHY WHAT?
WHY DO YOU WANT TO HELP US? BECAUSE I KNOW IT'S NOT OUT OF THE GOODNESS OF YOUR HEART.
NO, IT'S COOL.
I WANT TO HELP BECAUSE I NEED YOUR GWEN IF I'M GOING TO GET BACK TO MY WORLD.
MY FRIENDS ARE IN DANGER. I CAN'T STAY HERE. SO PLEASE. HELP ME HELP YOU HELP ME.

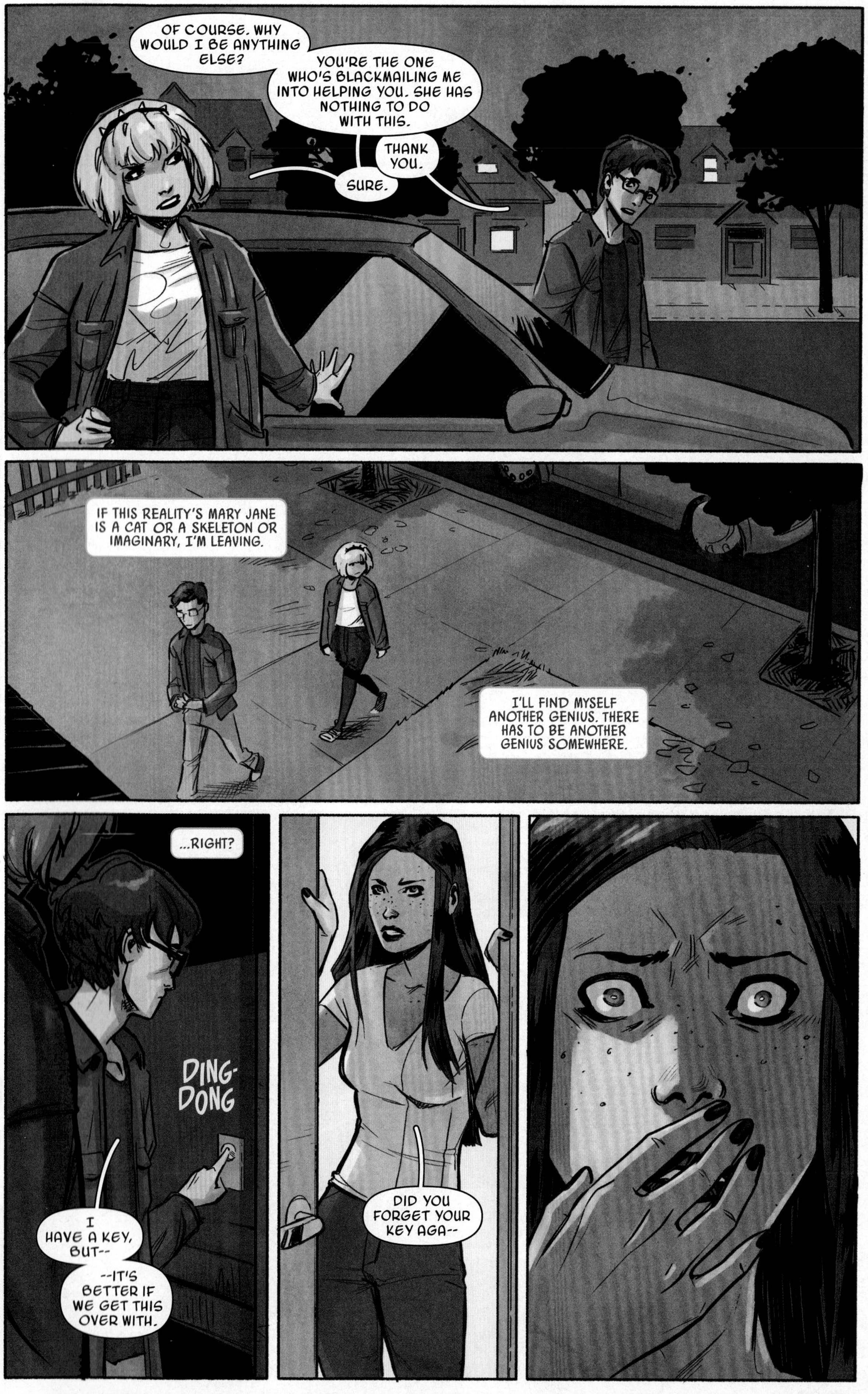
OF COURSE. WHY WOULD I BE ANYTHING ELSE?
YOU'RE THE ONE WHO'S BLACKMAILING ME INTO HELPING YOU. SHE HAS NOTHING TO DO WITH THIS.
THANK YOU.
SURE.
IF THIS REALITY'S MARY JANE IS A CAT OR A SKELETON OR IMAGINARY, I'M LEAVING.
I'LL FIND MYSELF ANOTHER GENIUS. THERE HAS TO BE ANOTHER GENIUS SOMEWHERE.
...RIGHT?
DING-DONG
I HAVE A KEY, BUT--
--IT'S BETTER IF WE GET THIS OVER WITH.
DID YOU FORGET YOUR KEY AGA--

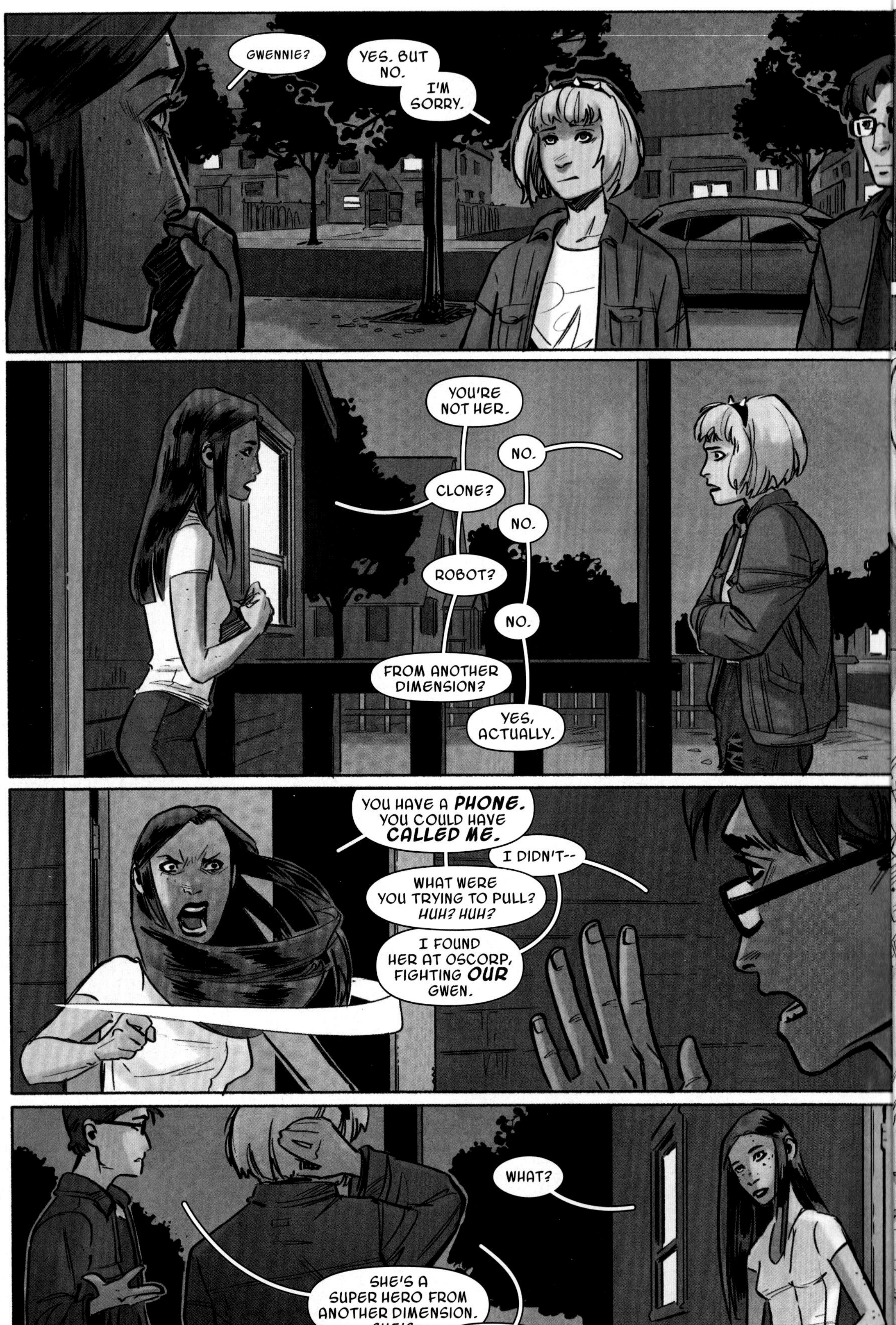
GWENNIE?
YES. BUT NO.
I'M SORRY.
YOU'RE NOT HER.
NO.
CLONE?
NO.
ROBOT?
NO.
FROM ANOTHER DIMENSION?
YES, ACTUALLY.
YOU HAVE A **PHONE.** YOU COULD HAVE **CALLED ME.**
I DIDN'T--
WHAT WERE YOU TRYING TO PULL? HUH? HUH?
I FOUND HER AT OSCORP, FIGHTING **OUR** GWEN.
WHAT?
SHE'S A SUPER HERO FROM ANOTHER DIMENSION. SHE'S--
I'M SPIDER-WOMAN.
MAYBE. I NEED A NEW CODE-NAME. BUT MOSTLY, YEAH.
SPIDER-WOMAN.

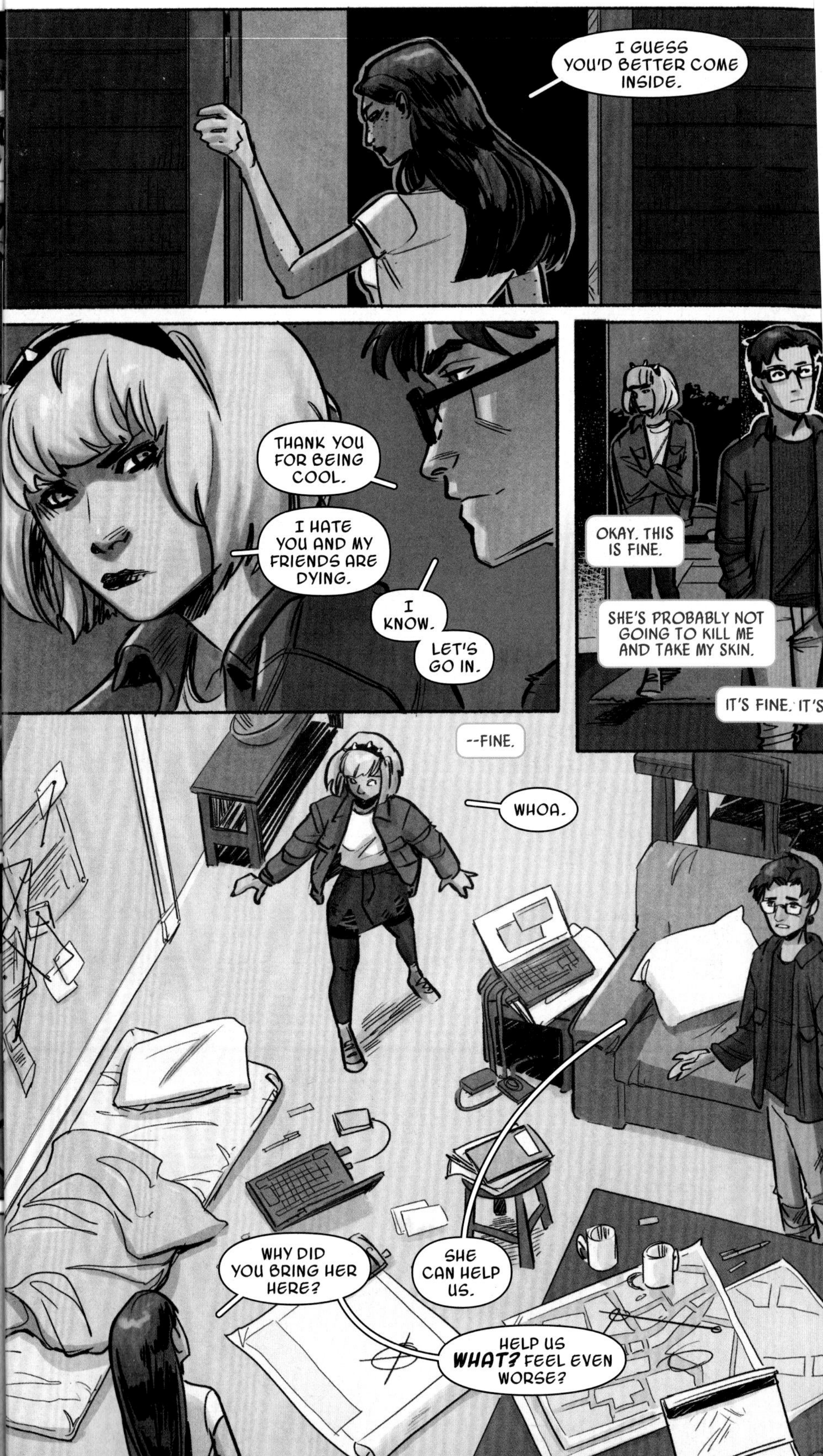
I GUESS YOU'D BETTER COME INSIDE.
THANK YOU FOR BEING COOL.
I HATE YOU AND MY FRIENDS ARE DYING.
I KNOW.
LET'S GO IN.
OKAY. THIS IS FINE.
SHE'S PROBABLY NOT GOING TO KILL ME AND TAKE MY SKIN.
IT'S FINE. IT'S--
--FINE.
WHOA.
WHY DID YOU BRING HER HERE?
SHE CAN HELP US.
HELP US **WHAT?** FEEL EVEN WORSE?

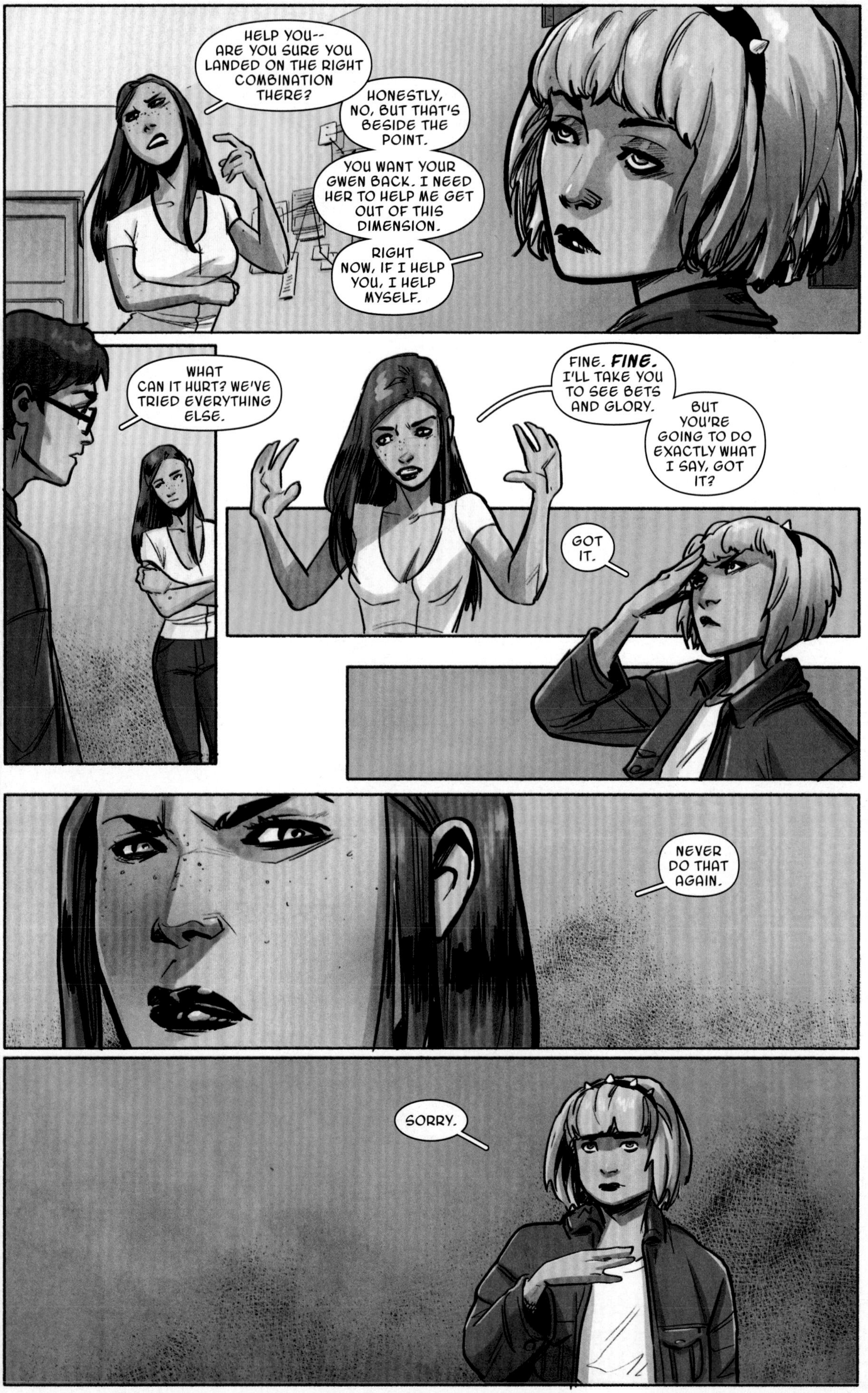
HELP YOU-- ARE YOU SURE YOU LANDED ON THE RIGHT COMBINATION THERE?
HONESTLY, NO, BUT THAT'S BESIDE THE POINT.
YOU WANT YOUR GWEN BACK. I NEED HER TO HELP ME GET OUT OF THIS DIMENSION.
RIGHT NOW, IF I HELP YOU, I HELP MYSELF.
WHAT CAN IT HURT? WE'VE TRIED EVERYTHING ELSE.
FINE. **FINE.** I'LL TAKE YOU TO SEE BETS AND GLORY.
BUT YOU'RE GOING TO DO EXACTLY WHAT I SAY, GOT IT?
GOT IT.
NEVER DO THAT AGAIN.
SORRY.

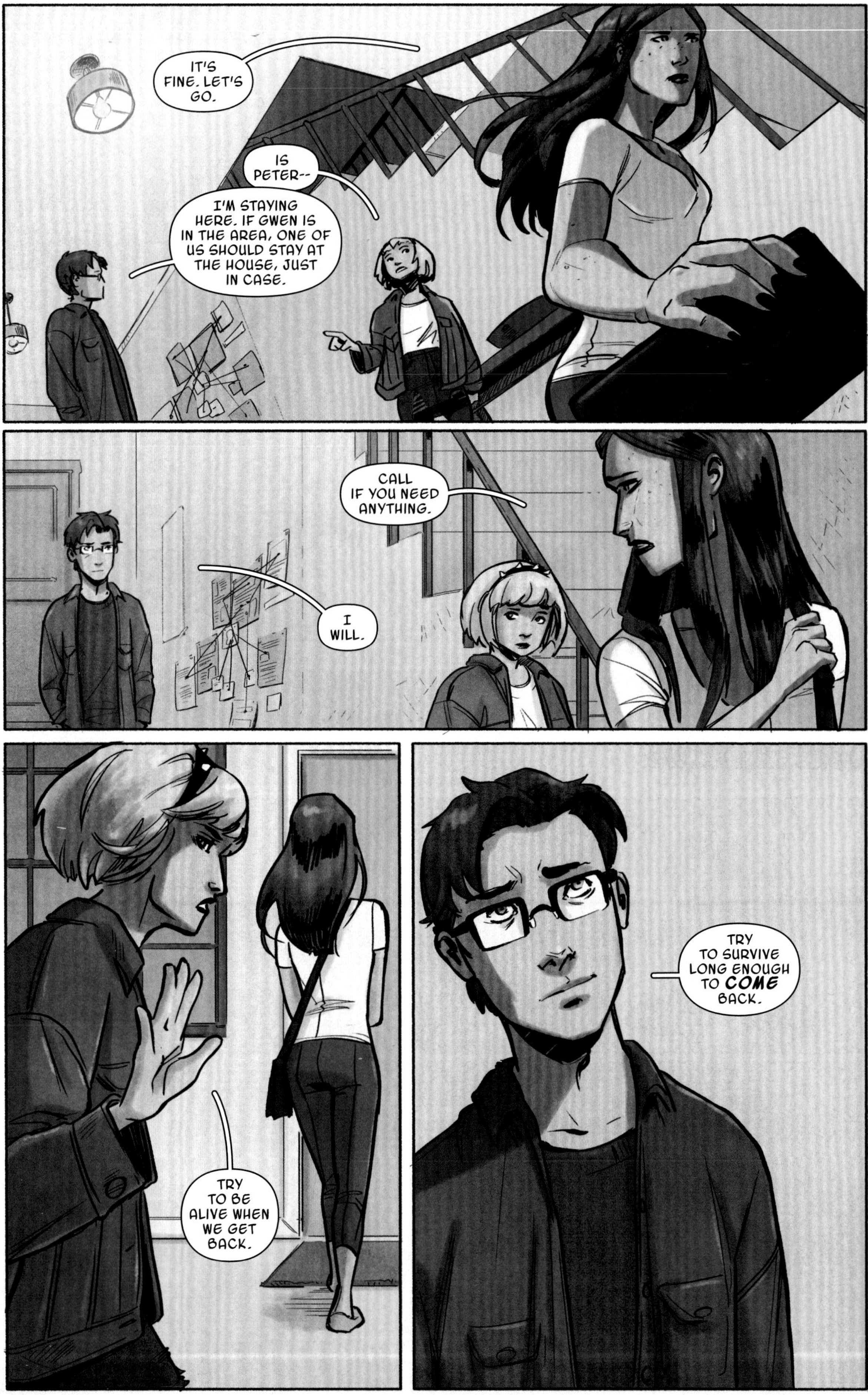
IT'S FINE. LET'S GO.
IS PETER--
I'M STAYING HERE. IF GWEN IS IN THE AREA, ONE OF US SHOULD STAY AT THE HOUSE, JUST IN CASE.
CALL IF YOU NEED ANYTHING.
I WILL.
TRY TO BE ALIVE WHEN WE GET BACK.
TRY TO SURVIVE LONG ENOUGH TO COME BACK.

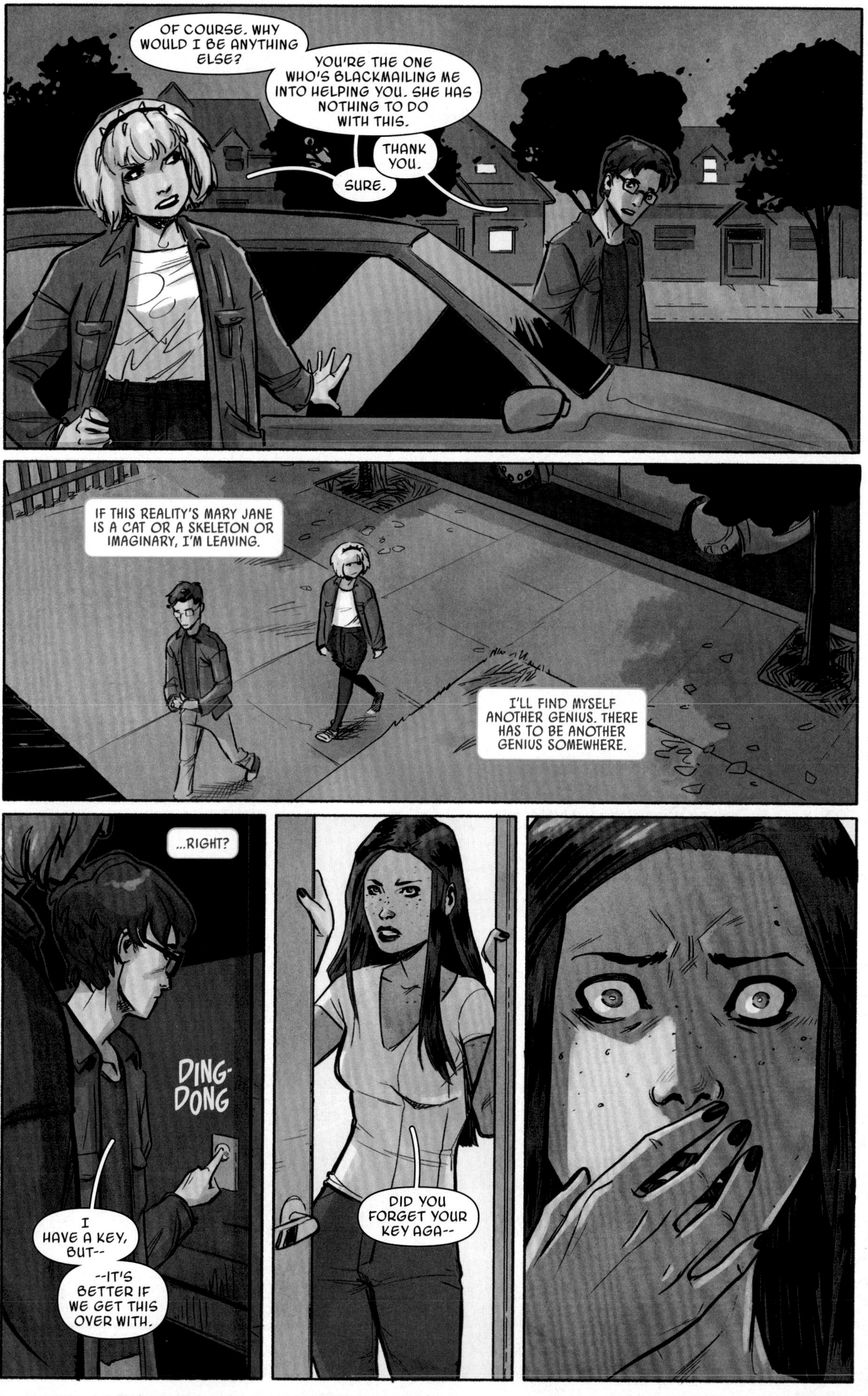
OF COURSE. WHY WOULD I BE ANYTHING ELSE?
YOU'RE THE ONE WHO'S BLACKMAILING ME INTO HELPING YOU. SHE HAS NOTHING TO DO WITH THIS.
THANK YOU.
SURE.
IF THIS REALITY'S MARY JANE IS A CAT OR A SKELETON OR IMAGINARY, I'M LEAVING.
I'LL FIND MYSELF ANOTHER GENIUS. THERE HAS TO BE ANOTHER GENIUS SOMEWHERE.
...RIGHT?
DING-DONG
I HAVE A KEY, BUT--
--IT'S BETTER IF WE GET THIS OVER WITH.
DID YOU FORGET YOUR KEY AGA--

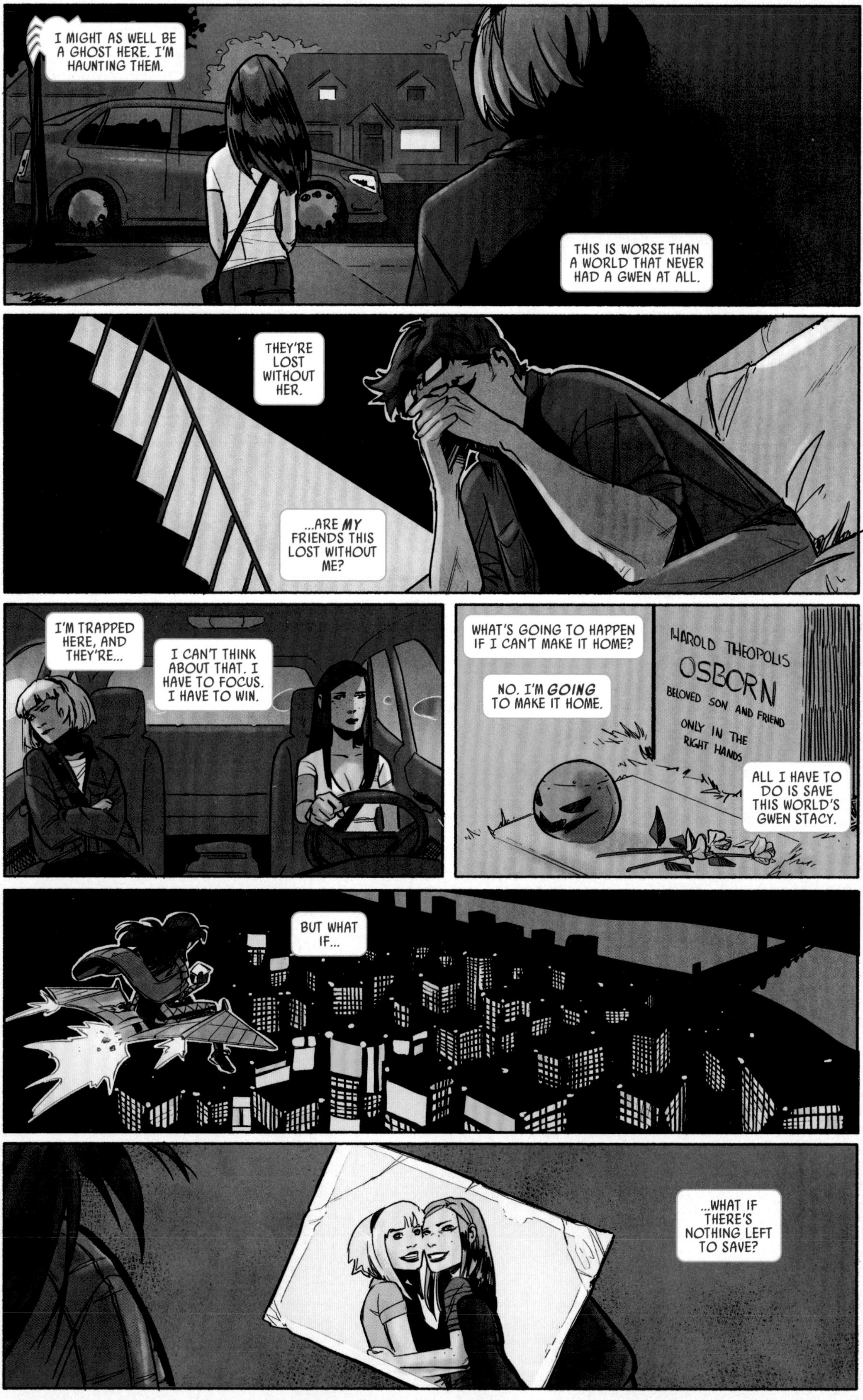
I MIGHT AS WELL BE A GHOST HERE. I'M HAUNTING THEM.
THIS IS WORSE THAN A WORLD THAT NEVER HAD A GWEN AT ALL.
THEY'RE LOST WITHOUT HER.
...ARE MY FRIENDS THIS LOST WITHOUT ME?
I'M TRAPPED HERE, AND THEY'RE...
I CAN'T THINK ABOUT THAT. I HAVE TO FOCUS. I HAVE TO WIN.
WHAT'S GOING TO HAPPEN IF I CAN'T MAKE IT HOME?
HAROLD THEOPOLIS OSBORN BELOVED SON AND FRIEND ONLY IN THE RIGHT HANDS
NO. I'M GOING TO MAKE IT HOME.
ALL I HAVE TO DO IS SAVE THIS WORLD'S GWEN STACY.
BUT WHAT IF...
...WHAT IF THERE'S NOTHING LEFT TO SAVE?

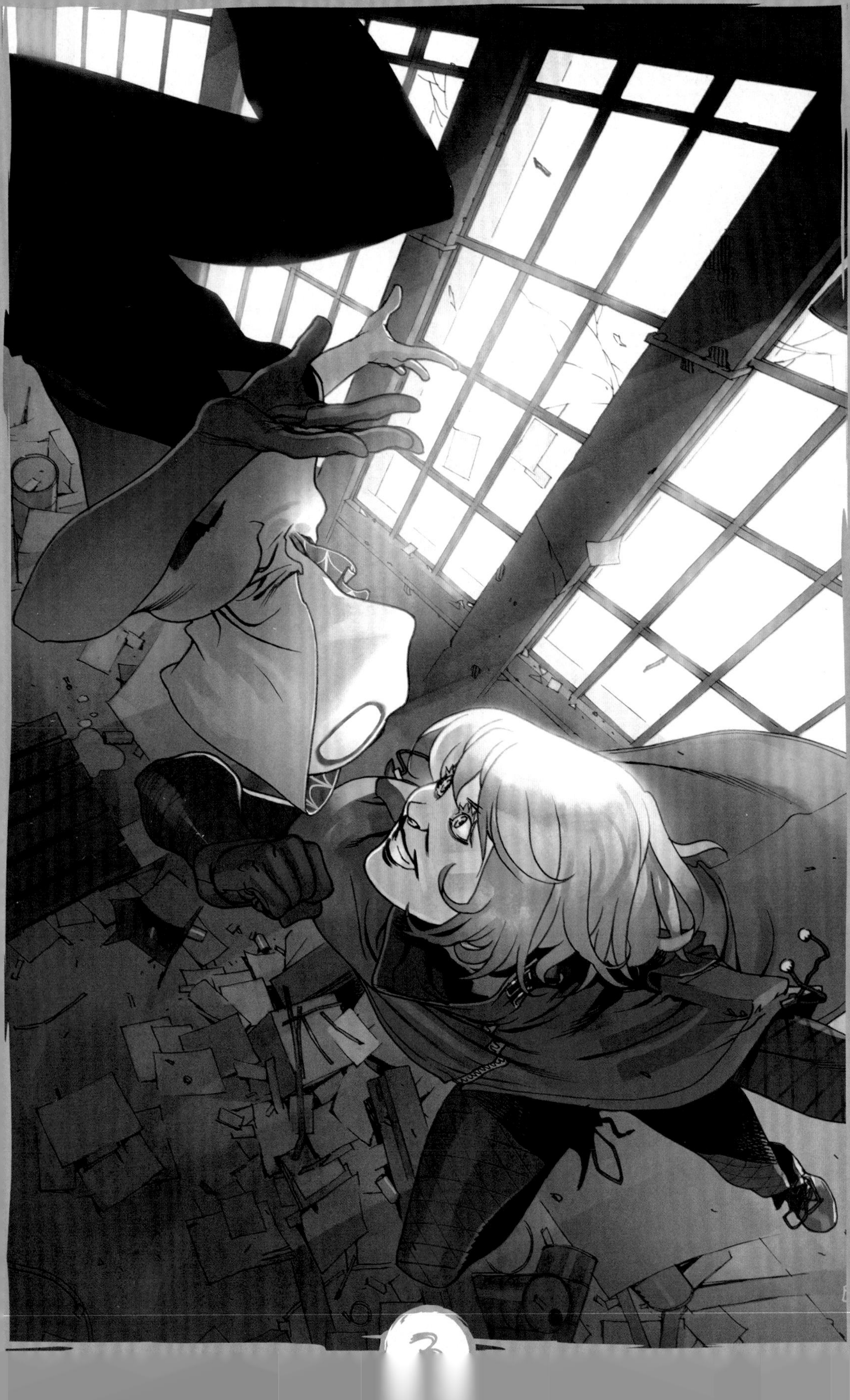

3

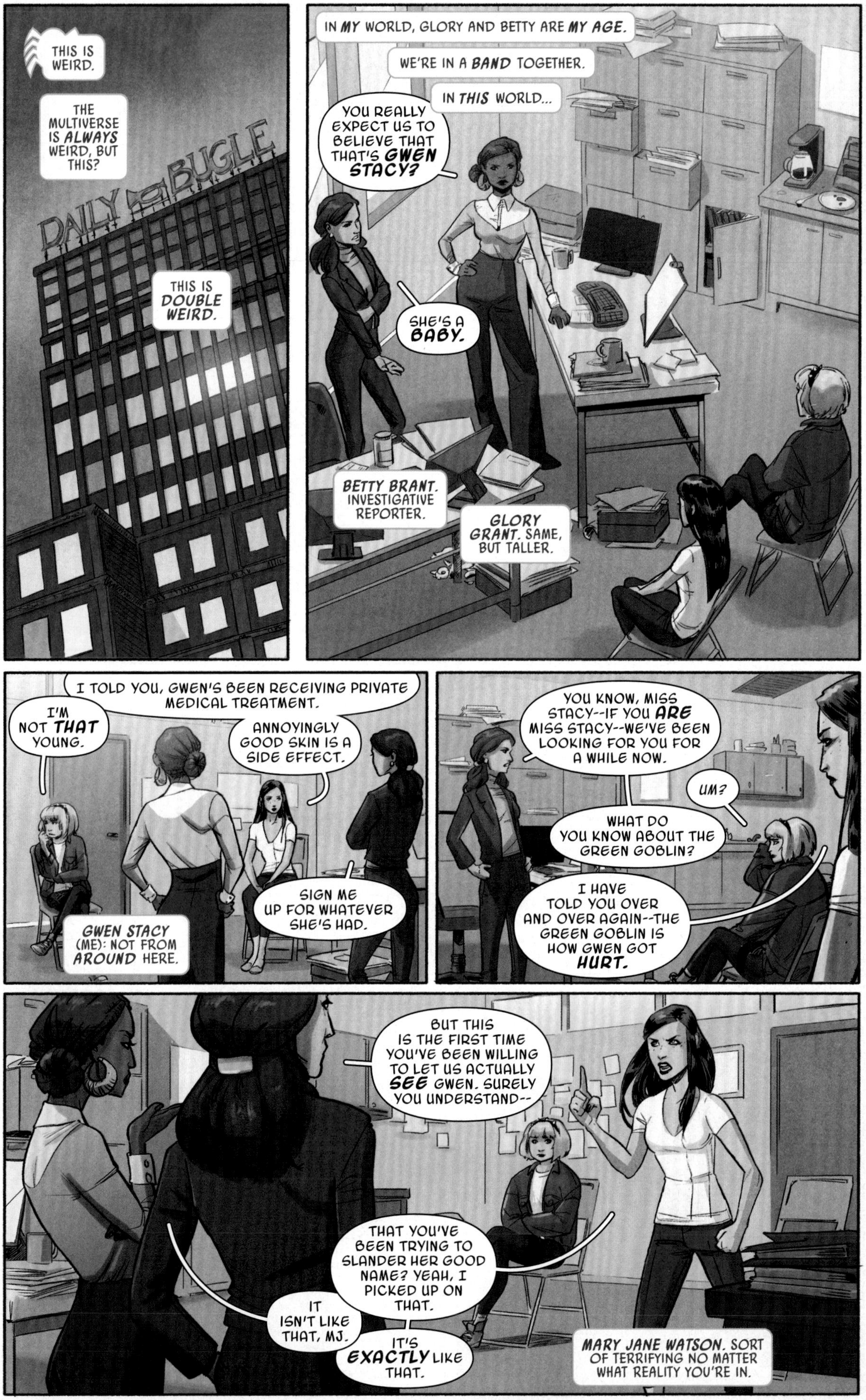

THIS IS WEIRD.
THE MULTIVERSE IS ALWAYS WEIRD, BUT THIS?
DAILY BUGLE
THIS IS DOUBLE WEIRD.
IN MY WORLD, GLORY AND BETTY ARE MY AGE.
WE'RE IN A BAND TOGETHER.
IN THIS WORLD...
YOU REALLY EXPECT US TO BELIEVE THAT THAT'S GWEN STACY?
SHE'S A BABY.
BETTY BRANT. INVESTIGATIVE REPORTER.
GLORY GRANT. SAME, BUT TALLER.
I TOLD YOU, GWEN'S BEEN RECEIVING PRIVATE MEDICAL TREATMENT.
I'M NOT THAT YOUNG.
ANNOYINGLY GOOD SKIN IS A SIDE EFFECT.
SIGN ME UP FOR WHATEVER SHE'S HAD.
GWEN STACY (ME): NOT FROM AROUND HERE.
YOU KNOW, MISS STACY--IF YOU ARE MISS STACY--WE'VE BEEN LOOKING FOR YOU FOR A WHILE NOW.
UM?
WHAT DO YOU KNOW ABOUT THE GREEN GOBLIN?
I HAVE TOLD YOU OVER AND OVER AGAIN--THE GREEN GOBLIN IS HOW GWEN GOT HURT.
BUT THIS IS THE FIRST TIME YOU'VE BEEN WILLING TO LET US ACTUALLY SEE GWEN. SURELY YOU UNDERSTAND--
THAT YOU'VE BEEN TRYING TO SLANDER HER GOOD NAME? YEAH, I PICKED UP ON THAT.
IT ISN'T LIKE THAT, MJ.
IT'S EXACTLY LIKE THAT.
MARY JANE WATSON. SORT OF TERRIFYING NO MATTER WHAT REALITY YOU'RE IN.

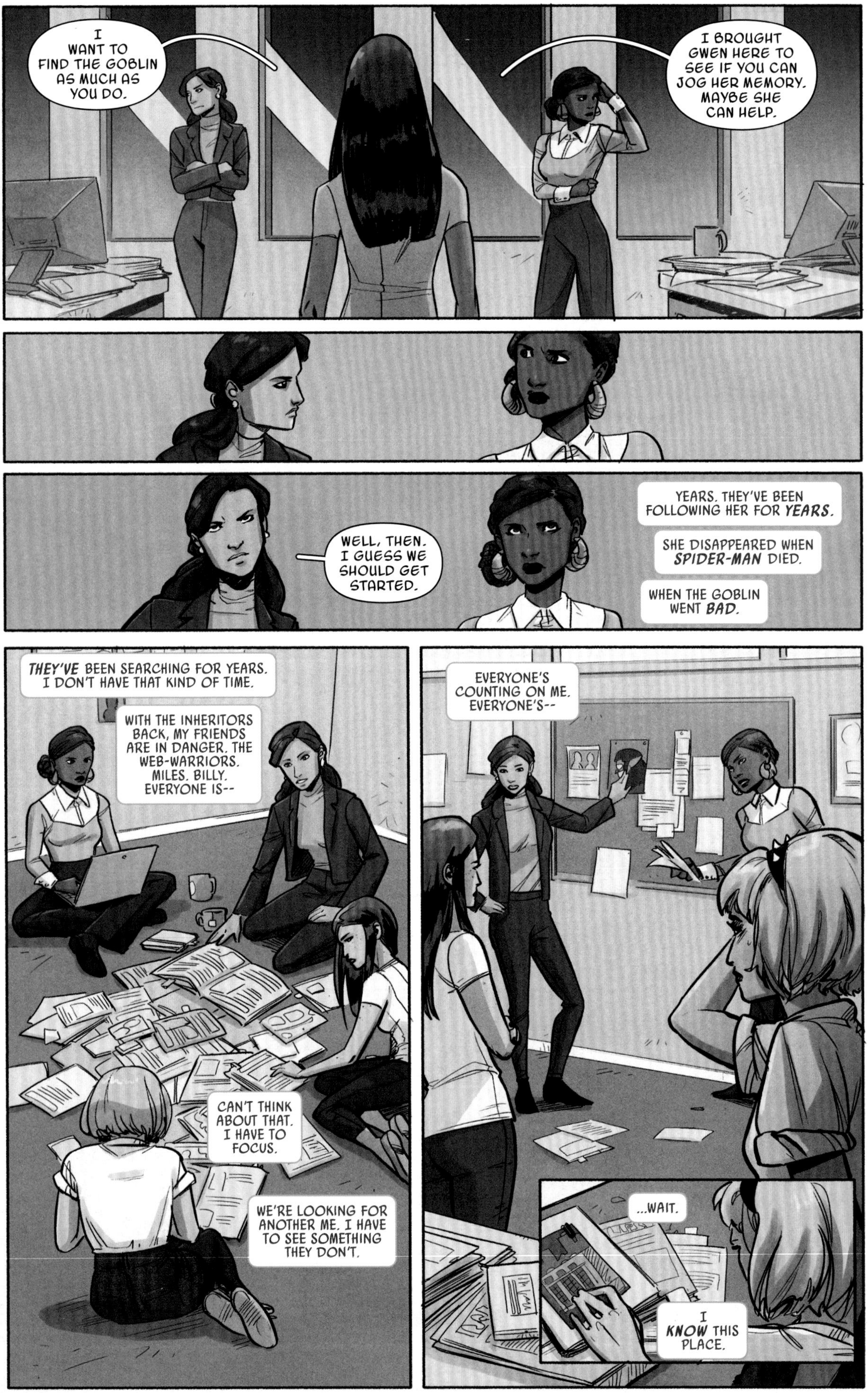
I WANT TO FIND THE GOBLIN AS MUCH AS YOU DO.
I BROUGHT GWEN HERE TO SEE IF YOU CAN JOG HER MEMORY. MAYBE SHE CAN HELP.
WELL, THEN. I GUESS WE SHOULD GET STARTED.
YEARS. THEY'VE BEEN FOLLOWING HER FOR YEARS.
SHE DISAPPEARED WHEN SPIDER-MAN DIED.
WHEN THE GOBLIN WENT BAD.
THEY'VE BEEN SEARCHING FOR YEARS. I DON'T HAVE THAT KIND OF TIME.
WITH THE INHERITORS BACK, MY FRIENDS ARE IN DANGER. THE WEB-WARRIORS. MILES. BILLY. EVERYONE IS--
CAN'T THINK ABOUT THAT. I HAVE TO FOCUS.
WE'RE LOOKING FOR ANOTHER ME. I HAVE TO SEE SOMETHING THEY DON'T.
EVERYONE'S COUNTING ON ME. EVERYONE'S--
...WAIT.
I KNOW THIS PLACE.

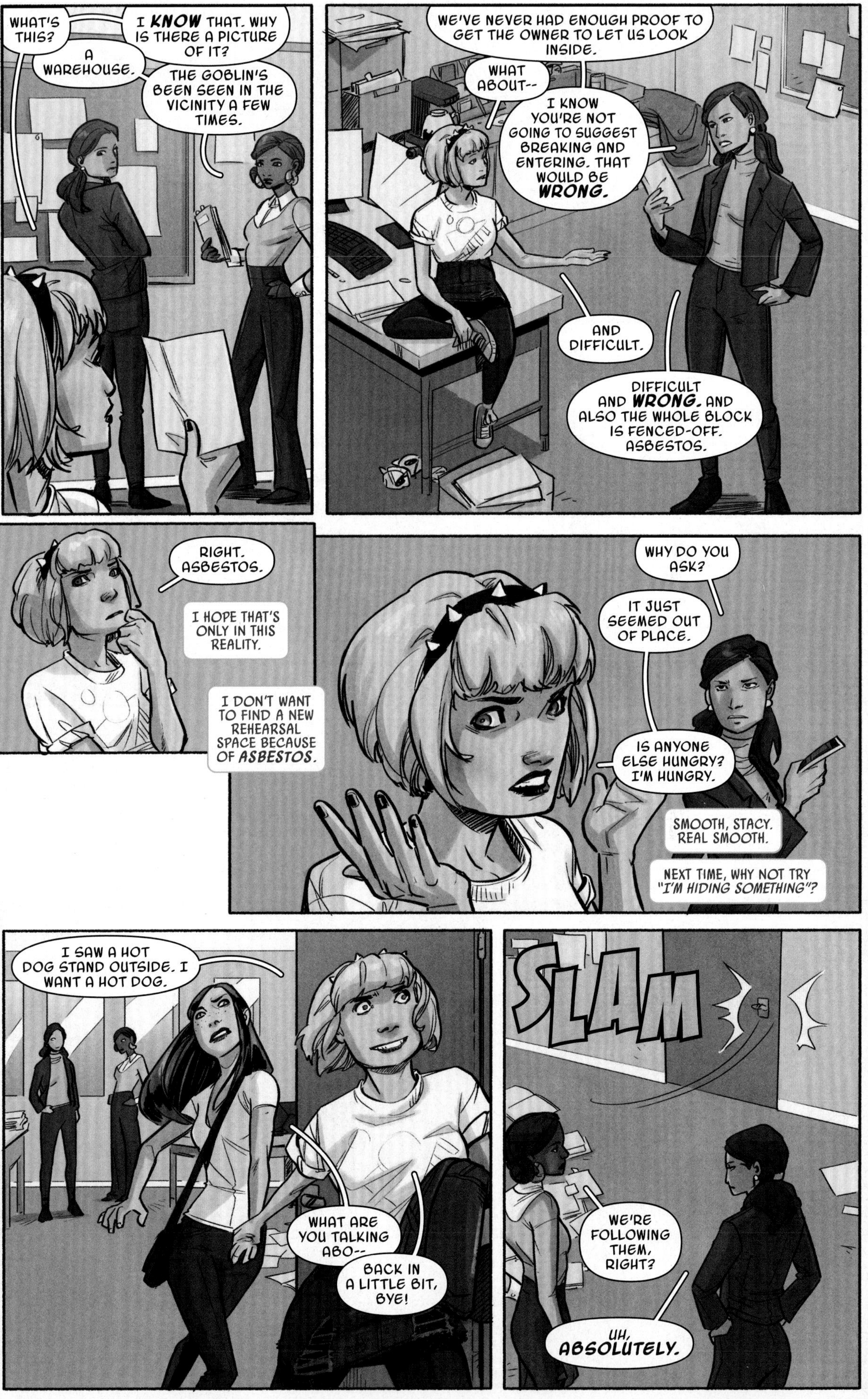
WHAT'S THIS?
A WAREHOUSE.
I KNOW THAT. WHY IS THERE A PICTURE OF IT?
THE GOBLIN'S BEEN SEEN IN THE VICINITY A FEW TIMES.
WE'VE NEVER HAD ENOUGH PROOF TO GET THE OWNER TO LET US LOOK INSIDE.
WHAT ABOUT--
I KNOW YOU'RE NOT GOING TO SUGGEST BREAKING AND ENTERING. THAT WOULD BE WRONG.
AND DIFFICULT.
DIFFICULT AND WRONG. AND ALSO THE WHOLE BLOCK IS FENCED-OFF. ASBESTOS.
RIGHT. ASBESTOS.
I HOPE THAT'S ONLY IN THIS REALITY.
I DON'T WANT TO FIND A NEW REHEARSAL SPACE BECAUSE OF ASBESTOS.
WHY DO YOU ASK?
IT JUST SEEMED OUT OF PLACE.
IS ANYONE ELSE HUNGRY? I'M HUNGRY.
SMOOTH, STACY. REAL SMOOTH.
NEXT TIME, WHY NOT TRY "I'M HIDING SOMETHING"?
I SAW A HOT DOG STAND OUTSIDE. I WANT A HOT DOG.
WHAT ARE YOU TALKING ABO--
BACK IN A LITTLE BIT, BYE!
SLAM
WE'RE FOLLOWING THEM, RIGHT?
UH, ABSOLUTELY.

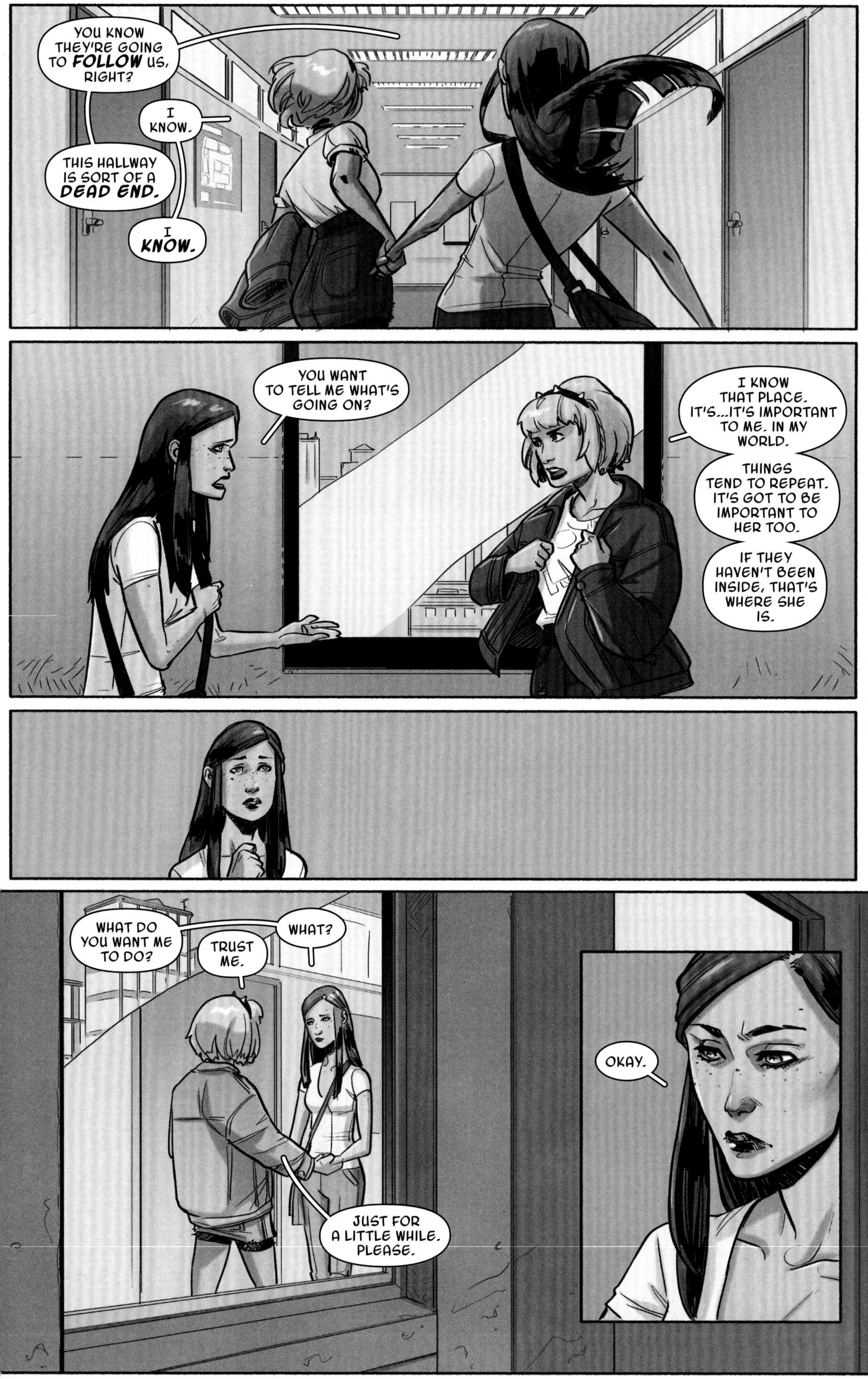
YOU KNOW THEY'RE GOING TO FOLLOW US, RIGHT?
I KNOW.
THIS HALLWAY IS SORT OF A DEAD END.
I KNOW.
YOU WANT TO TELL ME WHAT'S GOING ON?
I KNOW THAT PLACE. IT'S...IT'S IMPORTANT TO ME. IN MY WORLD.
THINGS TEND TO REPEAT. IT'S GOT TO BE IMPORTANT TO HER TOO.
IF THEY HAVEN'T BEEN INSIDE, THAT'S WHERE SHE IS.
WHAT DO YOU WANT ME TO DO?
TRUST ME.
WHAT?
JUST FOR A LITTLE WHILE. PLEASE.
OKAY.

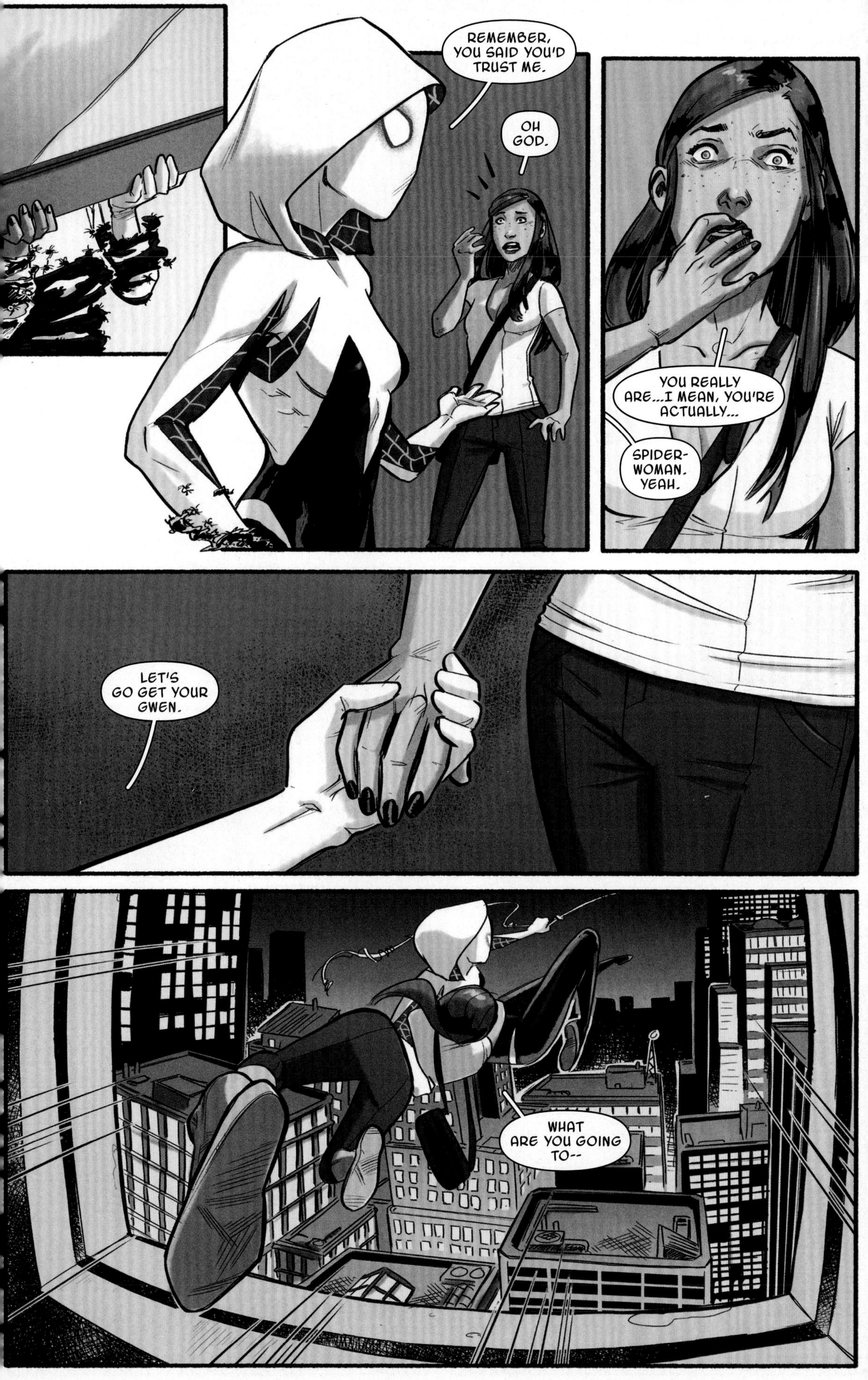
REMEMBER, YOU SAID YOU'D TRUST ME.
OH GOD.
YOU REALLY ARE...I MEAN, YOU'RE ACTUALLY...
SPIDER-WOMAN. YEAH.
LET'S GO GET YOUR GWEN.
WHAT ARE YOU GOING TO--

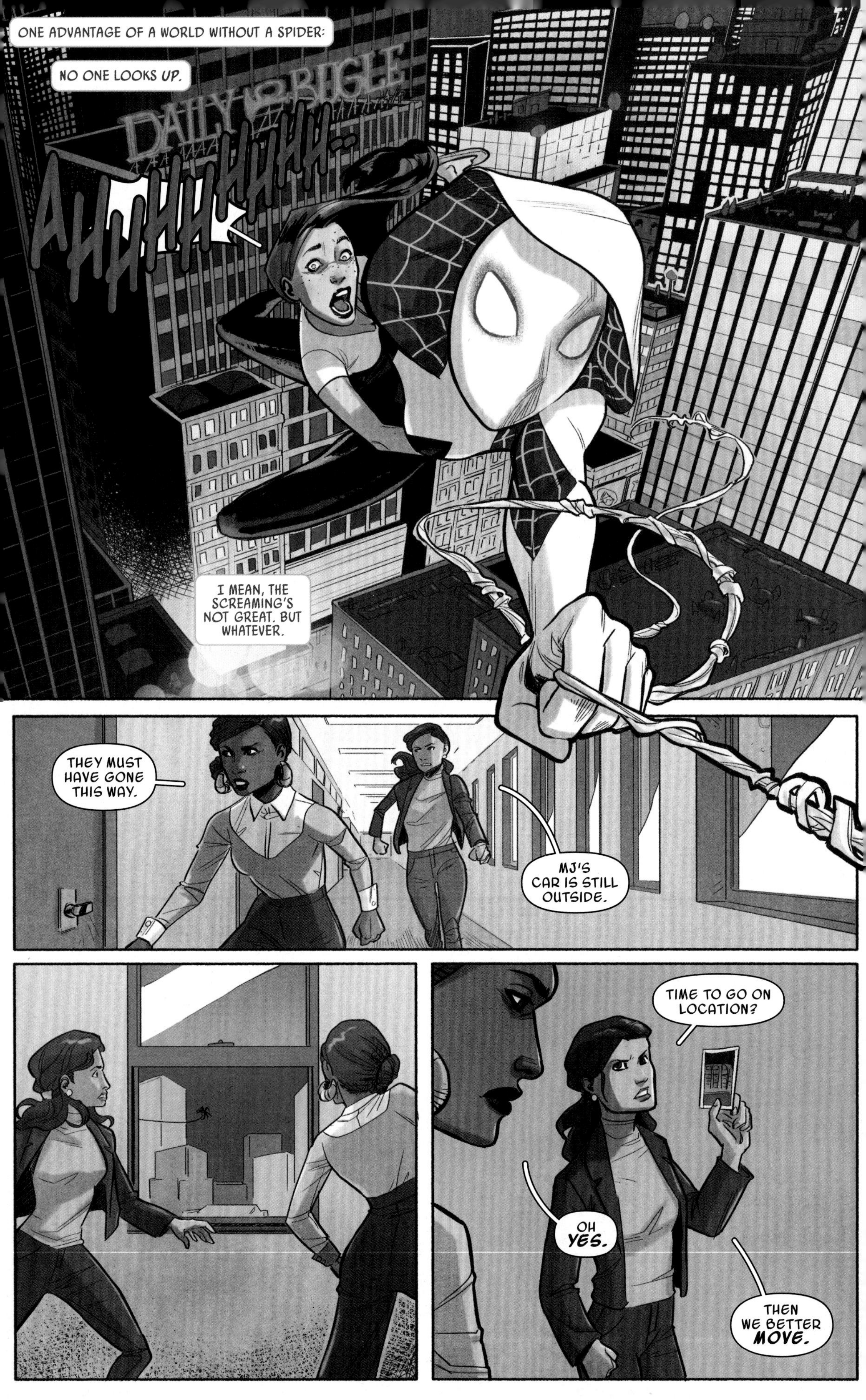
ONE ADVANTAGE OF A WORLD WITHOUT A SPIDER:
NO ONE LOOKS UP.
DAILY BUGLE
AHHHHHHHHH--
I MEAN, THE SCREAMING'S NOT GREAT. BUT WHATEVER.
THEY MUST HAVE GONE THIS WAY.
MJ'S CAR IS STILL OUTSIDE.
TIME TO GO ON LOCATION?
OH YES.
THEN WE BETTER MOVE.

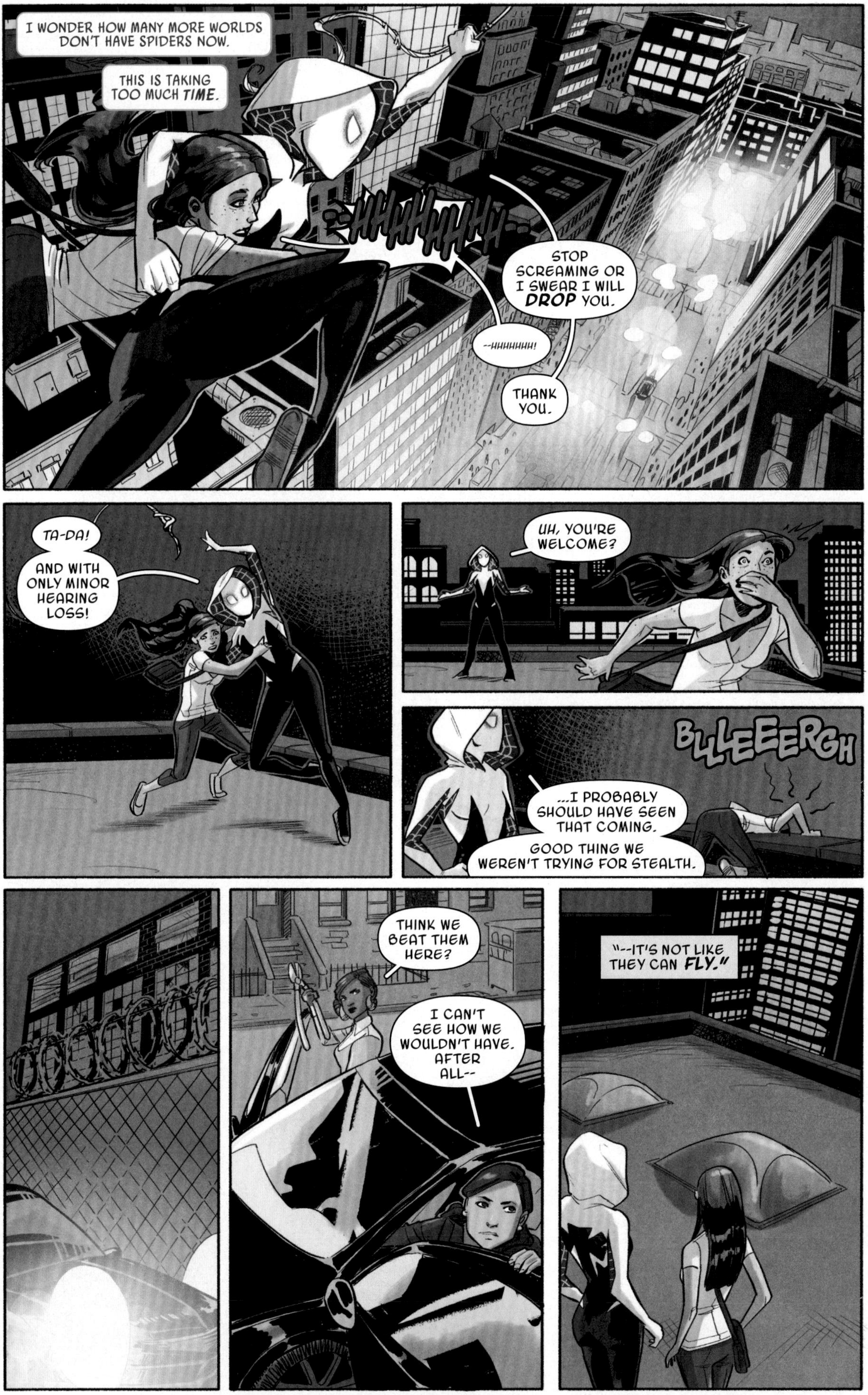
I WONDER HOW MANY MORE WORLDS DON'T HAVE SPIDERS NOW.
THIS IS TAKING TOO MUCH TIME.
E-HHHHHHHHH--
STOP SCREAMING OR I SWEAR I WILL DROP YOU.
--HHHHHHH!
THANK YOU.
TA-DA!
AND WITH ONLY MINOR HEARING LOSS!
UH, YOU'RE WELCOME?
BULEEERGH
...I PROBABLY SHOULD HAVE SEEN THAT COMING.
GOOD THING WE WEREN'T TRYING FOR STEALTH.
THINK WE BEAT THEM HERE?
I CAN'T SEE HOW WE WOULDN'T HAVE. AFTER ALL--
"--IT'S NOT LIKE THEY CAN FLY."

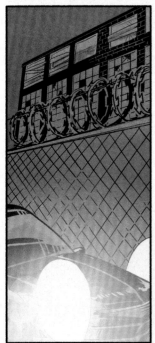

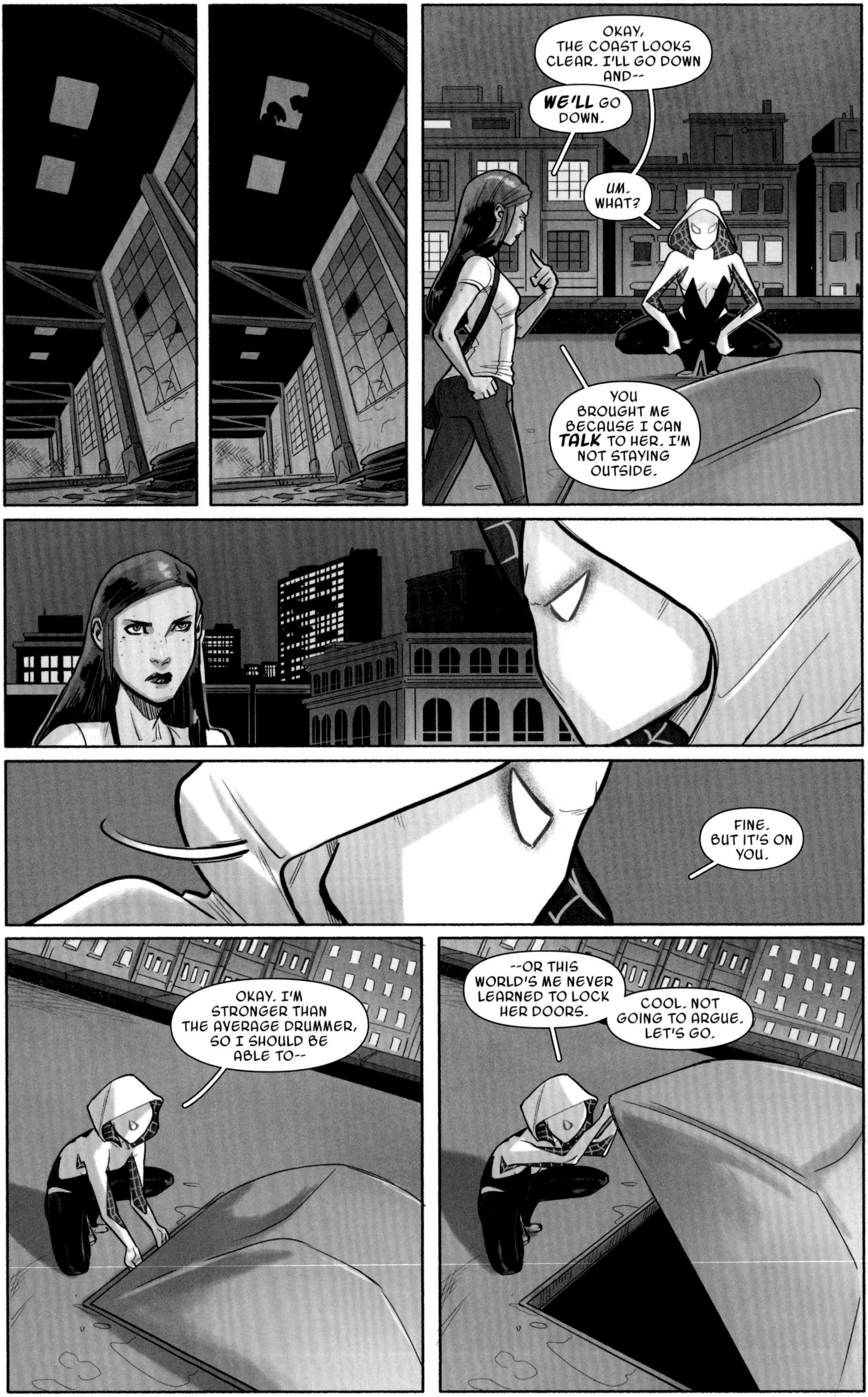
OKAY, THE COAST LOOKS CLEAR. I'LL GO DOWN AND--
WE'LL GO DOWN.
UM. WHAT?
YOU BROUGHT ME BECAUSE I CAN TALK TO HER. I'M NOT STAYING OUTSIDE.
FINE. BUT IT'S ON YOU.
OKAY. I'M STRONGER THAN THE AVERAGE DRUMMER, SO I SHOULD BE ABLE TO--
--OR THIS WORLD'S ME NEVER LEARNED TO LOCK HER DOORS.
COOL. NOT GOING TO ARGUE. LET'S GO.

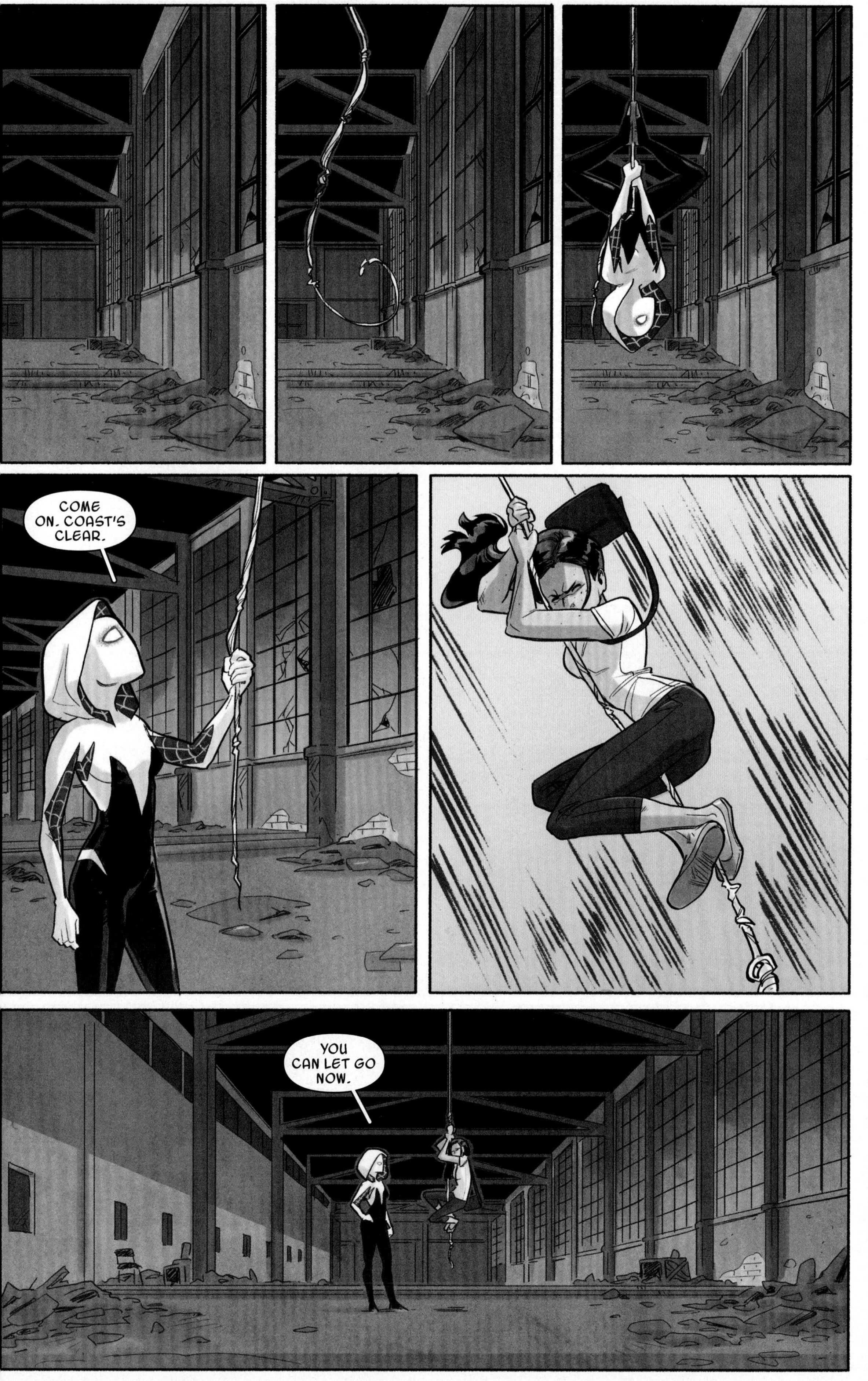
COME ON. COAST'S CLEAR.
YOU CAN LET GO NOW.

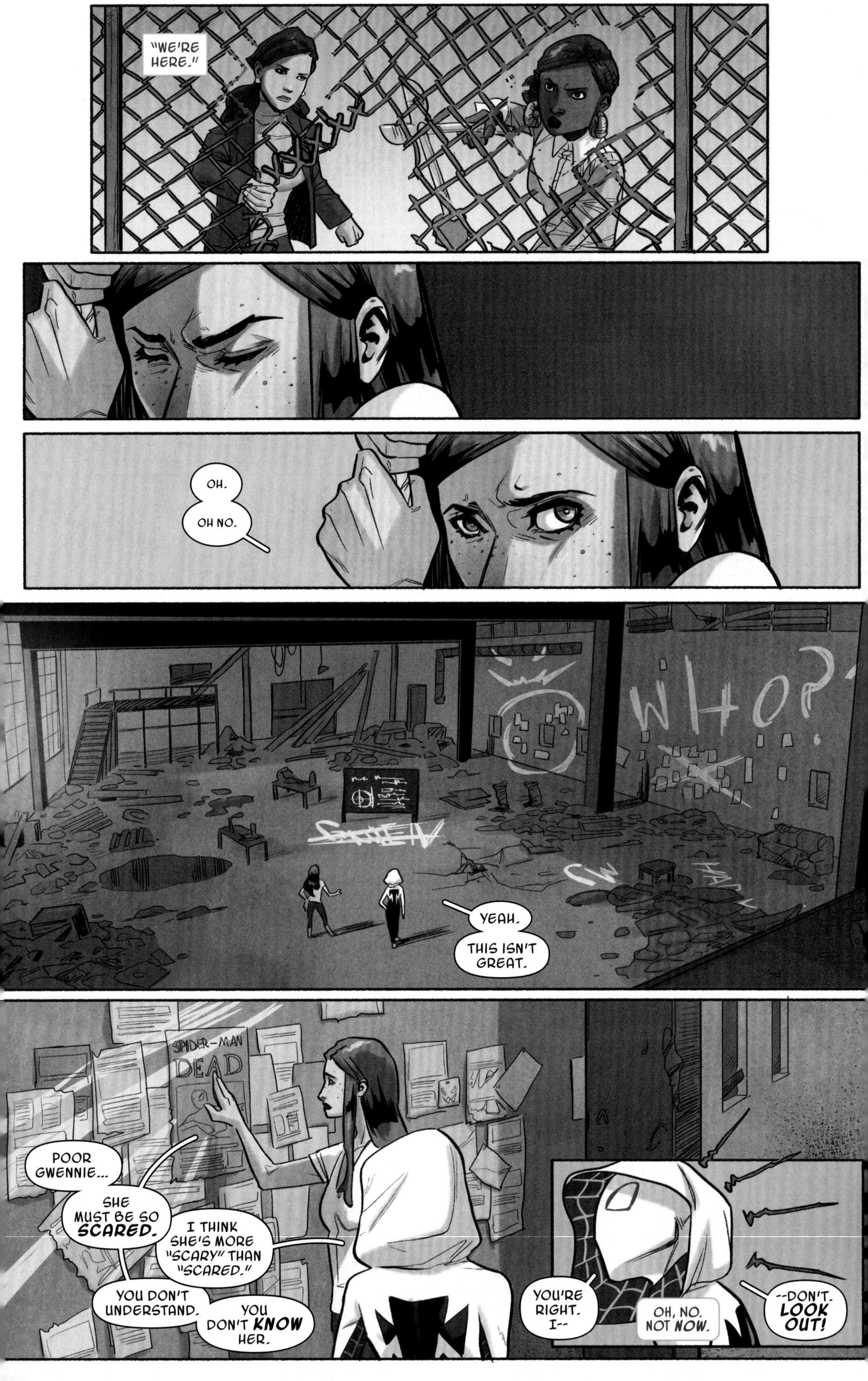
"WE'RE HERE."
OH.
OH NO.
YEAH.
THIS ISN'T GREAT.
SPIDER-MAN DEAD
POOR GWENNIE...
SHE MUST BE SO SCARED.
I THINK SHE'S MORE "SCARY" THAN "SCARED."
YOU DON'T UNDERSTAND.
YOU DON'T KNOW HER.
YOU'RE RIGHT. I--
OH, NO. NOT NOW.
--DON'T. LOOK OUT!

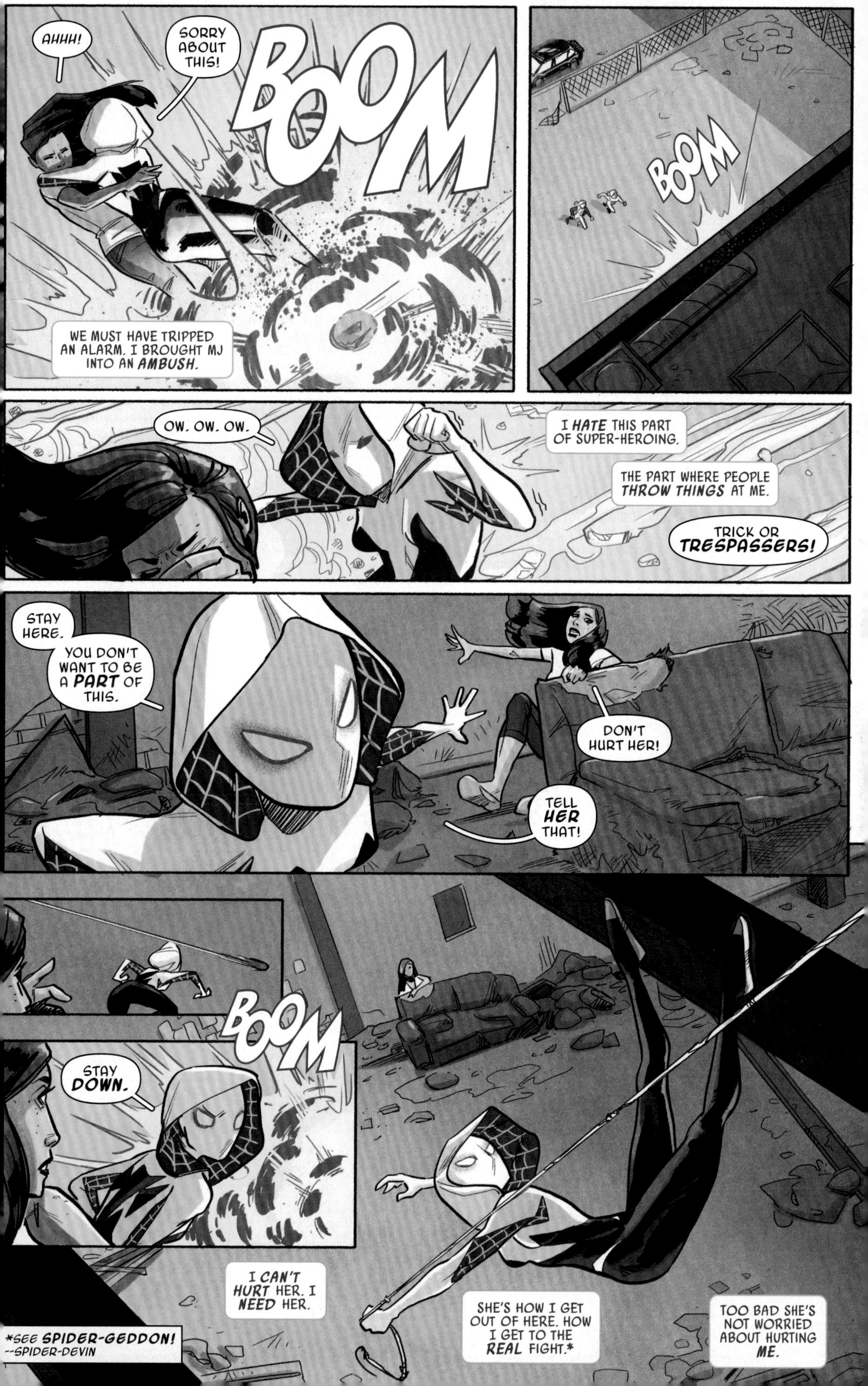
AHHH!
SORRY ABOUT THIS!
BOOM
WE MUST HAVE TRIPPED AN ALARM. I BROUGHT MJ INTO AN AMBUSH.
BOOM
OW. OW. OW.
I HATE THIS PART OF SUPER-HEROING.
THE PART WHERE PEOPLE THROW THINGS AT ME.
TRICK OR TRESPASSERS!
STAY HERE.
YOU DON'T WANT TO BE A PART OF THIS.
DON'T HURT HER!
TELL HER THAT!
BOOM
STAY DOWN.
I CAN'T HURT HER. I NEED HER.
SHE'S HOW I GET OUT OF HERE. HOW I GET TO THE REAL FIGHT.*
TOO BAD SHE'S NOT WORRIED ABOUT HURTING ME.
*SEE SPIDER-GEDDON! --SPIDER-DEVIN

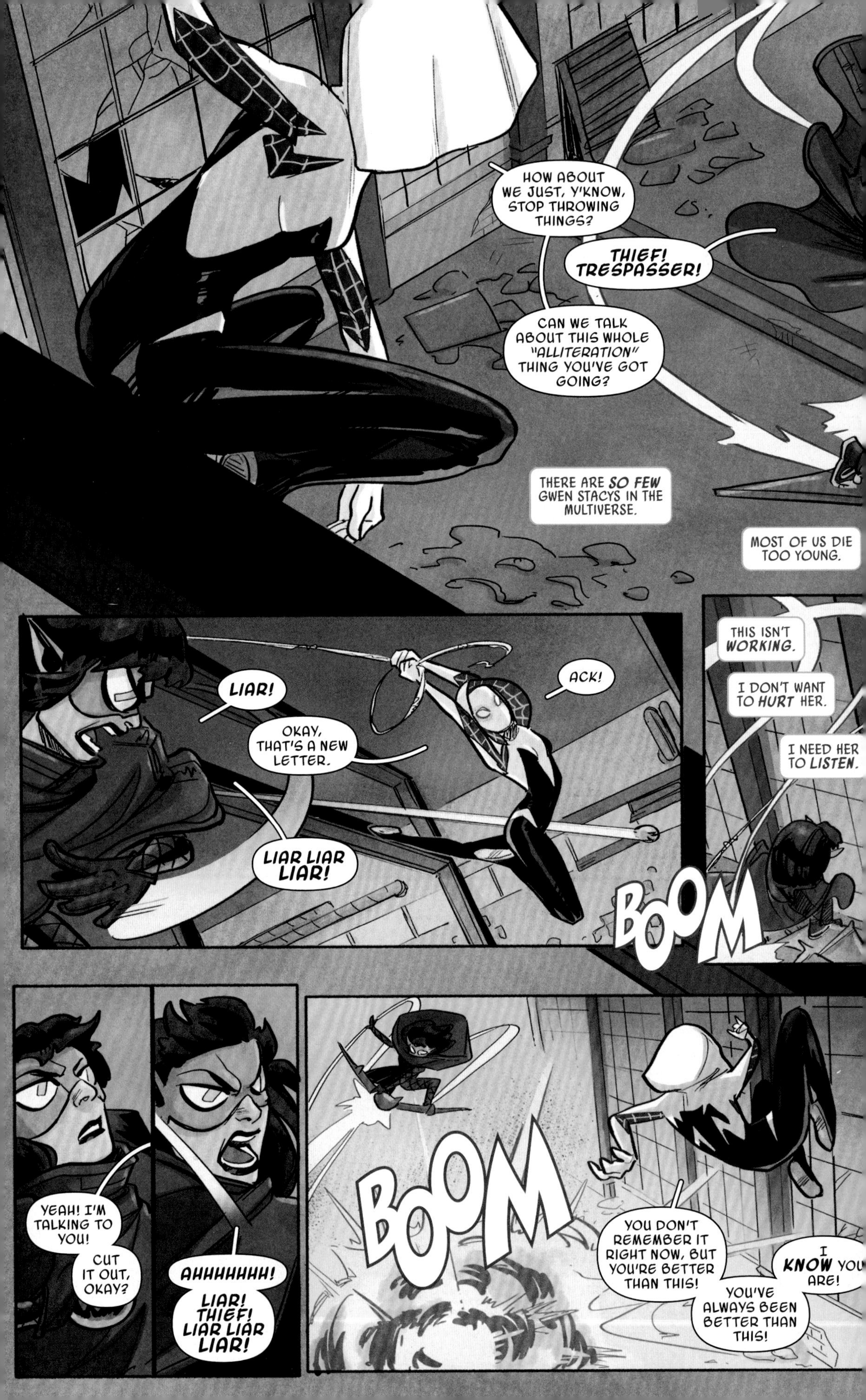
HOW ABOUT WE JUST, Y'KNOW, STOP THROWING THINGS?
THIEF! TRESPASSER!
CAN WE TALK ABOUT THIS WHOLE "ALLITERATION" THING YOU'VE GOT GOING?
THERE ARE SO FEW GWEN STACYS IN THE MULTIVERSE.
MOST OF US DIE TOO YOUNG.
LIAR!
OKAY, THAT'S A NEW LETTER.
ACK!
LIAR LIAR LIAR!
THIS ISN'T WORKING.
I DON'T WANT TO HURT HER.
I NEED HER TO LISTEN.
BOOM
YEAH! I'M TALKING TO YOU!
CUT IT OUT, OKAY?
AHHHHHHH!
LIAR! THIEF! LIAR LIAR LIAR!
BOOM
YOU DON'T REMEMBER IT RIGHT NOW, BUT YOU'RE BETTER THAN THIS!
I KNOW YOU ARE!
YOU'VE ALWAYS BEEN BETTER THAN THIS!

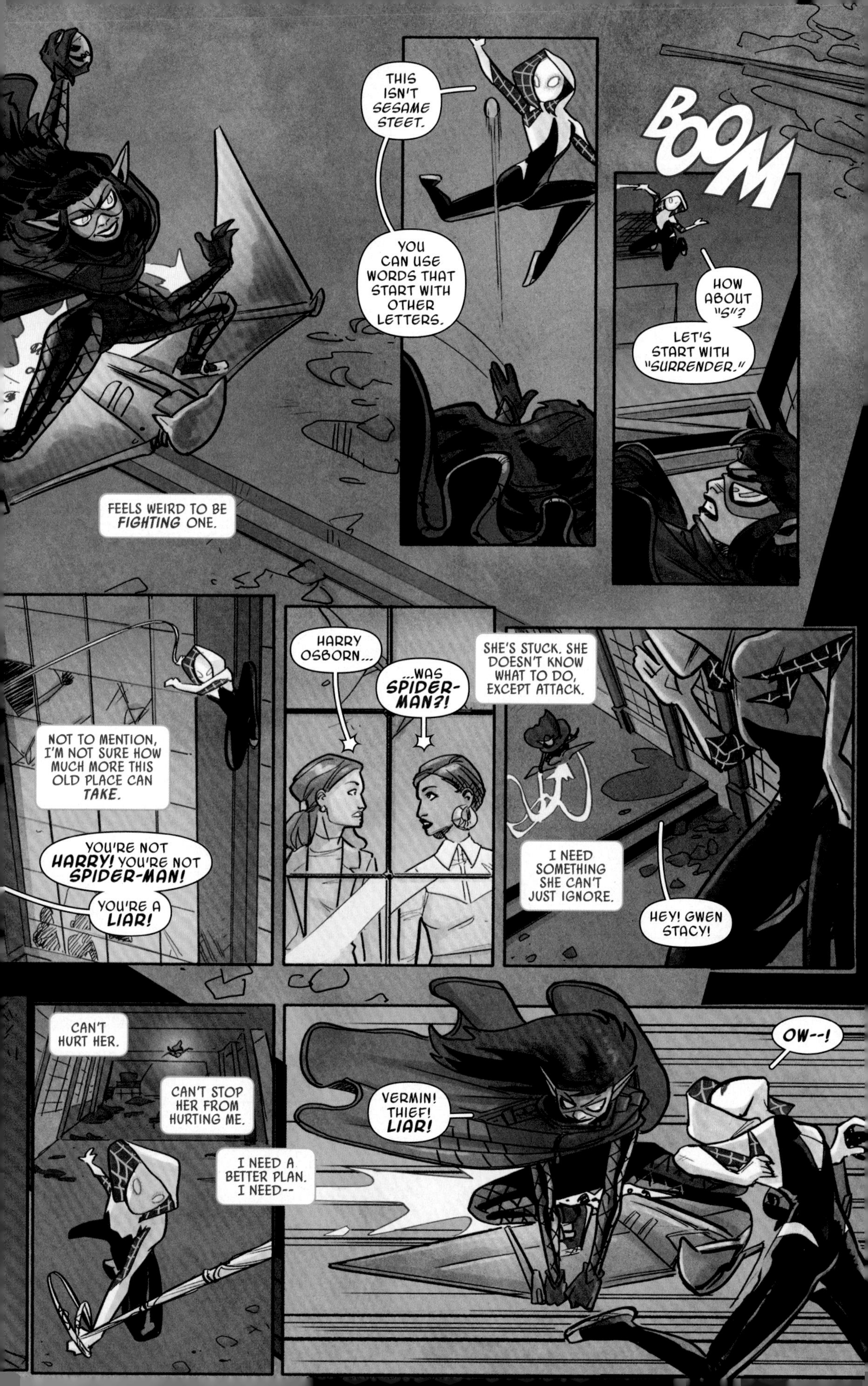
THIS ISN'T SESAME STEET.
YOU CAN USE WORDS THAT START WITH OTHER LETTERS.
BOOM
HOW ABOUT "S"?
LET'S START WITH "SURRENDER."
FEELS WEIRD TO BE *FIGHTING* ONE.
NOT TO MENTION, I'M NOT SURE HOW MUCH MORE THIS OLD PLACE CAN *TAKE*.
YOU'RE NOT **HARRY!** YOU'RE NOT **SPIDER-MAN!**
YOU'RE A **LIAR!**
HARRY OSBORN...
...WAS **SPIDER-MAN?!**
SHE'S STUCK. SHE DOESN'T KNOW WHAT TO DO, EXCEPT ATTACK.
I NEED SOMETHING SHE CAN'T JUST IGNORE.
HEY! GWEN STACY!
CAN'T HURT HER.
CAN'T STOP HER FROM HURTING ME.
I NEED A BETTER PLAN. I NEED--
VERMIN! THIEF! **LIAR!**
OW--!

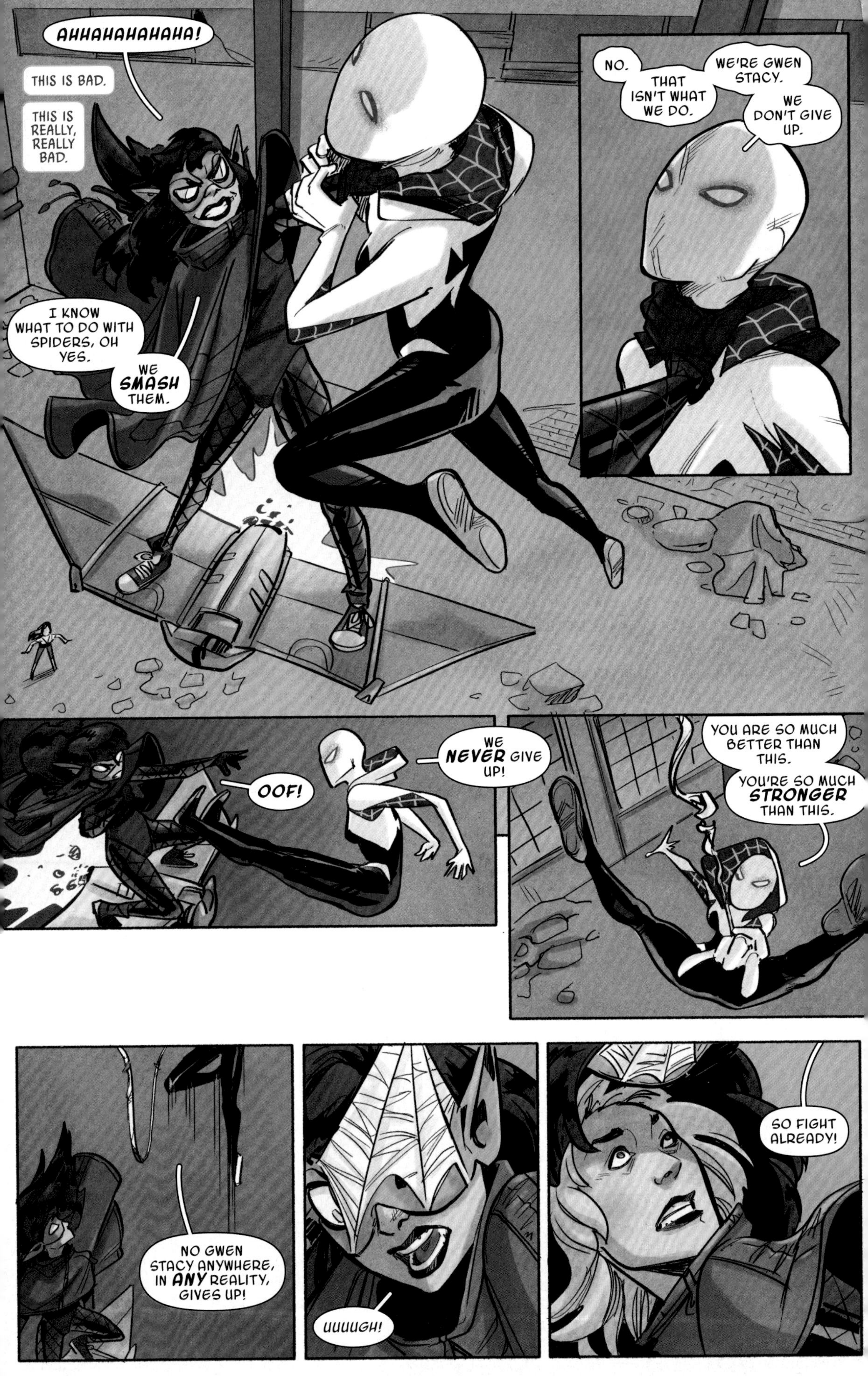
AHHAHAHAHAHA!
THIS IS BAD.
THIS IS REALLY, REALLY BAD.
I KNOW WHAT TO DO WITH SPIDERS, OH YES.
WE **SMASH** THEM.
NO.
THAT ISN'T WHAT WE DO.
WE'RE GWEN STACY.
WE DON'T GIVE UP.
OOF!
WE **NEVER** GIVE UP!
YOU ARE SO MUCH BETTER THAN THIS.
YOU'RE SO MUCH **STRONGER** THAN THIS.
NO GWEN STACY ANYWHERE, IN **ANY** REALITY, GIVES UP!
UUUUGH!
SO FIGHT ALREADY!

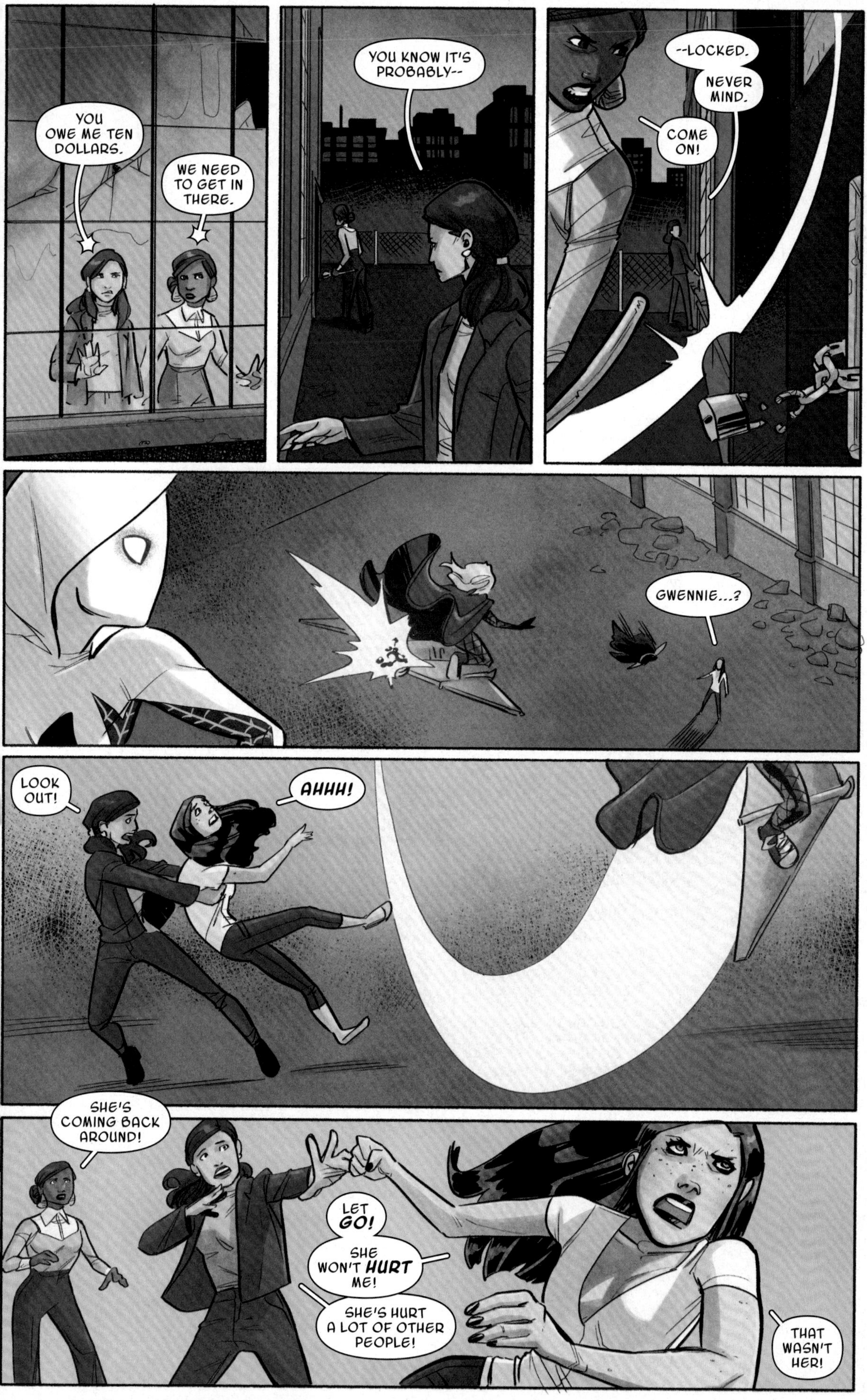
YOU OWE ME TEN DOLLARS.
WE NEED TO GET IN THERE.
YOU KNOW IT'S PROBABLY--
--LOCKED.
NEVER MIND.
COME ON!
GWENNIE...?
LOOK OUT!
AHHH!
SHE'S COMING BACK AROUND!
LET GO!
SHE WON'T HURT ME!
SHE'S HURT A LOT OF OTHER PEOPLE!
THAT WASN'T HER!

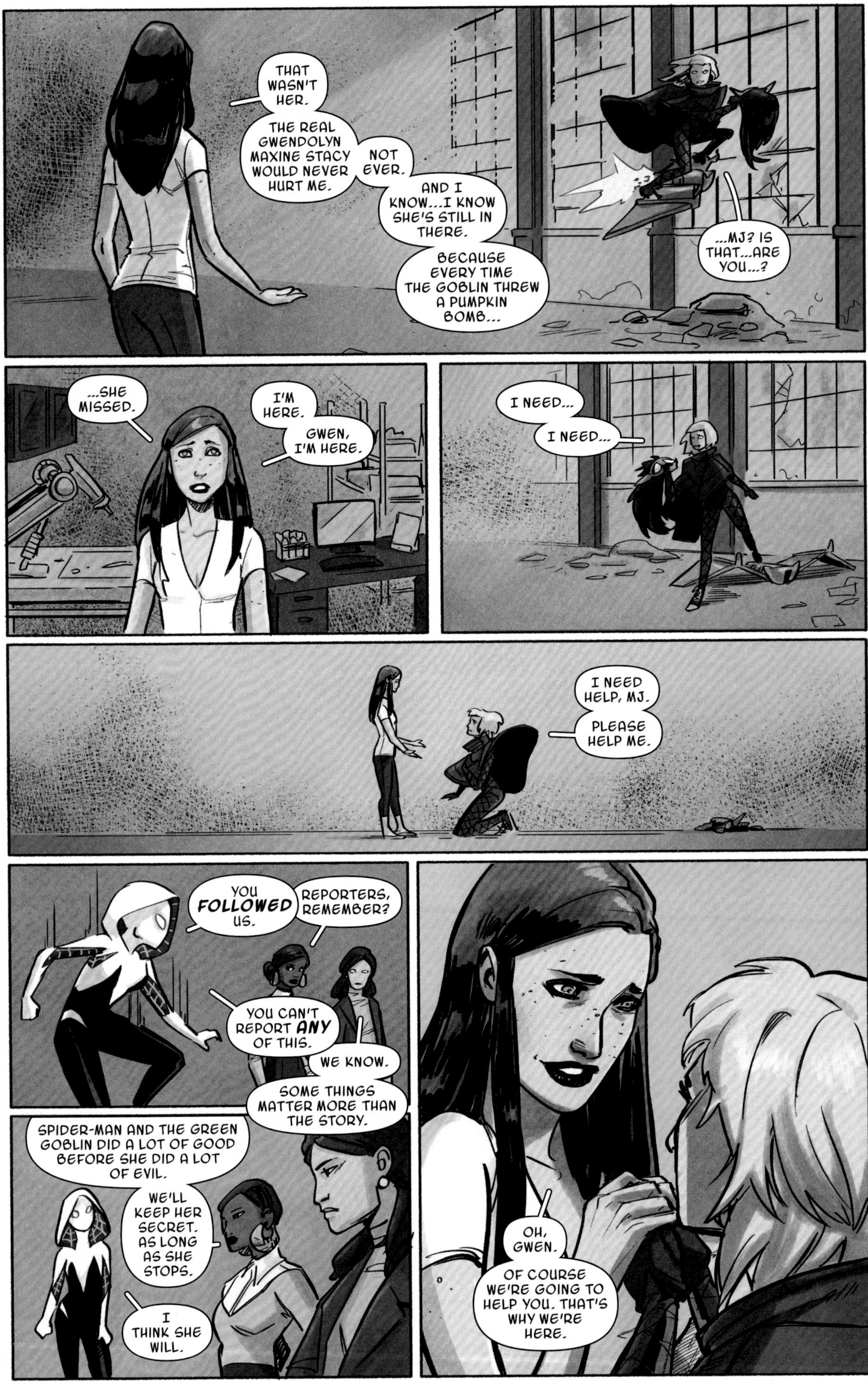
THAT WASN'T HER.
THE REAL GWENDOLYN MAXINE STACY WOULD NEVER HURT ME.
NOT EVER.
AND I KNOW...I KNOW SHE'S STILL IN THERE.
BECAUSE EVERY TIME THE GOBLIN THREW A PUMPKIN BOMB...
...MJ? IS THAT...ARE YOU...?
...SHE MISSED.
I'M HERE.
GWEN, I'M HERE.
I NEED...
I NEED...
I NEED HELP, MJ.
PLEASE HELP ME.
YOU **FOLLOWED** US.
REPORTERS, REMEMBER?
YOU CAN'T REPORT **ANY** OF THIS.
WE KNOW.
SOME THINGS MATTER MORE THAN THE STORY.
SPIDER-MAN AND THE GREEN GOBLIN DID A LOT OF GOOD BEFORE SHE DID A LOT OF EVIL.
WE'LL KEEP HER SECRET. AS LONG AS SHE STOPS.
I THINK SHE WILL.
OH, GWEN.
OF COURSE WE'RE GOING TO HELP YOU. THAT'S WHY WE'RE HERE.

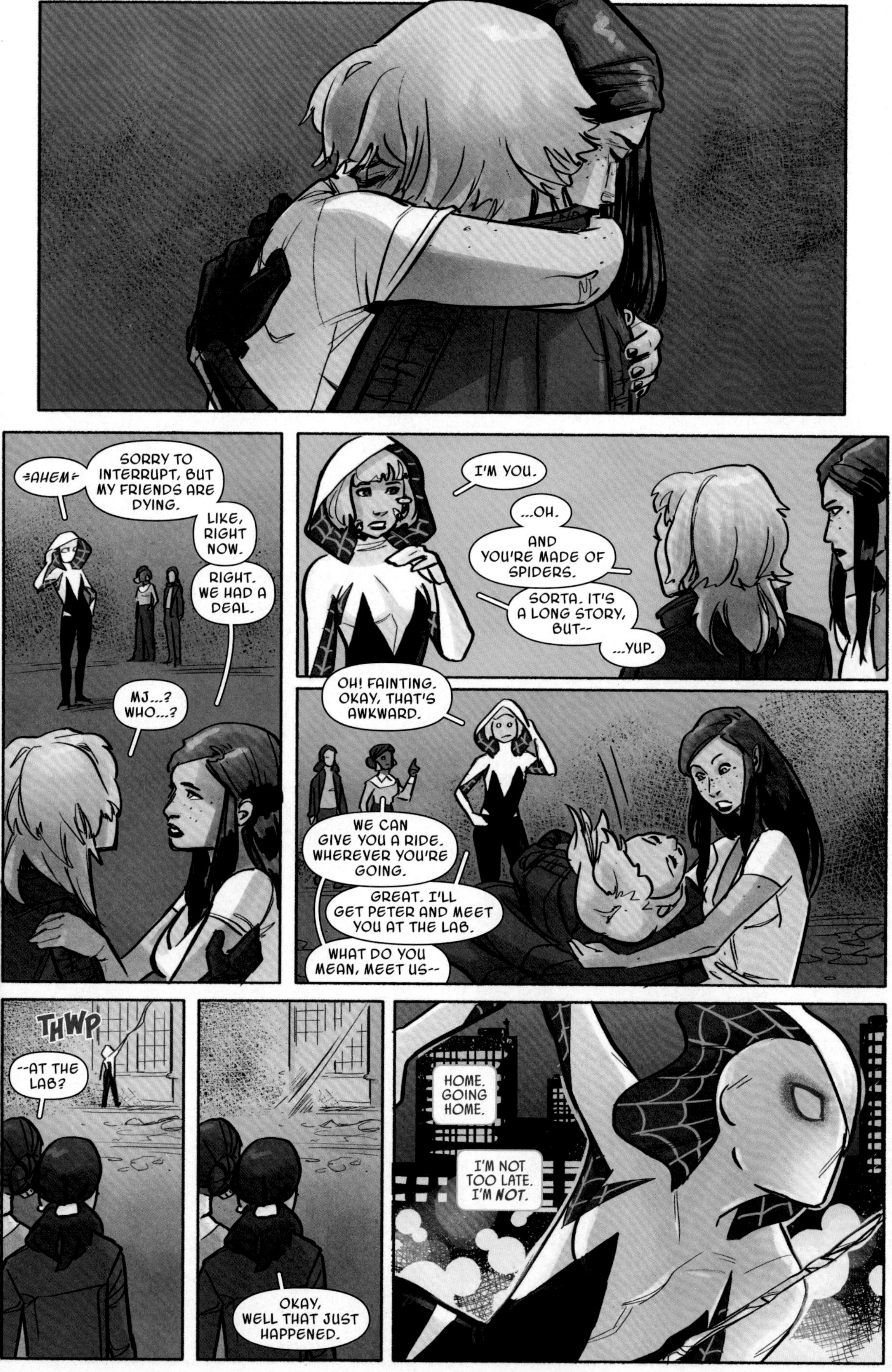

AHEM
SORRY TO INTERRUPT, BUT MY FRIENDS ARE DYING.
LIKE, RIGHT NOW.
RIGHT. WE HAD A DEAL.
MJ...? WHO...?
I'M YOU.
...OH.
AND YOU'RE MADE OF SPIDERS.
SORTA. IT'S A LONG STORY, BUT--
...YUP.
OH! FAINTING. OKAY, THAT'S AWKWARD.
WE CAN GIVE YOU A RIDE. WHEREVER YOU'RE GOING.
GREAT. I'LL GET PETER AND MEET YOU AT THE LAB.
WHAT DO YOU MEAN, MEET US--
THWP
--AT THE LAB?
OKAY, WELL THAT JUST HAPPENED.
HOME. GOING HOME.
I'M NOT TOO LATE. I'M NOT.

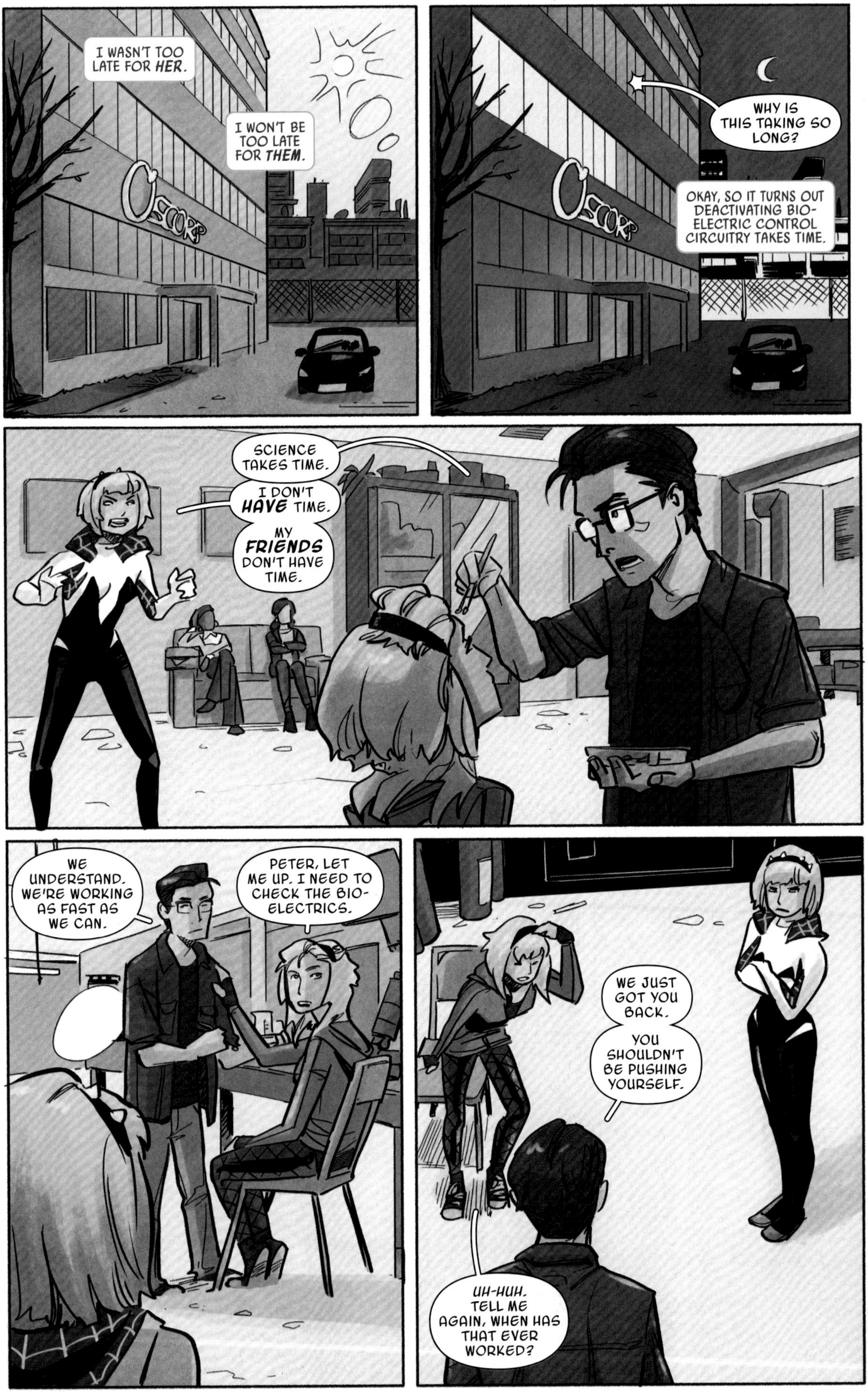
I WASN'T TOO LATE FOR HER.
I WON'T BE TOO LATE FOR THEM.
OSCORP
WHY IS THIS TAKING SO LONG?
OKAY, SO IT TURNS OUT DEACTIVATING BIO-ELECTRIC CONTROL CIRCUITRY TAKES TIME.
SCIENCE TAKES TIME.
I DON'T HAVE TIME.
MY FRIENDS DON'T HAVE TIME.
WE UNDERSTAND. WE'RE WORKING AS FAST AS WE CAN.
PETER, LET ME UP. I NEED TO CHECK THE BIO-ELECTRICS.
WE JUST GOT YOU BACK.
YOU SHOULDN'T BE PUSHING YOURSELF.
UH-HUH. TELL ME AGAIN, WHEN HAS THAT EVER WORKED?

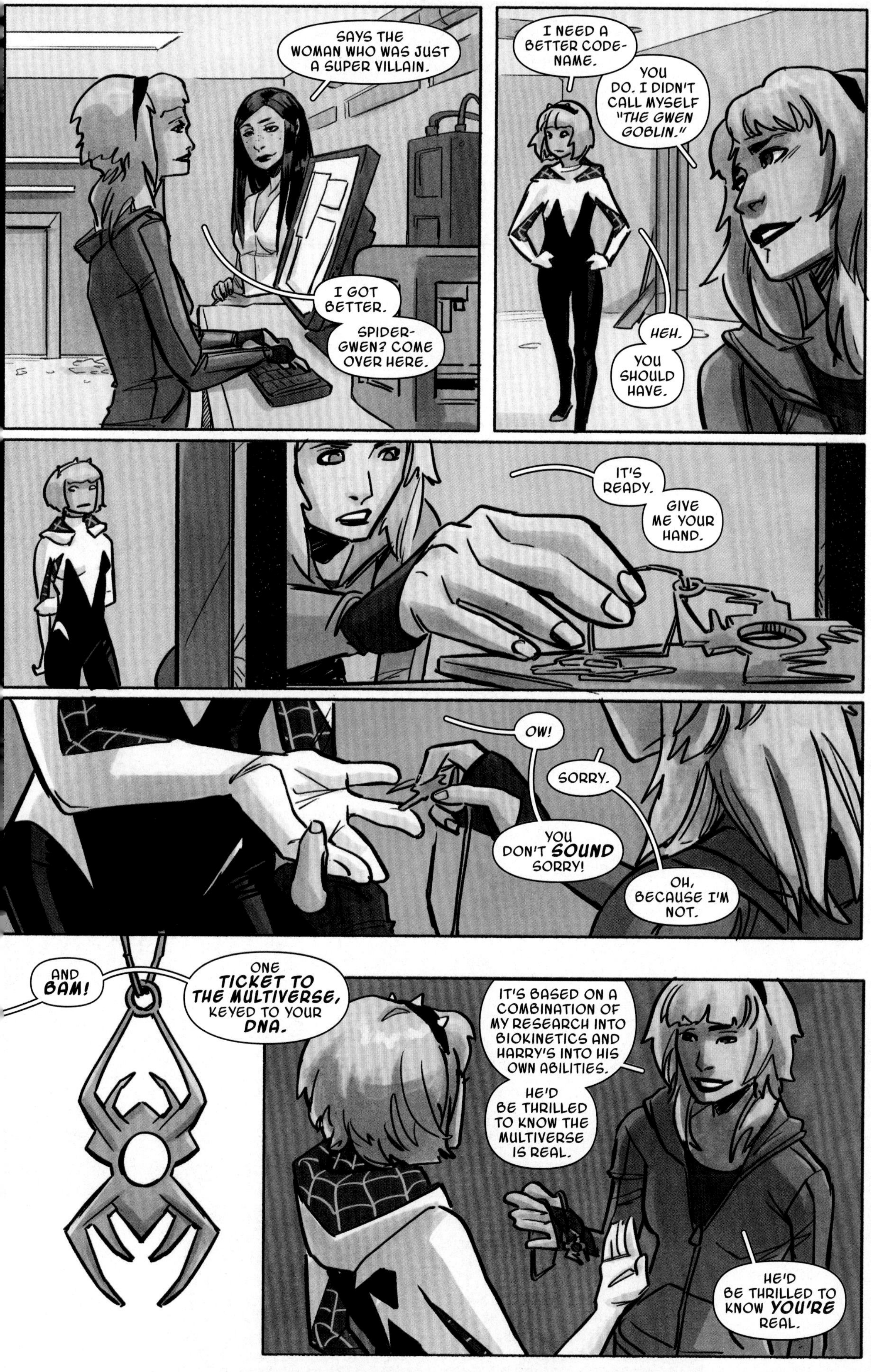
SAYS THE WOMAN WHO WAS JUST A SUPER VILLAIN.
I GOT BETTER.
SPIDER-GWEN? COME OVER HERE.
I NEED A BETTER CODE-NAME.
YOU DO. I DIDN'T CALL MYSELF "THE GWEN GOBLIN."
HEH.
YOU SHOULD HAVE.
IT'S READY.
GIVE ME YOUR HAND.
OW!
SORRY.
YOU DON'T SOUND SORRY!
OH, BECAUSE I'M NOT.
AND BAM!
ONE TICKET TO THE MULTIVERSE, KEYED TO YOUR DNA.
IT'S BASED ON A COMBINATION OF MY RESEARCH INTO BIOKINETICS AND HARRY'S INTO HIS OWN ABILITIES.
HE'D BE THRILLED TO KNOW THE MULTIVERSE IS REAL.
HE'D BE THRILLED TO KNOW YOU'RE REAL.

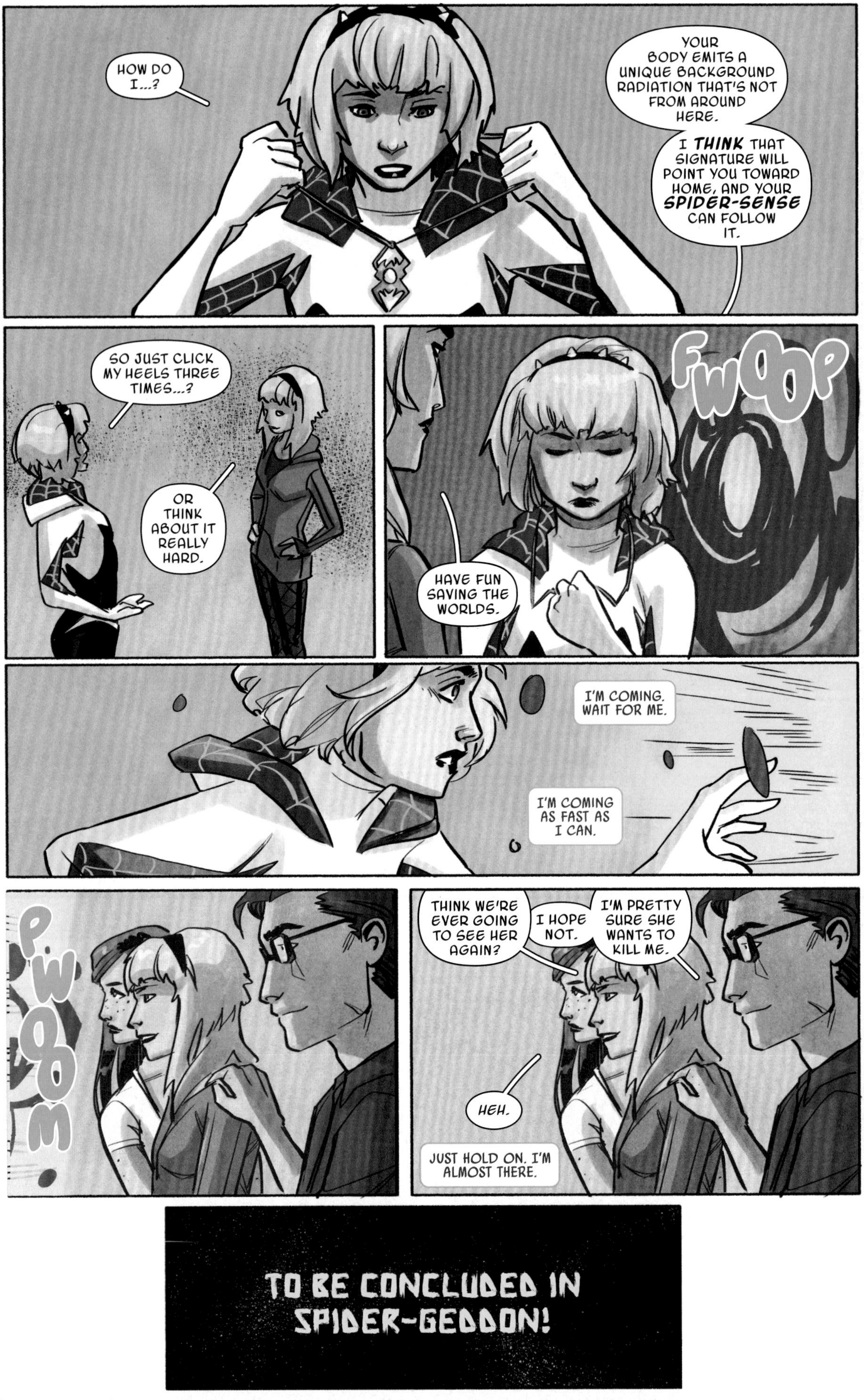
HOW DO I...?
YOUR BODY EMITS A UNIQUE BACKGROUND RADIATION THAT'S NOT FROM AROUND HERE.
I *THINK* THAT SIGNATURE WILL POINT YOU TOWARD HOME, AND YOUR *SPIDER-SENSE* CAN FOLLOW IT.
SO JUST CLICK MY HEELS THREE TIMES...?
OR THINK ABOUT IT REALLY HARD.
FWOOOP
HAVE FUN SAVING THE WORLDS.
I'M COMING. WAIT FOR ME.
I'M COMING AS FAST AS I CAN.
PWOOOM
THINK WE'RE EVER GOING TO SEE HER AGAIN?
I HOPE NOT.
I'M PRETTY SURE SHE WANTS TO KILL ME.
HEH.
JUST HOLD ON. I'M ALMOST THERE.
TO BE CONCLUDED IN SPIDER-GEDDON!

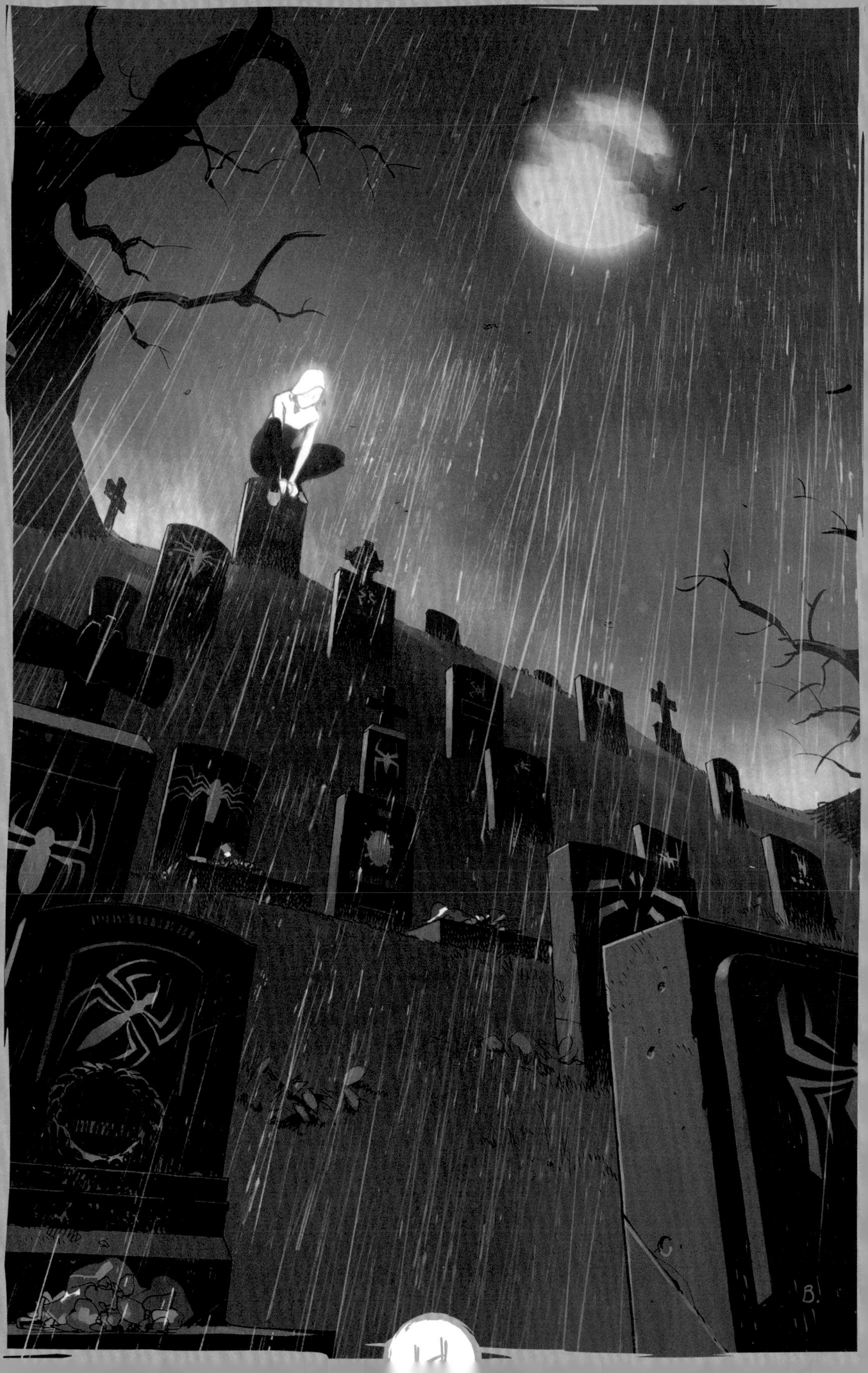

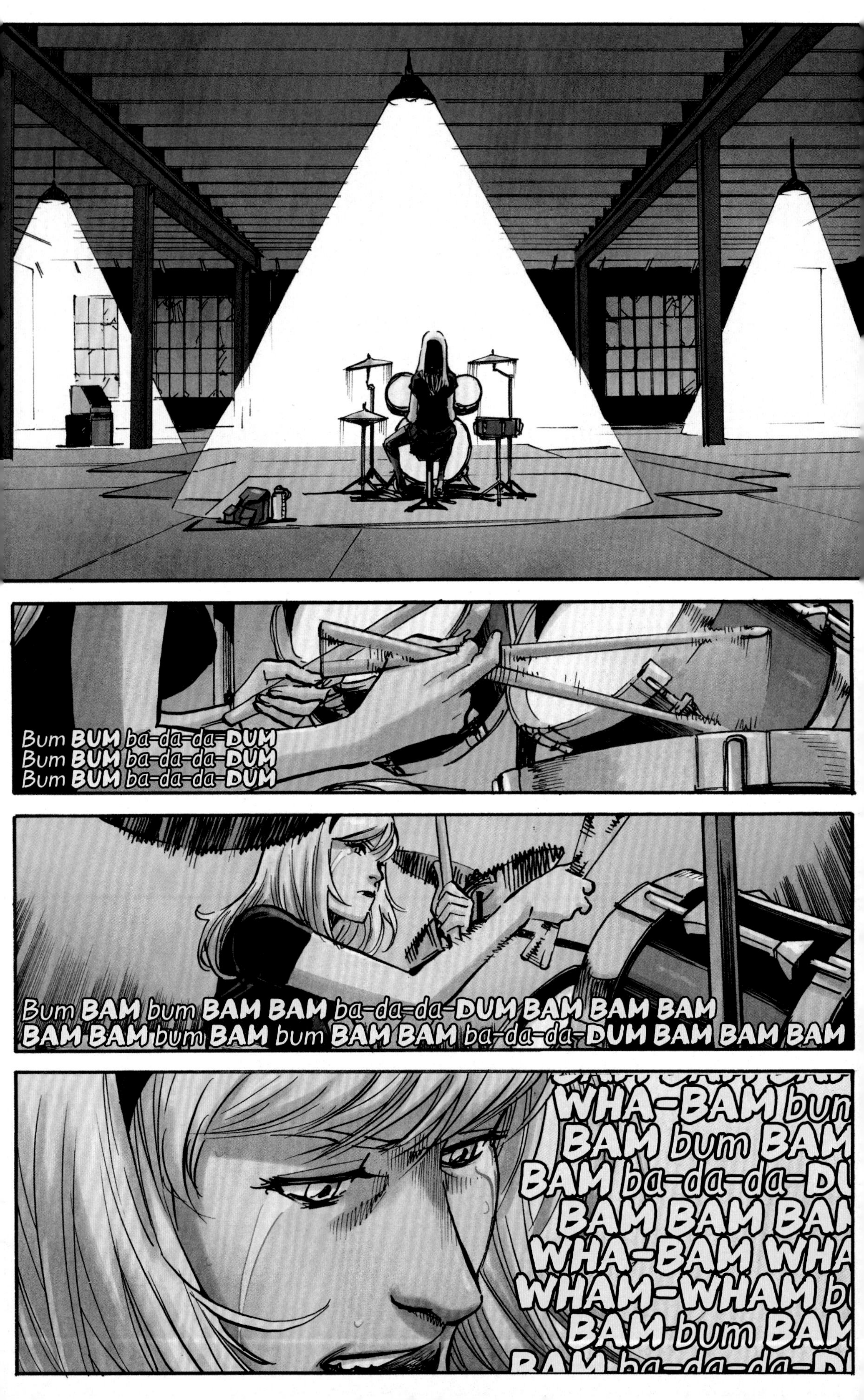
Bum BUM ba-da-da-DUM
Bum BUM ba-da-da-DUM
Bum BUM ba-da-da-DUM
Bum BAM bum BAM BAM ba-da-da-DUM BAM BAM BAM
BAM BAM bum BAM bum BAM BAM ba-da-da-DUM BAM BAM BAM
WHA-BAM
BAM bum
BAM ba-da-da-
BAM BAM
WHA-BAM
WHAM-WHAM
BAM bum

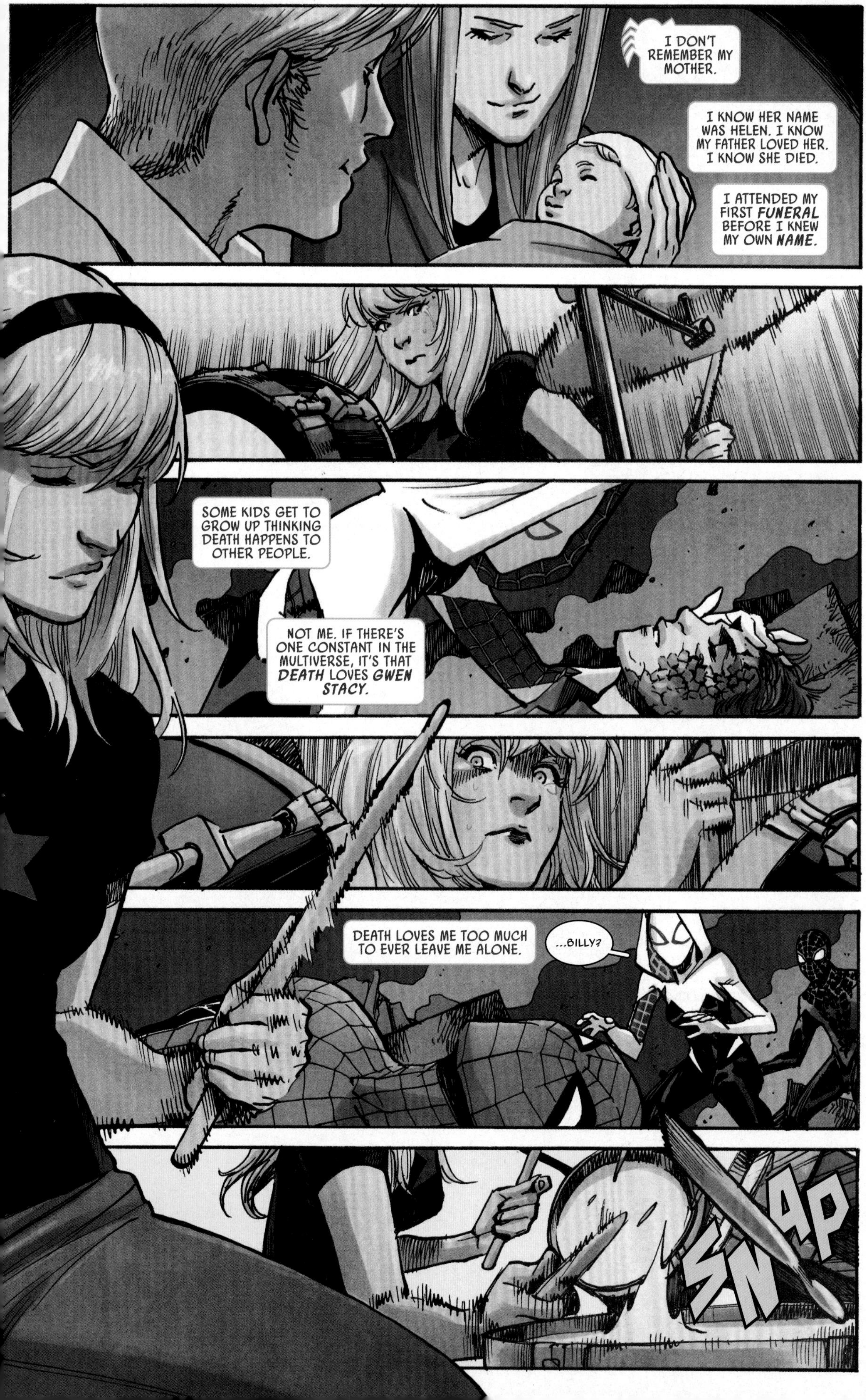
I DON'T REMEMBER MY MOTHER.
I KNOW HER NAME WAS HELEN. I KNOW MY FATHER LOVED HER. I KNOW SHE DIED.
I ATTENDED MY FIRST FUNERAL BEFORE I KNEW MY OWN NAME.
SOME KIDS GET TO GROW UP THINKING DEATH HAPPENS TO OTHER PEOPLE.
NOT ME. IF THERE'S ONE CONSTANT IN THE MULTIVERSE, IT'S THAT DEATH LOVES GWEN STACY.
DEATH LOVES ME TOO MUCH TO EVER LEAVE ME ALONE.
...BILLY?
SNAP

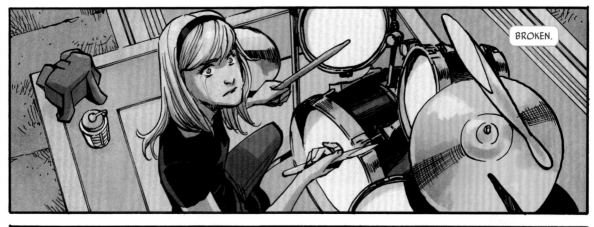

BROKEN.

EVERYTHING'S *BROKEN*.

IT'S NOT SUPPOSED TO BE LIKE THIS.

WE'RE *HEROES*. WE'RE *FIGHTERS*.

WE'RE SUPPOSED TO *WIN*.

WE PAY, YES, ABSOLUTELY.

EVERYTHING COSTS. EVERYTHING HAS TO COST.

BUT THIS COST TOO MUCH. EVERYTHING'S BROKEN.

GWEN?

...WHAT.

IT'S TIME, GWEN. ARE YOU READY?

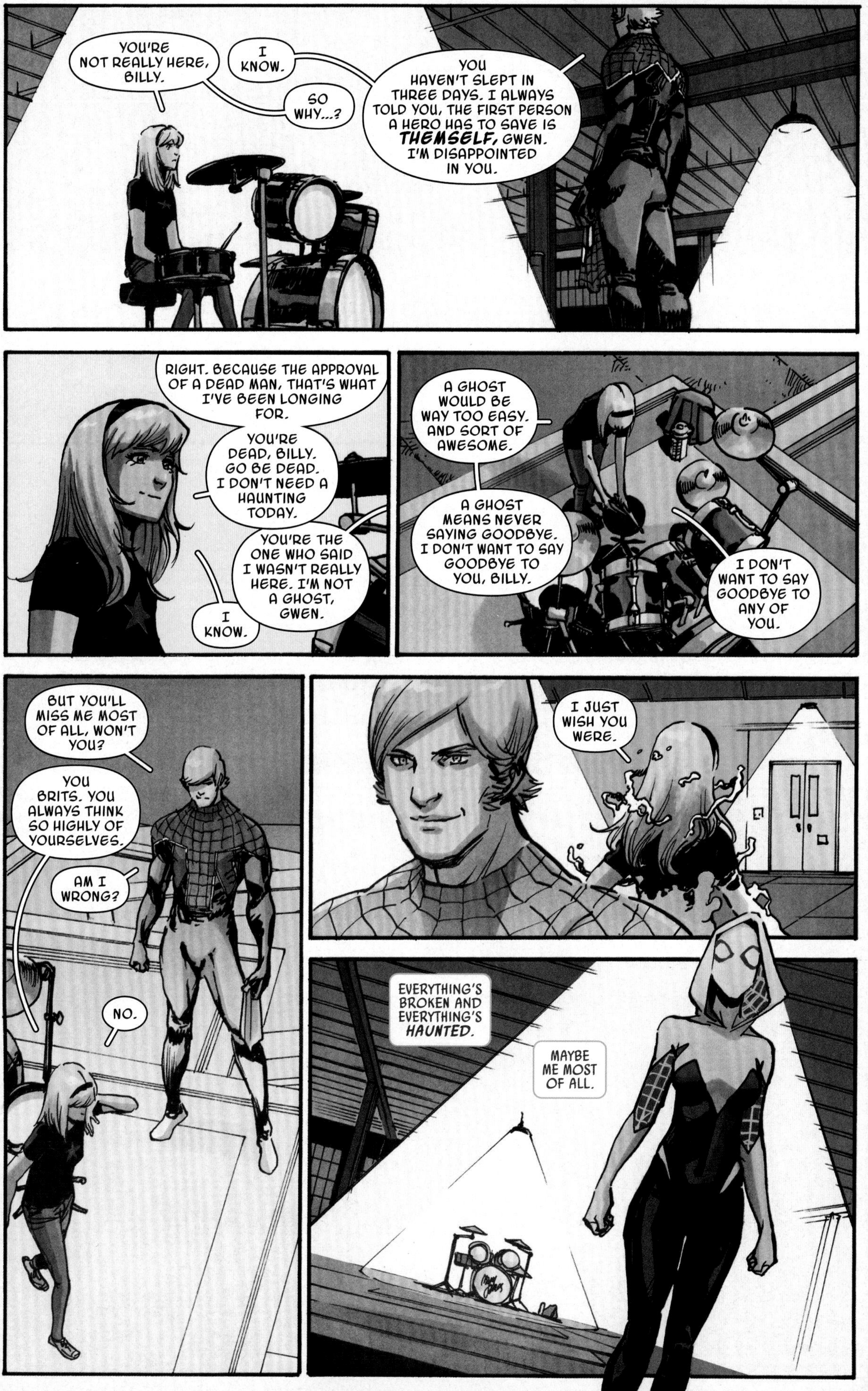
YOU'RE NOT REALLY HERE, BILLY.
I KNOW.
SO WHY...?
YOU HAVEN'T SLEPT IN THREE DAYS. I ALWAYS TOLD YOU, THE FIRST PERSON A HERO HAS TO SAVE IS THEMSELF, GWEN. I'M DISAPPOINTED IN YOU.
RIGHT. BECAUSE THE APPROVAL OF A DEAD MAN, THAT'S WHAT I'VE BEEN LONGING FOR.
YOU'RE DEAD, BILLY. GO BE DEAD. I DON'T NEED A HAUNTING TODAY.
YOU'RE THE ONE WHO SAID I WASN'T REALLY HERE. I'M NOT A GHOST, GWEN.
I KNOW.
A GHOST WOULD BE WAY TOO EASY. AND SORT OF AWESOME.
A GHOST MEANS NEVER SAYING GOODBYE. I DON'T WANT TO SAY GOODBYE TO YOU, BILLY.
I DON'T WANT TO SAY GOODBYE TO ANY OF YOU.
BUT YOU'LL MISS ME MOST OF ALL, WON'T YOU?
YOU BRITS. YOU ALWAYS THINK SO HIGHLY OF YOURSELVES.
AM I WRONG?
NO.
I JUST WISH YOU WERE.
EVERYTHING'S BROKEN AND EVERYTHING'S HAUNTED.
MAYBE ME MOST OF ALL.

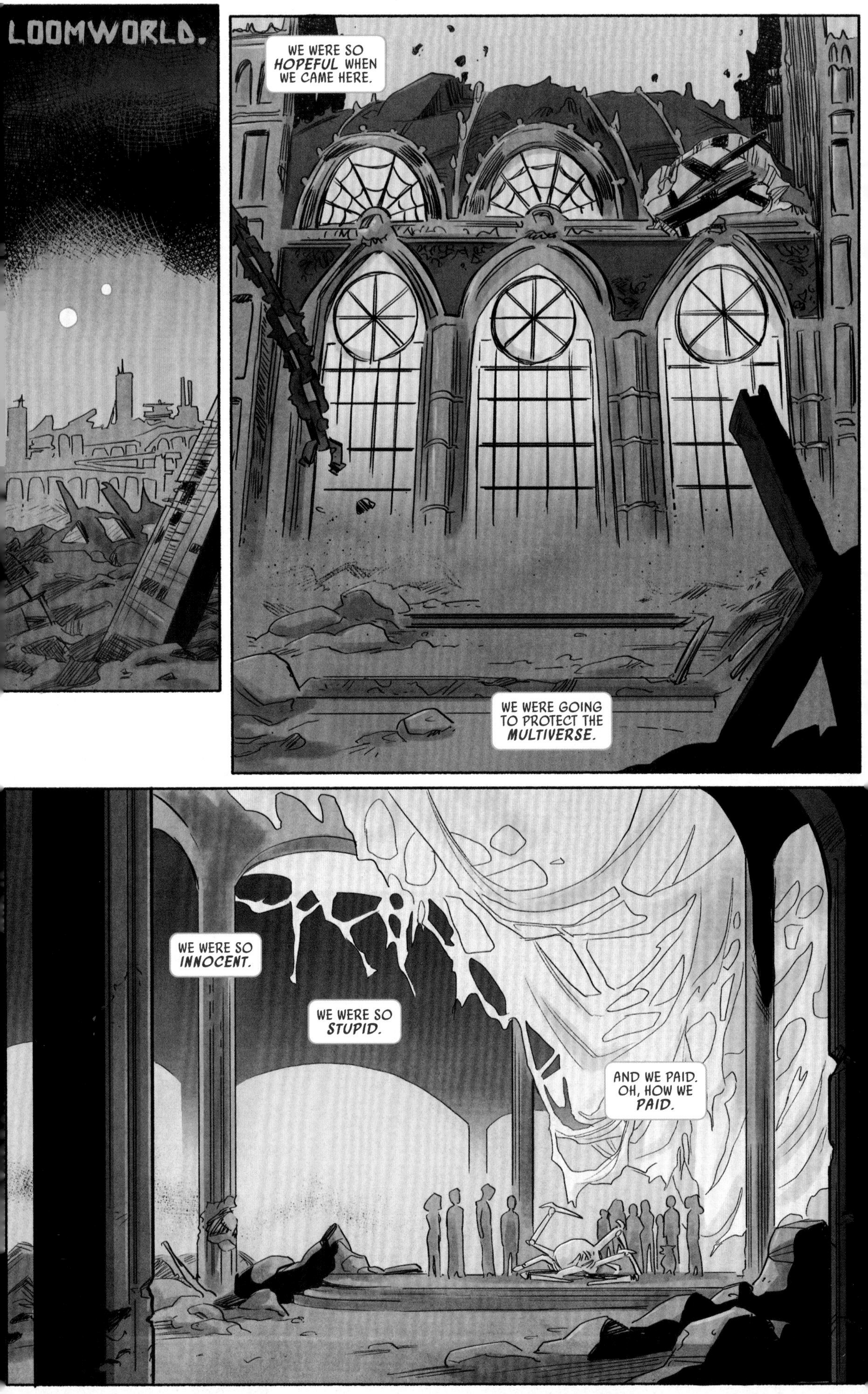
LOOMWORLD.
WE WERE SO HOPEFUL WHEN WE CAME HERE.
WE WERE GOING TO PROTECT THE MULTIVERSE.
WE WERE SO INNOCENT.
WE WERE SO STUPID.
AND WE PAID. OH, HOW WE PAID.

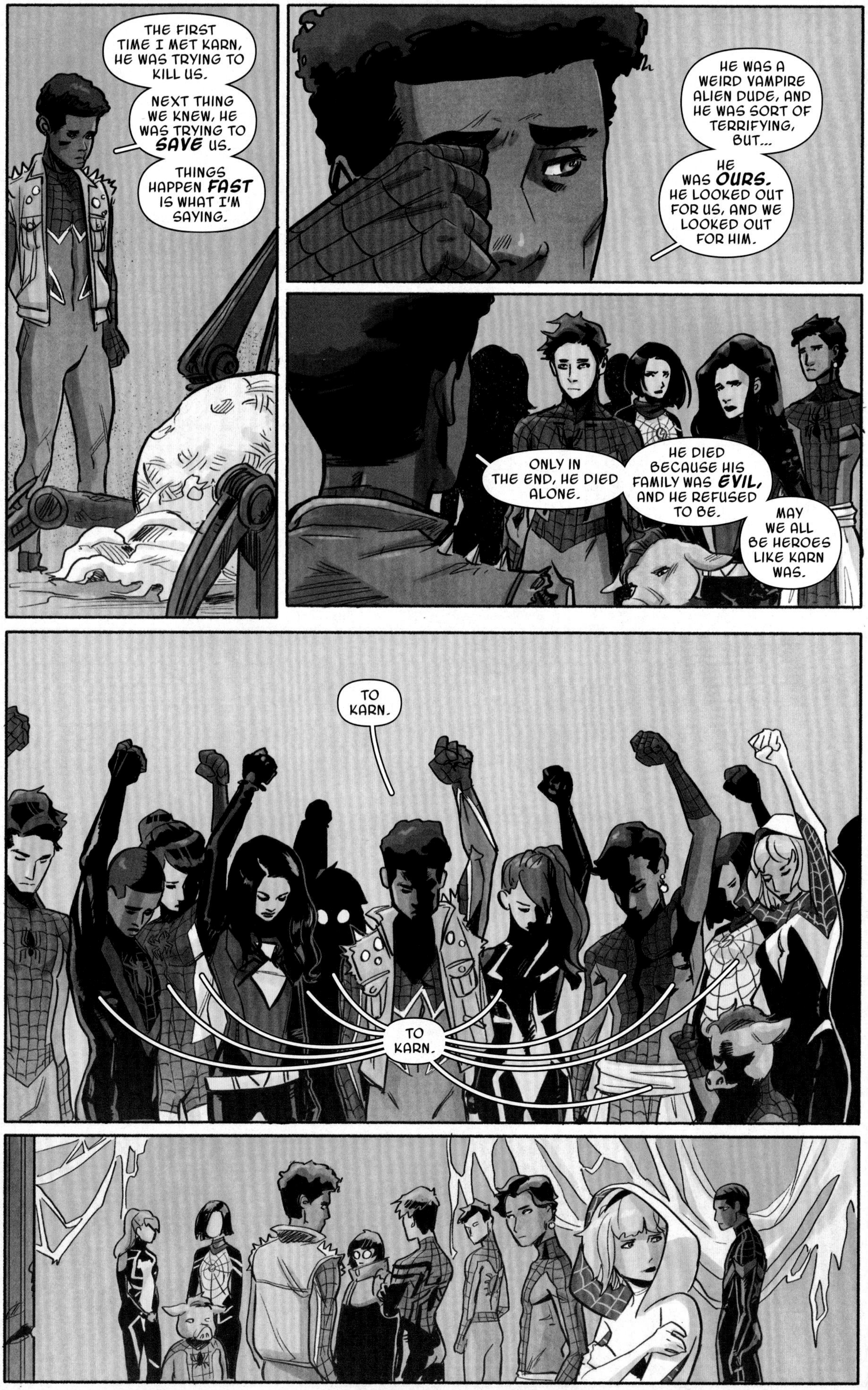
THE FIRST TIME I MET KARN, HE WAS TRYING TO KILL US.
NEXT THING WE KNEW, HE WAS TRYING TO SAVE US.
THINGS HAPPEN FAST IS WHAT I'M SAYING.
HE WAS A WEIRD VAMPIRE ALIEN DUDE, AND HE WAS SORT OF TERRIFYING, BUT...
HE WAS OURS. HE LOOKED OUT FOR US, AND WE LOOKED OUT FOR HIM.
ONLY IN THE END, HE DIED ALONE.
HE DIED BECAUSE HIS FAMILY WAS EVIL, AND HE REFUSED TO BE.
MAY WE ALL BE HEROES LIKE KARN WAS.
TO KARN.
TO KARN.

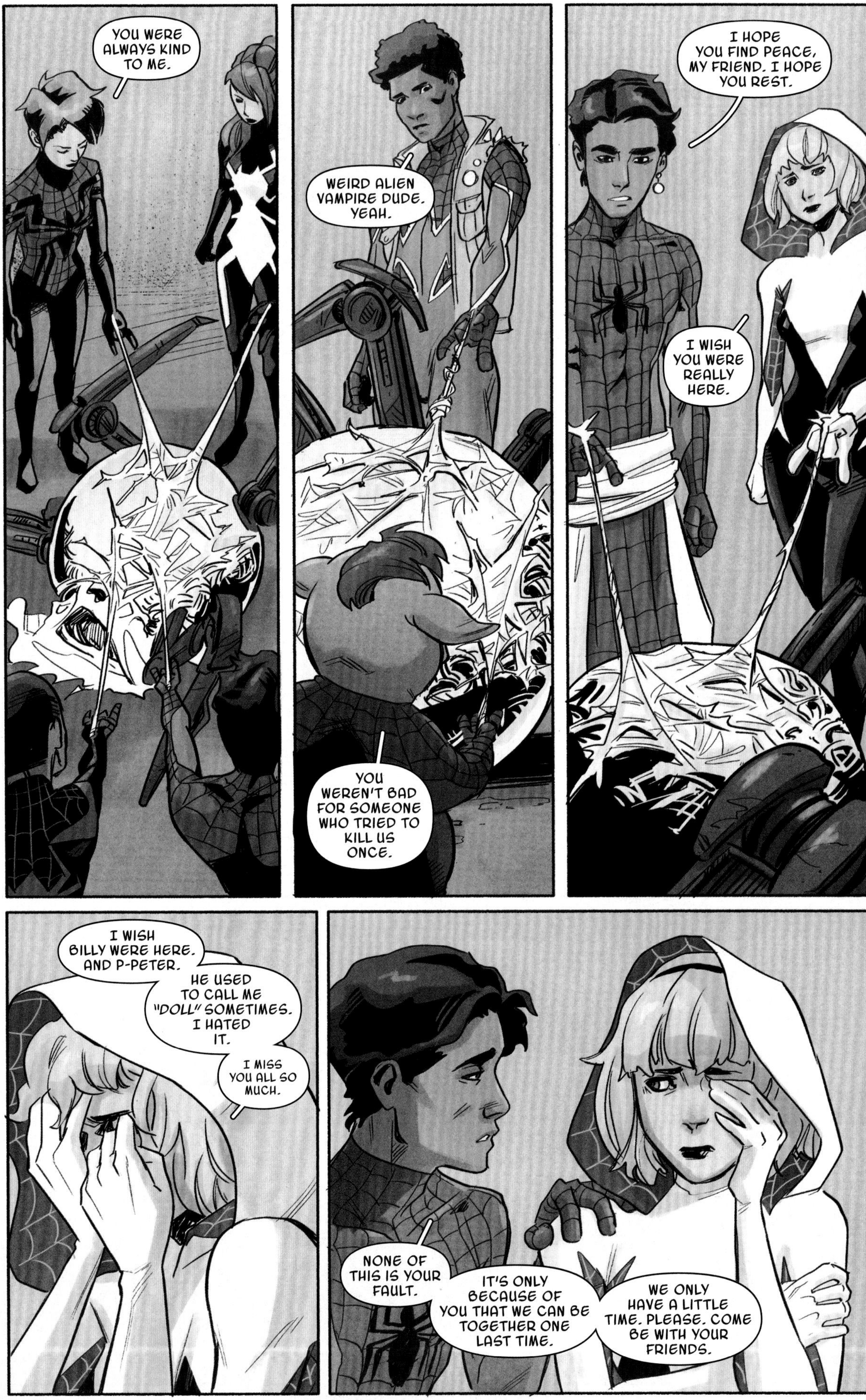
YOU WERE ALWAYS KIND TO ME.
WEIRD ALIEN VAMPIRE DUDE. YEAH.
YOU WEREN'T BAD FOR SOMEONE WHO TRIED TO KILL US ONCE.
I HOPE YOU FIND PEACE, MY FRIEND. I HOPE YOU REST.
I WISH YOU WERE REALLY HERE.
I WISH BILLY WERE HERE. AND P-PETER.
HE USED TO CALL ME "DOLL" SOMETIMES. I HATED IT.
I MISS YOU ALL SO MUCH.
NONE OF THIS IS YOUR FAULT.
IT'S ONLY BECAUSE OF YOU THAT WE CAN BE TOGETHER ONE LAST TIME.
WE ONLY HAVE A LITTLE TIME. PLEASE. COME BE WITH YOUR FRIENDS.

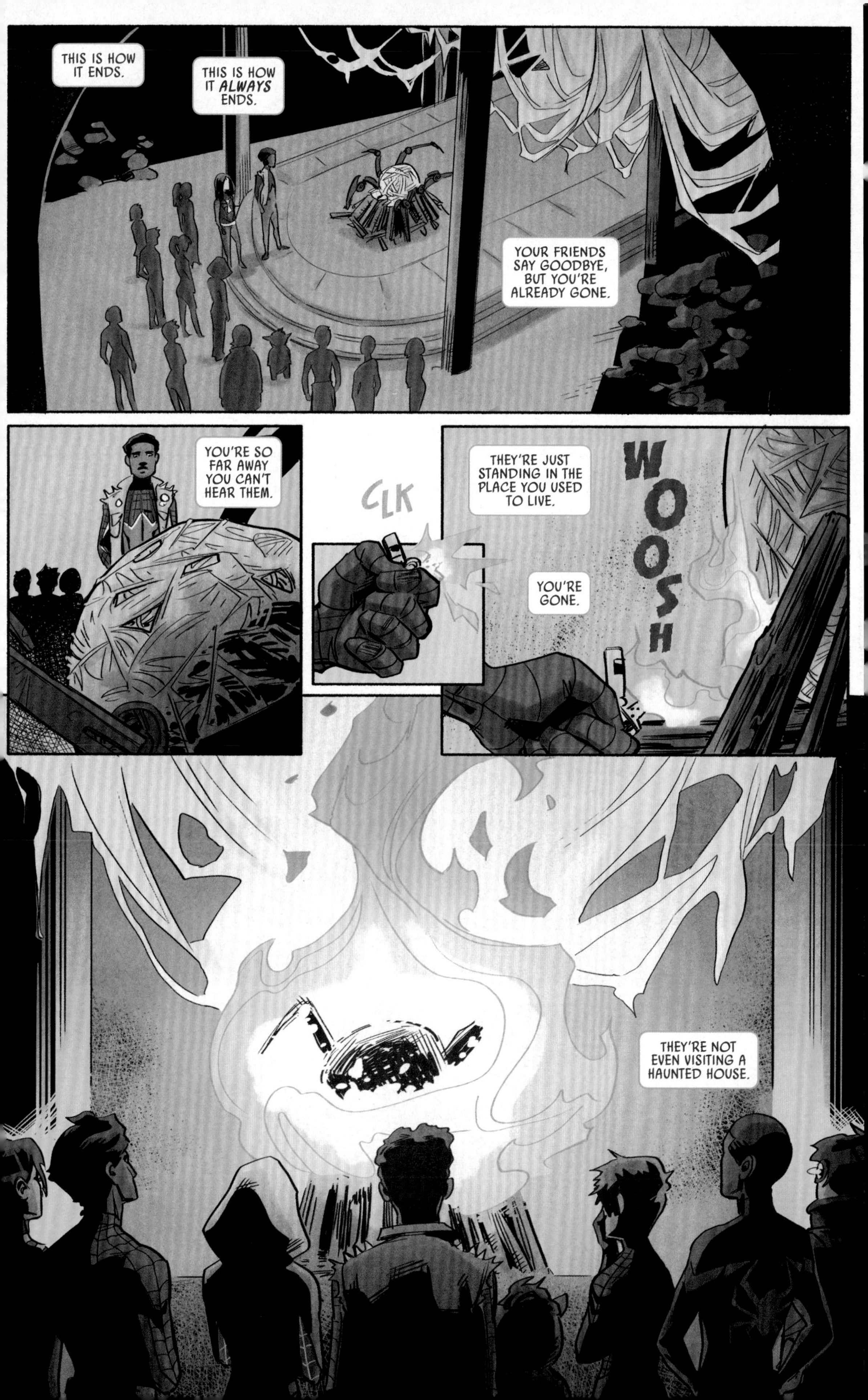
THIS IS HOW IT ENDS.
THIS IS HOW IT ALWAYS ENDS.
YOUR FRIENDS SAY GOODBYE, BUT YOU'RE ALREADY GONE.
YOU'RE SO FAR AWAY YOU CAN'T HEAR THEM.
CLK
THEY'RE JUST STANDING IN THE PLACE YOU USED TO LIVE.
WOOSH
YOU'RE GONE.
THEY'RE NOT EVEN VISITING A HAUNTED HOUSE.

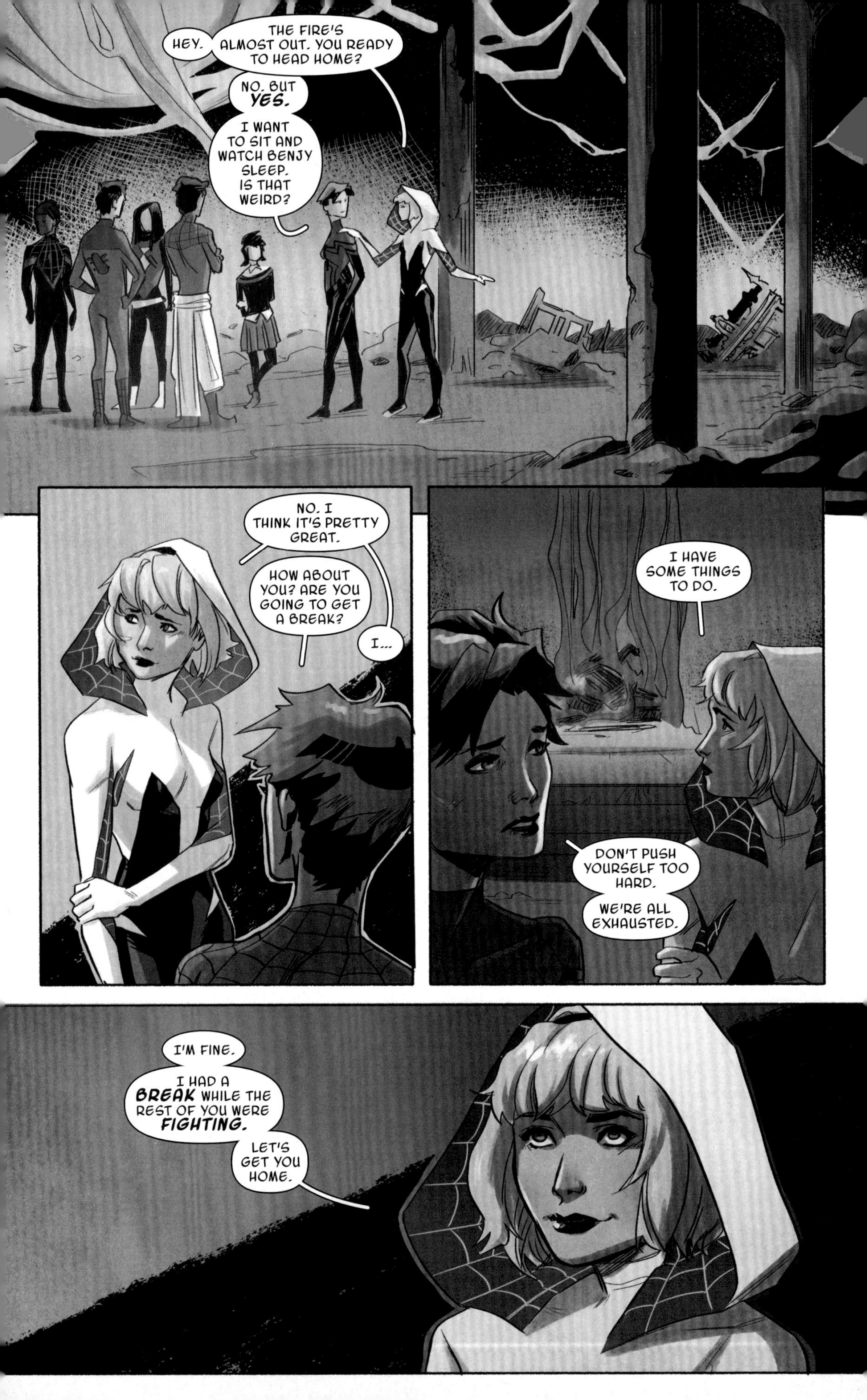
HEY.
THE FIRE'S ALMOST OUT. YOU READY TO HEAD HOME?
NO. BUT YES.
I WANT TO SIT AND WATCH BENJY SLEEP. IS THAT WEIRD?
NO. I THINK IT'S PRETTY GREAT.
HOW ABOUT YOU? ARE YOU GOING TO GET A BREAK?
I...
I HAVE SOME THINGS TO DO.
DON'T PUSH YOURSELF TOO HARD.
WE'RE ALL EXHAUSTED.
I'M FINE.
I HAD A BREAK WHILE THE REST OF YOU WERE FIGHTING.
LET'S GET YOU HOME.

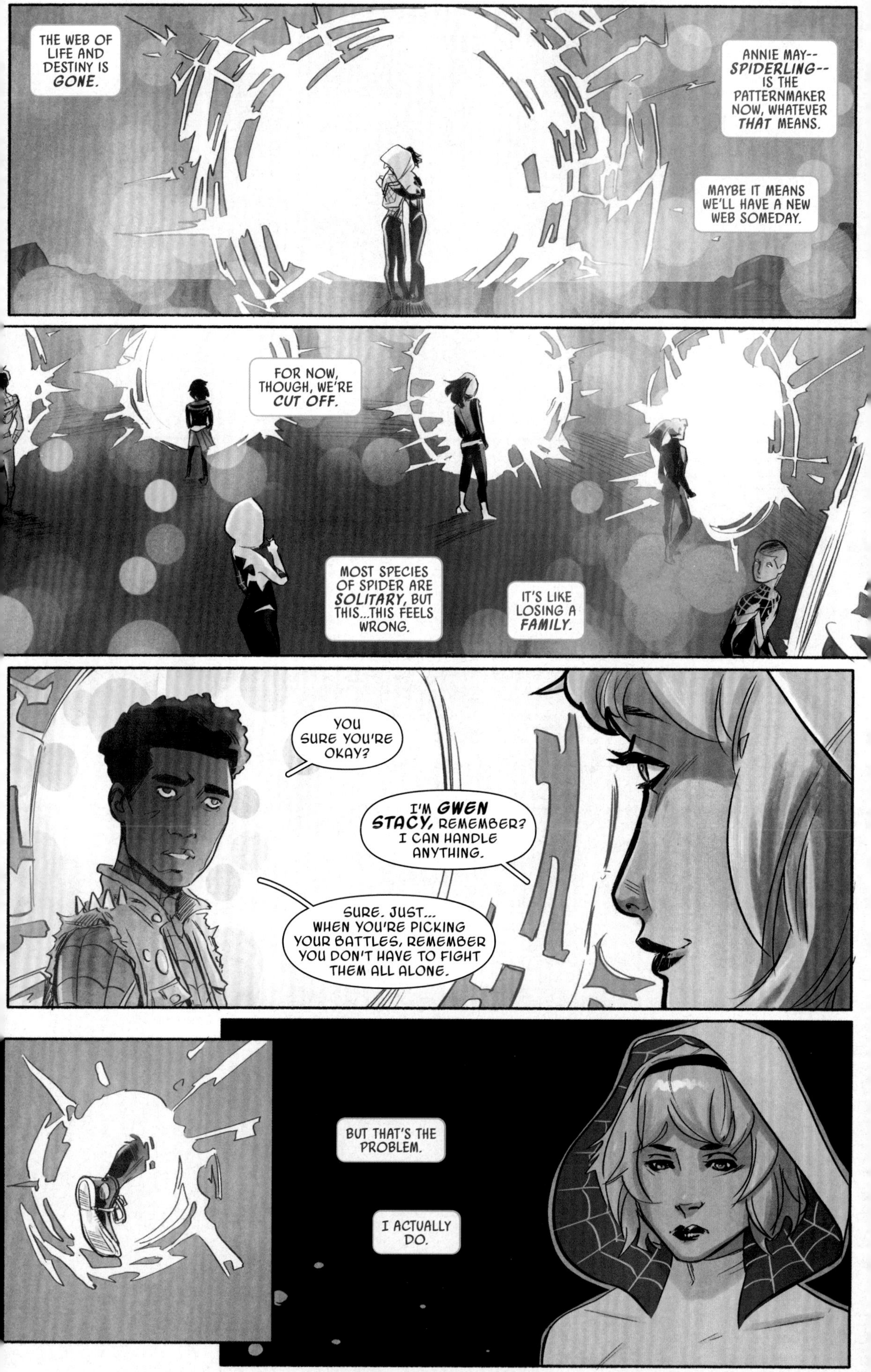

THE WEB OF LIFE AND DESTINY IS GONE.
ANNIE MAY-- SPIDERLING-- IS THE PATTERNMAKER NOW, WHATEVER THAT MEANS.
MAYBE IT MEANS WE'LL HAVE A NEW WEB SOMEDAY.
FOR NOW, THOUGH, WE'RE CUT OFF.
MOST SPECIES OF SPIDER ARE SOLITARY, BUT THIS...THIS FEELS WRONG.
IT'S LIKE LOSING A FAMILY.
YOU SURE YOU'RE OKAY?
I'M GWEN STACY, REMEMBER? I CAN HANDLE ANYTHING.
SURE. JUST... WHEN YOU'RE PICKING YOUR BATTLES, REMEMBER YOU DON'T HAVE TO FIGHT THEM ALL ALONE.
BUT THAT'S THE PROBLEM.
I ACTUALLY DO.

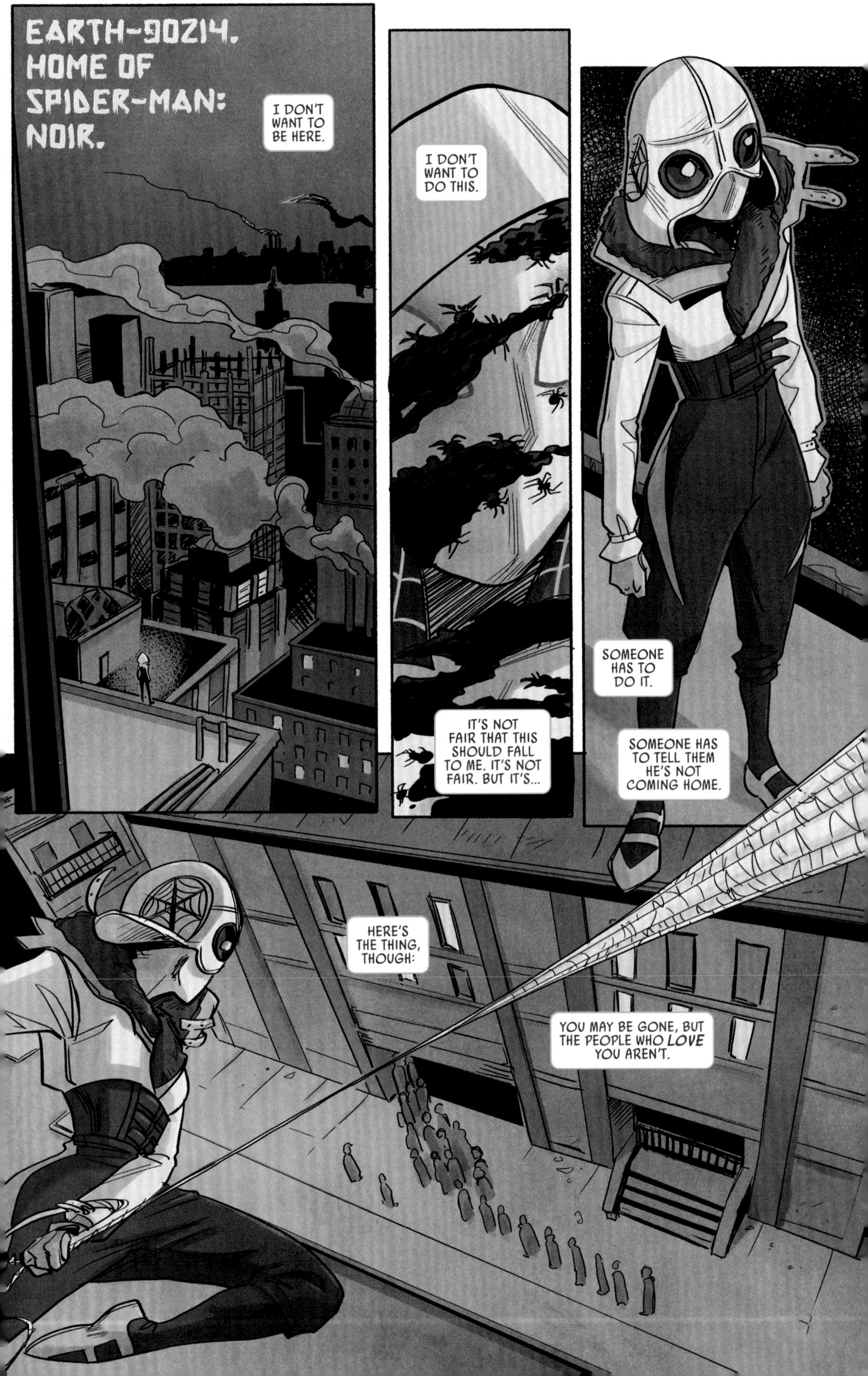
EARTH-90214. HOME OF SPIDER-MAN: NOIR.
I DON'T WANT TO BE HERE.
I DON'T WANT TO DO THIS.
IT'S NOT FAIR THAT THIS SHOULD FALL TO ME. IT'S NOT FAIR. BUT IT'S...
SOMEONE HAS TO DO IT.
SOMEONE HAS TO TELL THEM HE'S NOT COMING HOME.
HERE'S THE THING, THOUGH:
YOU MAY BE GONE, BUT THE PEOPLE WHO *LOVE* YOU AREN'T.

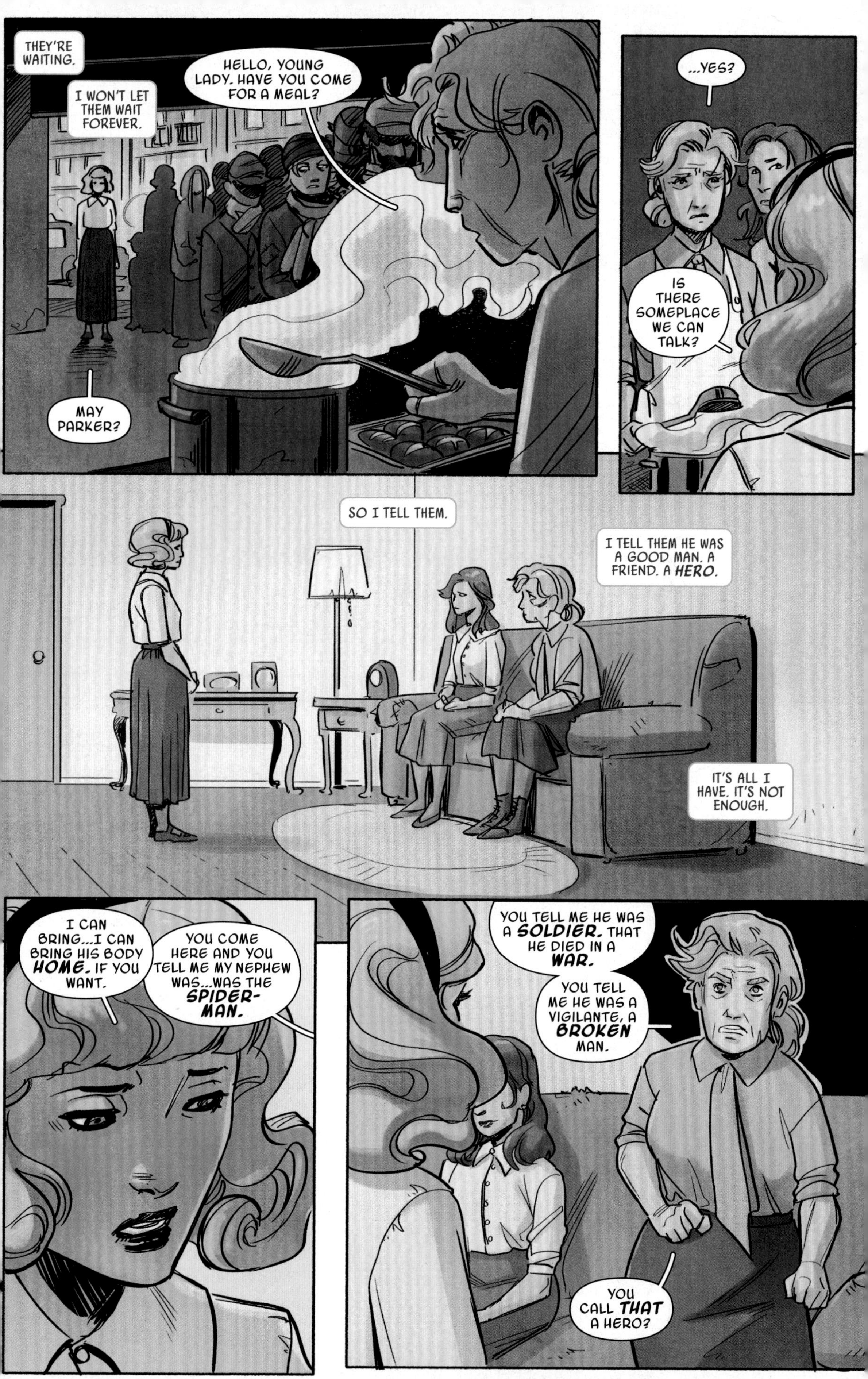
THEY'RE WAITING.
I WON'T LET THEM WAIT FOREVER.
HELLO, YOUNG LADY. HAVE YOU COME FOR A MEAL?
MAY PARKER?
...YES?
IS THERE SOMEPLACE WE CAN TALK?
SO I TELL THEM.
I TELL THEM HE WAS A GOOD MAN. A FRIEND. A HERO.
IT'S ALL I HAVE. IT'S NOT ENOUGH.
I CAN BRING...I CAN BRING HIS BODY HOME. IF YOU WANT.
YOU COME HERE AND YOU TELL ME MY NEPHEW WAS...WAS THE SPIDER-MAN.
YOU TELL ME HE WAS A SOLDIER. THAT HE DIED IN A WAR.
YOU TELL ME HE WAS A VIGILANTE, A BROKEN MAN.
YOU CALL THAT A HERO?

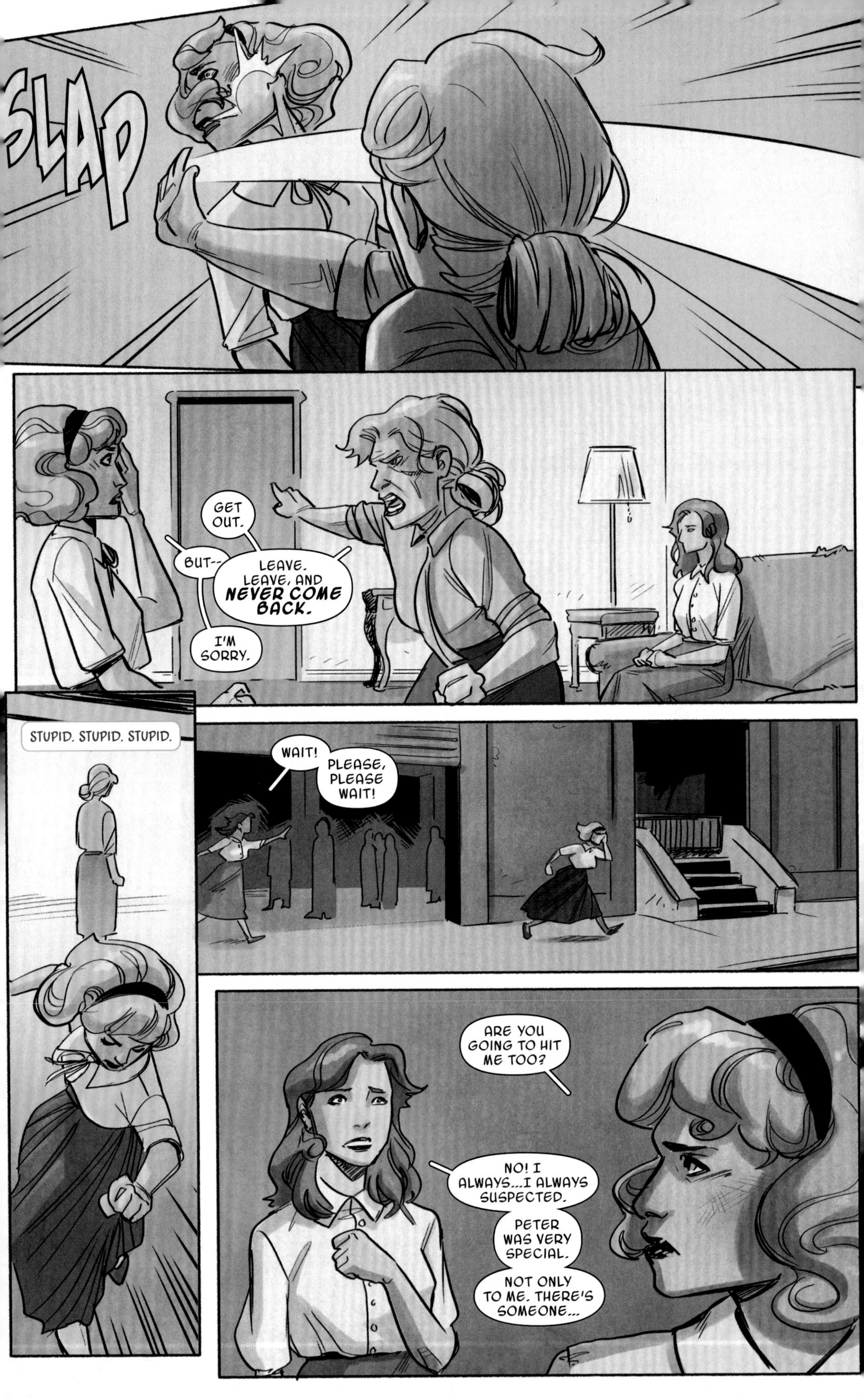
SLAP
GET OUT.
BUT--
LEAVE. LEAVE, AND NEVER COME BACK.
I'M SORRY.
STUPID. STUPID. STUPID.
WAIT!
PLEASE, PLEASE WAIT!
ARE YOU GOING TO HIT ME TOO?
NO! I ALWAYS...I ALWAYS SUSPECTED.
PETER WAS VERY SPECIAL.
NOT ONLY TO ME. THERE'S SOMEONE...

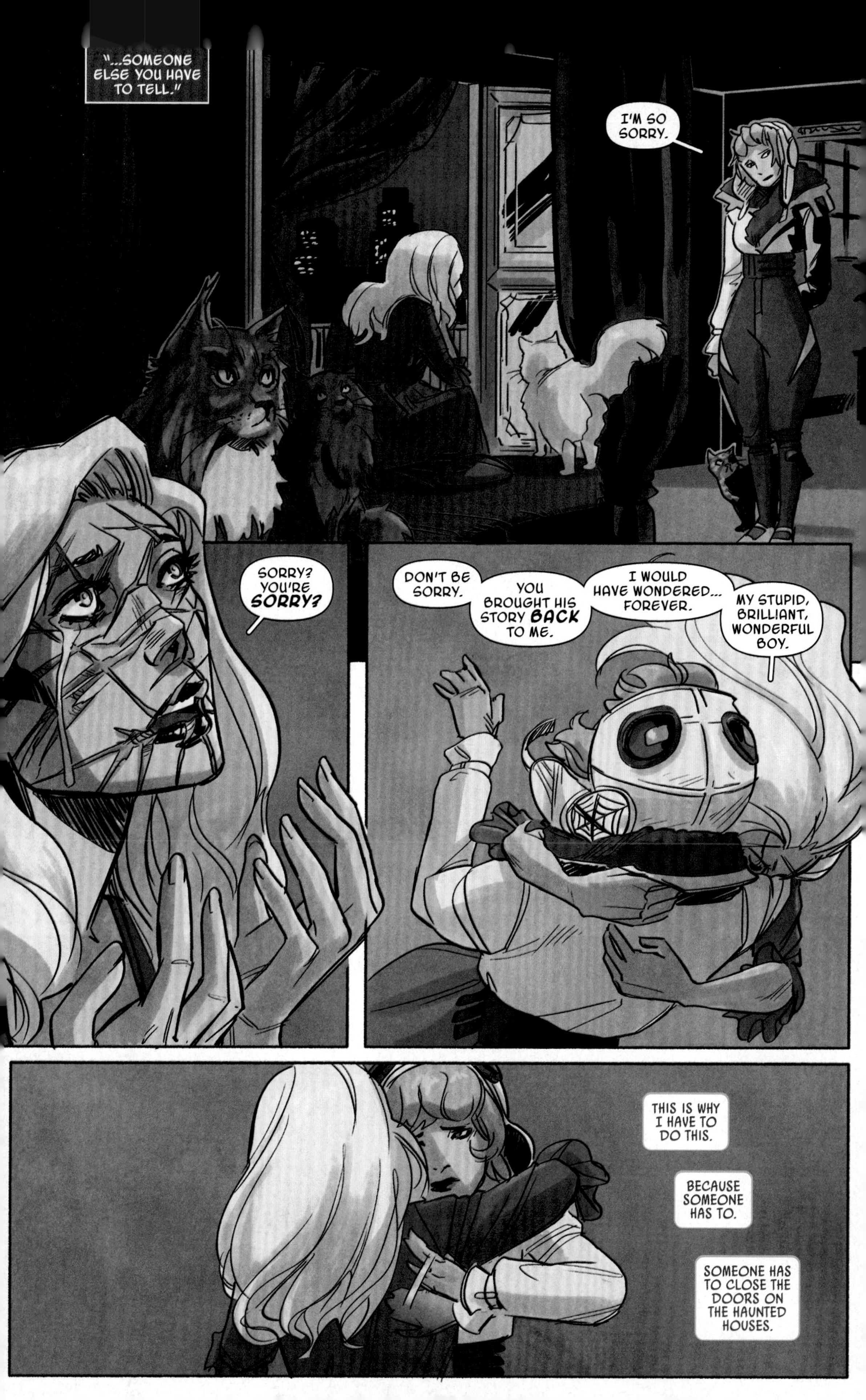
"...SOMEONE ELSE YOU HAVE TO TELL."
I'M SO SORRY.
SORRY? YOU'RE SORRY?
DON'T BE SORRY.
YOU BROUGHT HIS STORY BACK TO ME.
I WOULD HAVE WONDERED... FOREVER.
MY STUPID, BRILLIANT, WONDERFUL BOY.
THIS IS WHY I HAVE TO DO THIS.
BECAUSE SOMEONE HAS TO.
SOMEONE HAS TO CLOSE THE DOORS ON THE HAUNTED HOUSES.

EARTH-803. HOME OF THE LADY SPIDER.

SOMEONE HAS TO LET THE GHOSTS GO.

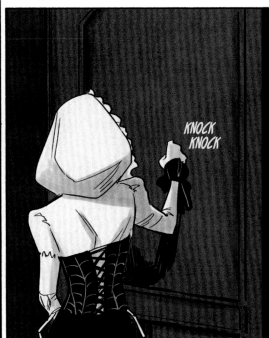

KNOCK KNOCK

GWEN! WHAT A DELIGHTFUL--

WAIT. WHERE ARE THE *OTHERS?*

WHY ARE YOU HERE? HAS SOMETHING HAPPENED?

GIVE ME A MOMENT. I'LL RETRIEVE MY ARMS, AND--

SOMEONE HAS TO LET THEM REST.

MARY. IT'S ALREADY OVER.

OH, *BILLY.*

OH, YOU BEAUTIFUL FOOL.

"WHEN I FIRST MET BILLY BRADDOCK, I THOUGHT HE WAS A BIT OF A SWOT."

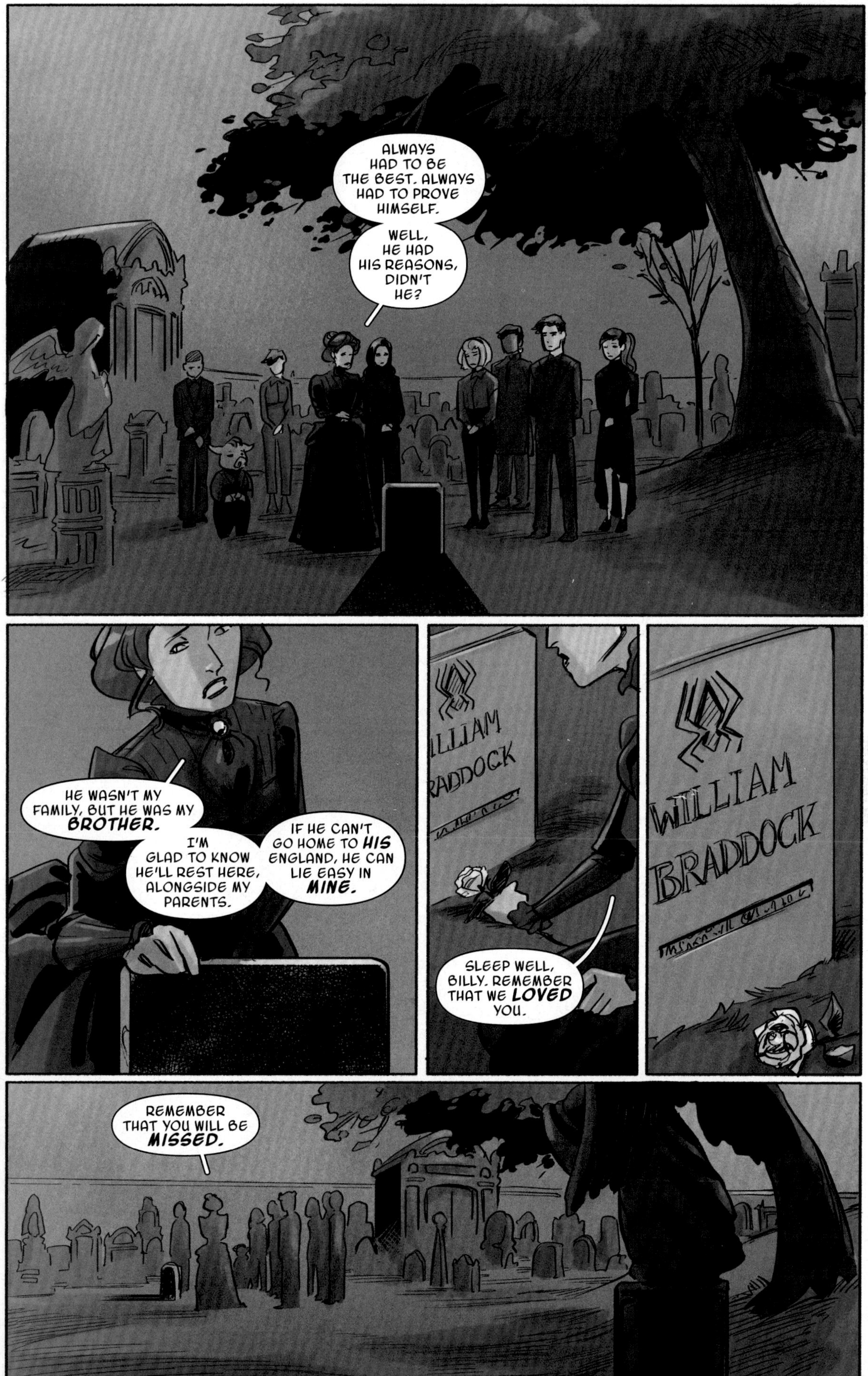
ALWAYS HAD TO BE THE BEST. ALWAYS HAD TO PROVE HIMSELF.
WELL, HE HAD HIS REASONS, DIDN'T HE?
HE WASN'T MY FAMILY, BUT HE WAS MY **BROTHER.**
I'M GLAD TO KNOW HE'LL REST HERE, ALONGSIDE MY PARENTS.
IF HE CAN'T GO HOME TO **HIS** ENGLAND, HE CAN LIE EASY IN **MINE.**
WILLIAM BRADDOCK
SLEEP WELL, BILLY. REMEMBER THAT WE **LOVED** YOU.
WILLIAM BRADDOCK
REMEMBER THAT YOU WILL BE **MISSED.**

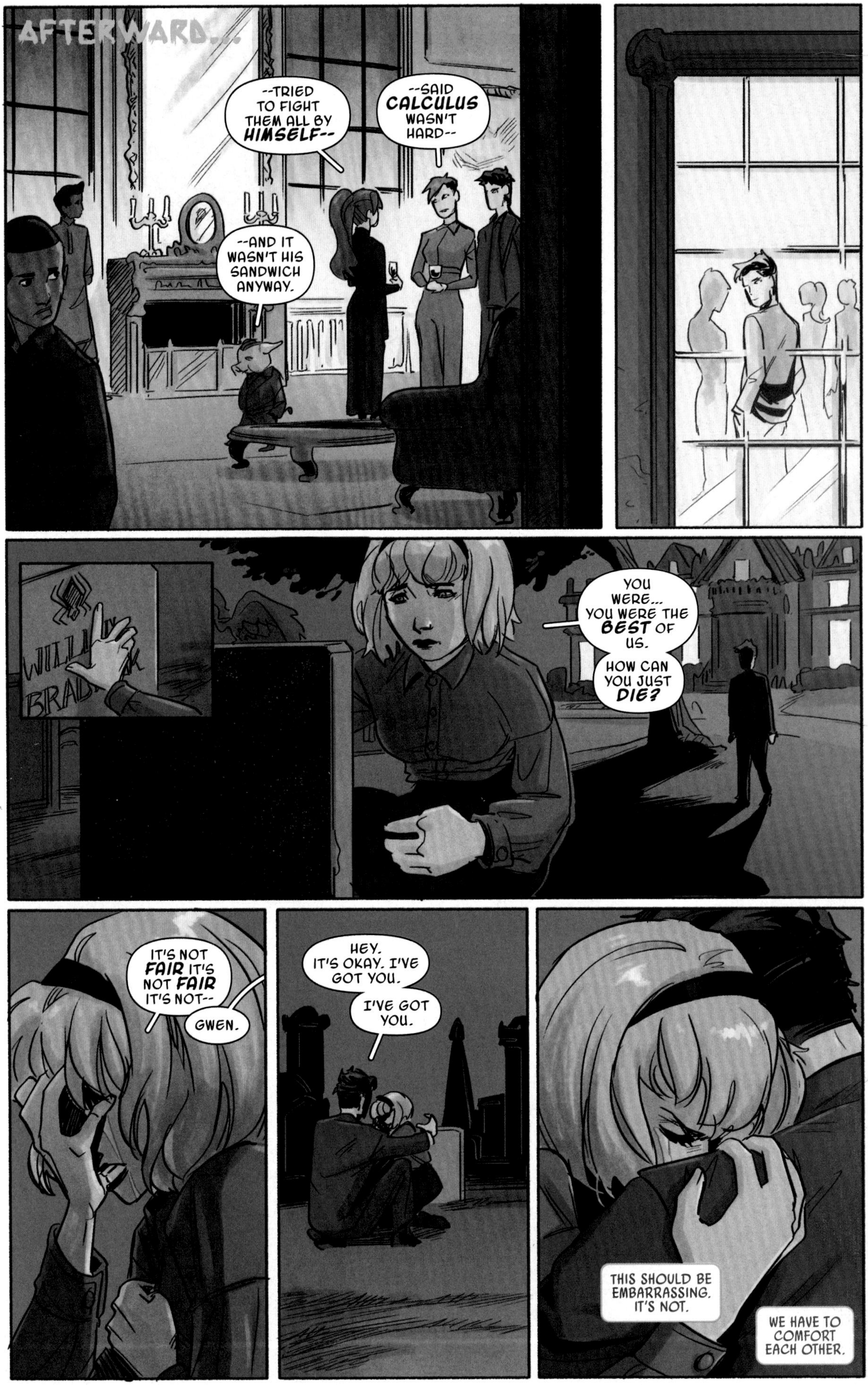
AFTERWARD...
--TRIED TO FIGHT THEM ALL BY HIMSELF--
--SAID CALCULUS WASN'T HARD--
--AND IT WASN'T HIS SANDWICH ANYWAY.
YOU WERE... YOU WERE THE BEST OF US.
HOW CAN YOU JUST DIE?
IT'S NOT FAIR IT'S NOT FAIR IT'S NOT--
GWEN.
HEY. IT'S OKAY. I'VE GOT YOU.
I'VE GOT YOU.
THIS SHOULD BE EMBARRASSING. IT'S NOT.
WE HAVE TO COMFORT EACH OTHER.

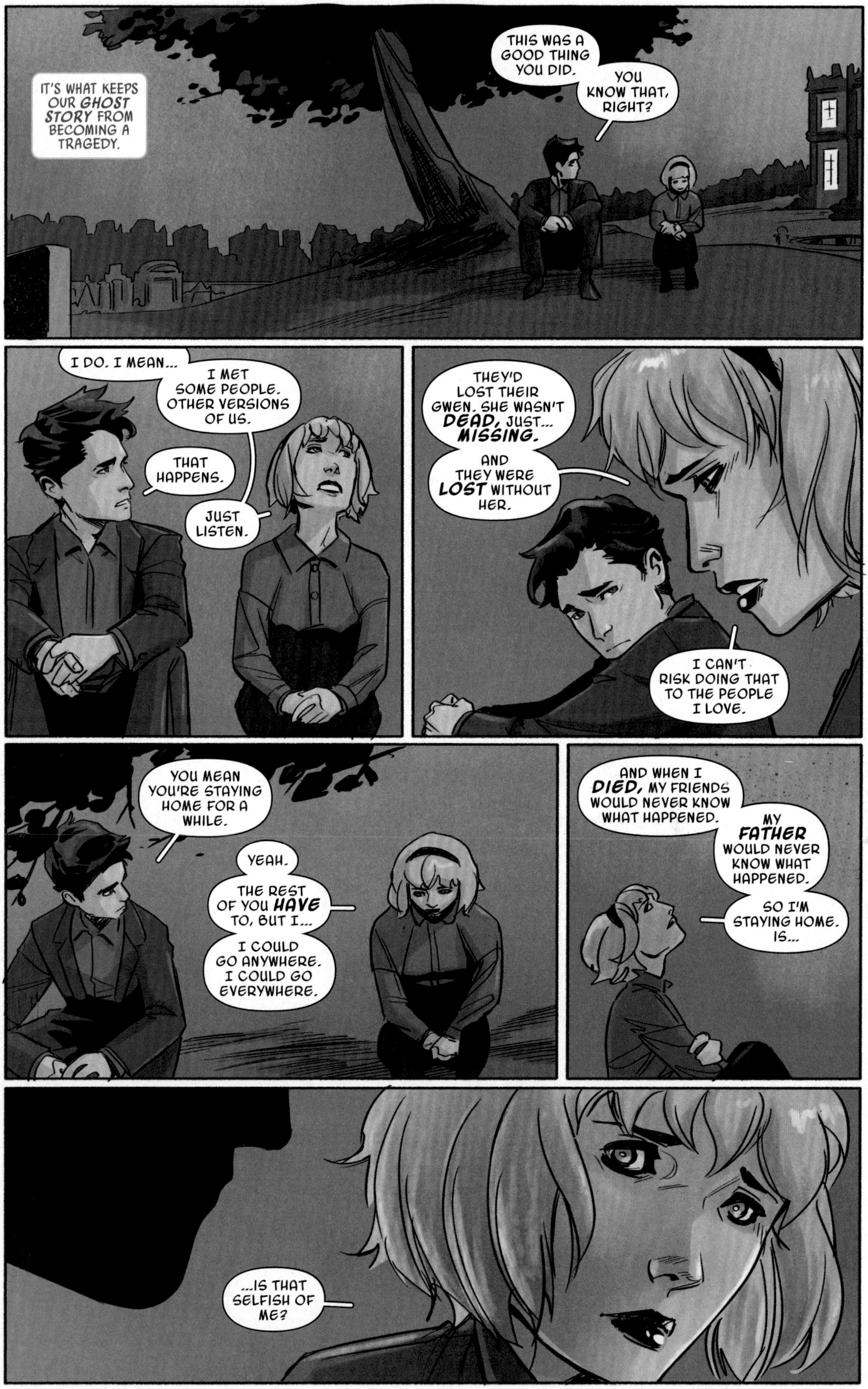
IT'S WHAT KEEPS OUR GHOST STORY FROM BECOMING A TRAGEDY.
THIS WAS A GOOD THING YOU DID.
YOU KNOW THAT, RIGHT?
I DO. I MEAN...
I MET SOME PEOPLE. OTHER VERSIONS OF US.
THAT HAPPENS.
JUST LISTEN.
THEY'D LOST THEIR GWEN. SHE WASN'T DEAD, JUST... MISSING.
AND THEY WERE LOST WITHOUT HER.
I CAN'T RISK DOING THAT TO THE PEOPLE I LOVE.
YOU MEAN YOU'RE STAYING HOME FOR A WHILE.
YEAH.
THE REST OF YOU HAVE TO, BUT I...
I COULD GO ANYWHERE. I COULD GO EVERYWHERE.
AND WHEN I DIED, MY FRIENDS WOULD NEVER KNOW WHAT HAPPENED.
MY FATHER WOULD NEVER KNOW WHAT HAPPENED.
SO I'M STAYING HOME. IS...
...IS THAT SELFISH OF ME?

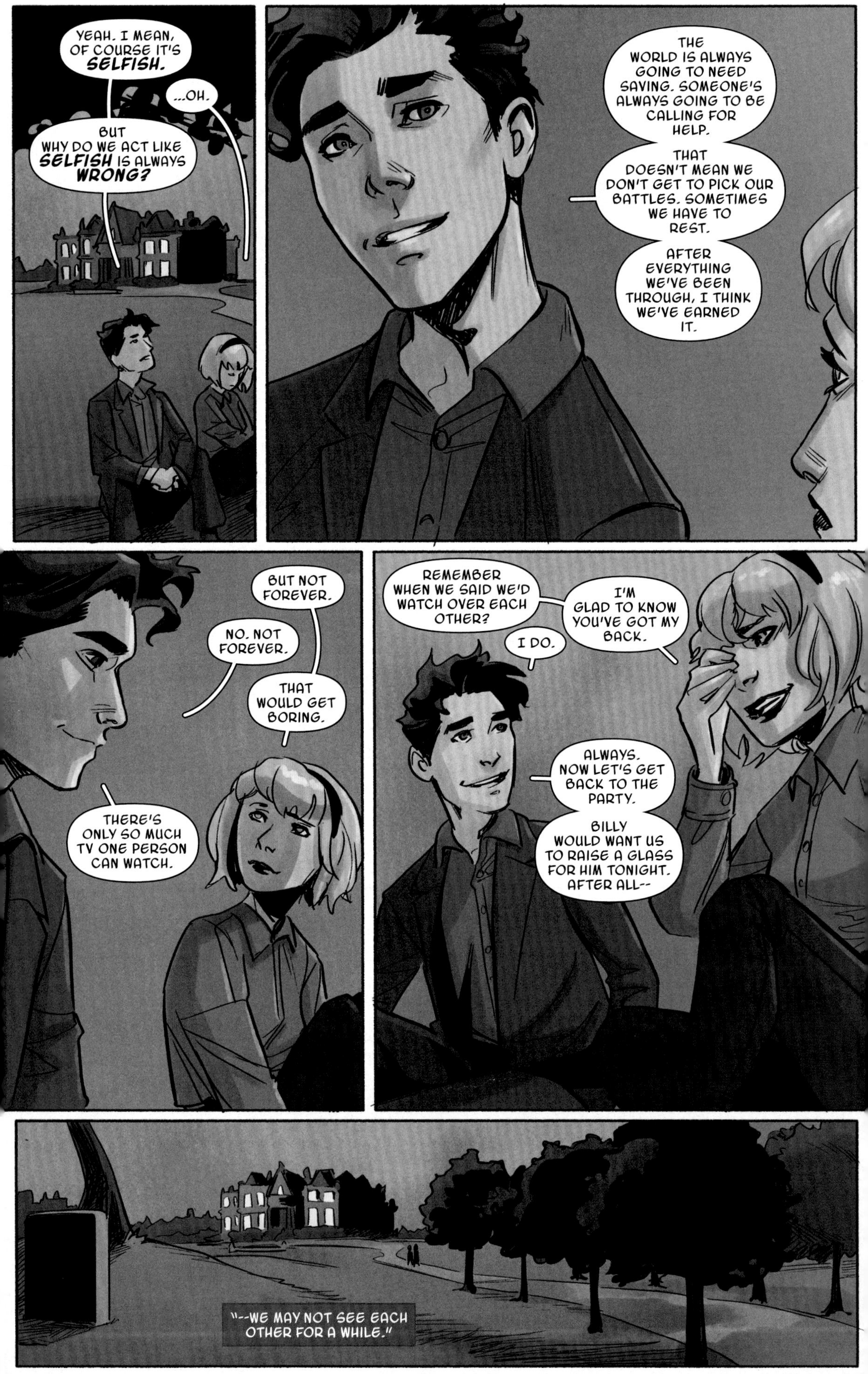
YEAH. I MEAN, OF COURSE IT'S **SELFISH.**
...OH.
BUT WHY DO WE ACT LIKE **SELFISH** IS ALWAYS **WRONG?**
THE WORLD IS ALWAYS GOING TO NEED SAVING. SOMEONE'S ALWAYS GOING TO BE CALLING FOR HELP.
THAT DOESN'T MEAN WE DON'T GET TO PICK OUR BATTLES. SOMETIMES WE HAVE TO REST.
AFTER EVERYTHING WE'VE BEEN THROUGH, I THINK WE'VE EARNED IT.
BUT NOT FOREVER.
NO. NOT FOREVER.
THAT WOULD GET BORING.
THERE'S ONLY SO MUCH TV ONE PERSON CAN WATCH.
REMEMBER WHEN WE SAID WE'D WATCH OVER EACH OTHER?
I DO.
I'M GLAD TO KNOW YOU'VE GOT MY BACK.
ALWAYS. NOW LET'S GET BACK TO THE PARTY.
BILLY WOULD WANT US TO RAISE A GLASS FOR HIM TONIGHT. AFTER ALL--
"--WE MAY NOT SEE EACH OTHER FOR A WHILE."

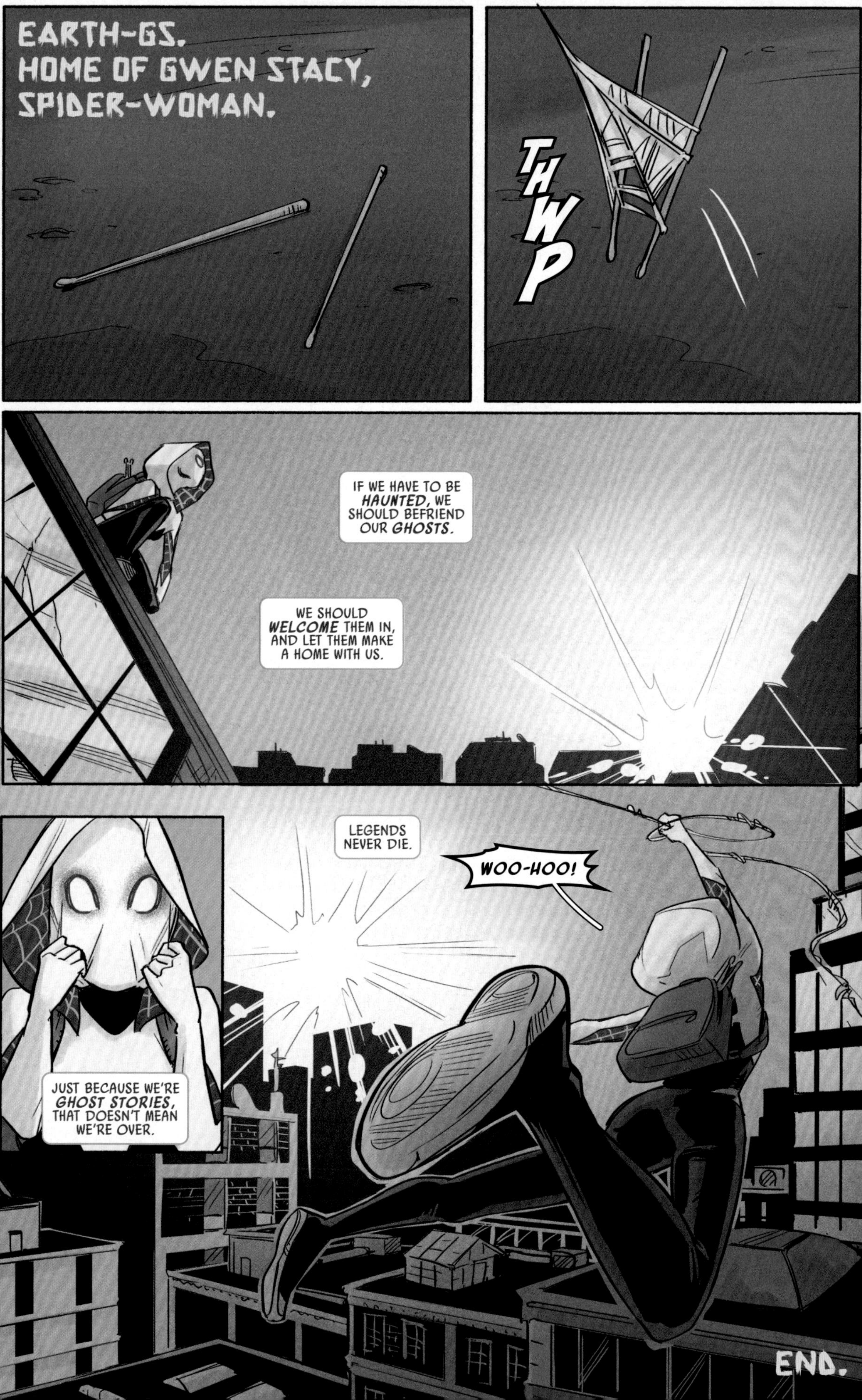
EARTH-65. HOME OF GWEN STACY, SPIDER-WOMAN.
THWP
IF WE HAVE TO BE HAUNTED, WE SHOULD BEFRIEND OUR GHOSTS.
WE SHOULD WELCOME THEM IN, AND LET THEM MAKE A HOME WITH US.
JUST BECAUSE WE'RE GHOST STORIES, THAT DOESN'T MEAN WE'RE OVER.
LEGENDS NEVER DIE.
WOO-HOO!
END.

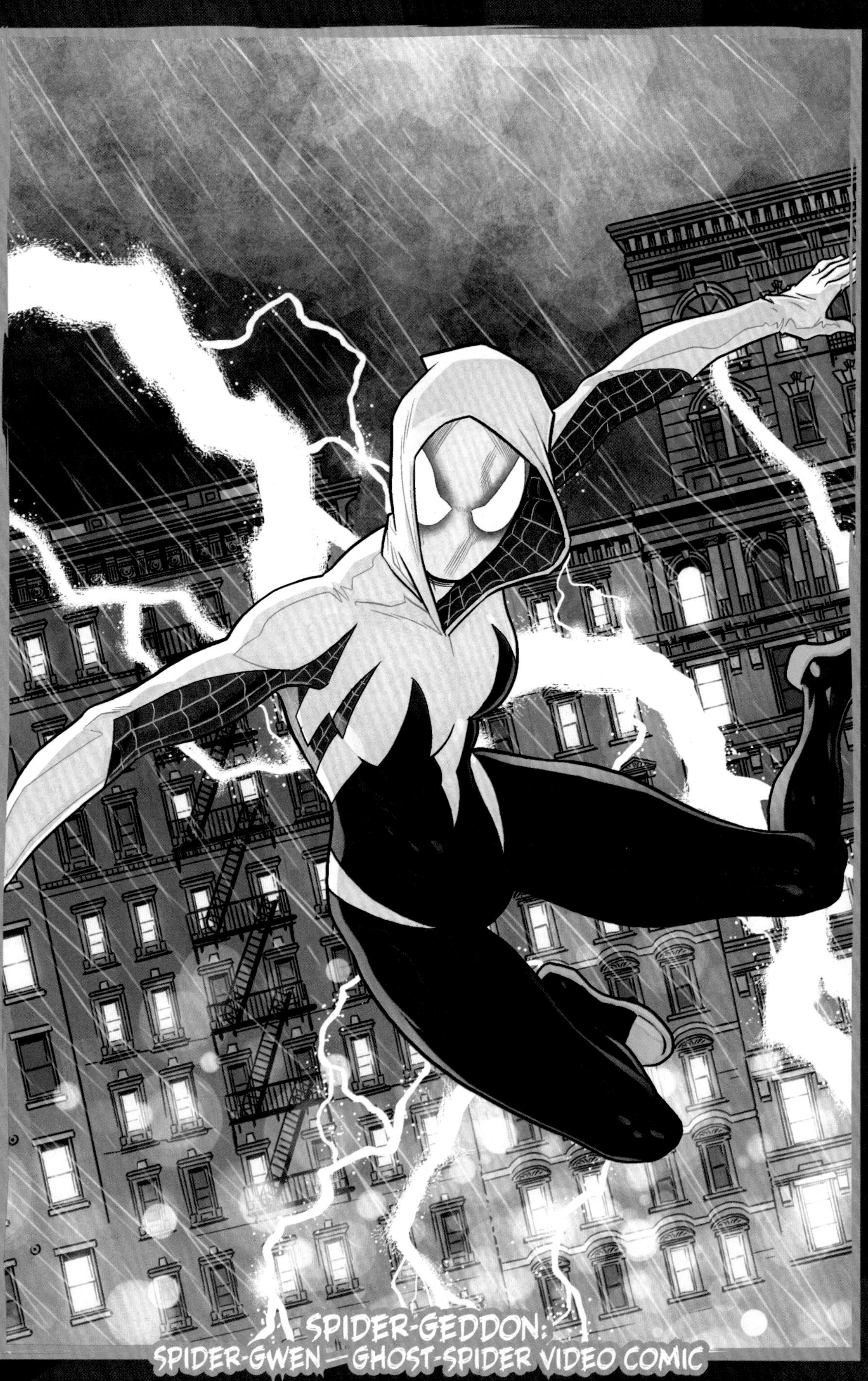
SPIDER-GEDDON:
SPIDER-GWEN — GHOST-SPIDER VIDEO COMIC

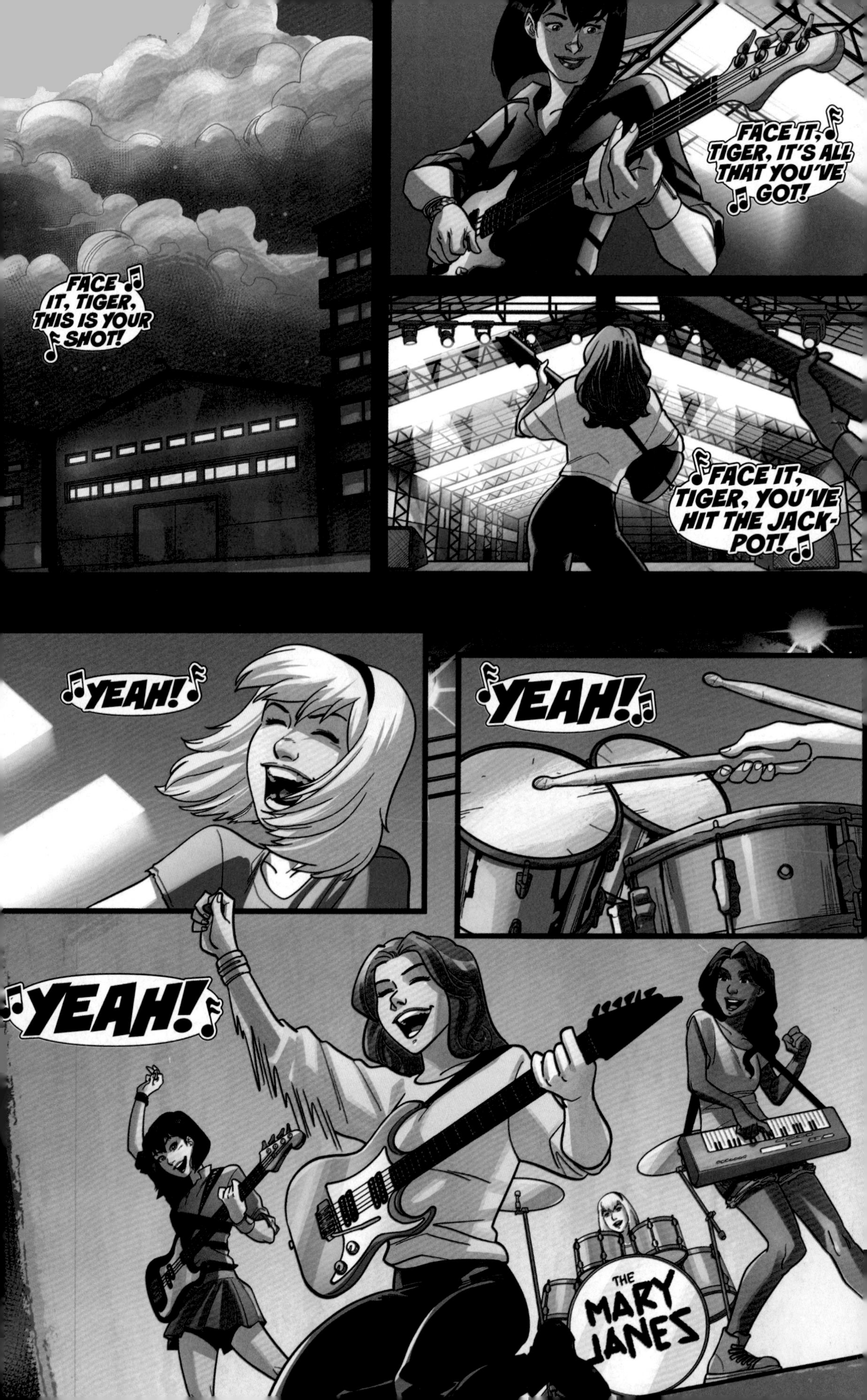
FACE IT, TIGER, THIS IS YOUR SHOT!
FACE IT, TIGER, IT'S ALL THAT YOU'VE GOT!
FACE IT, TIGER, YOU'VE HIT THE JACK-POT!
YEAH!
YEAH!
YEAH!
THE MARY JANES

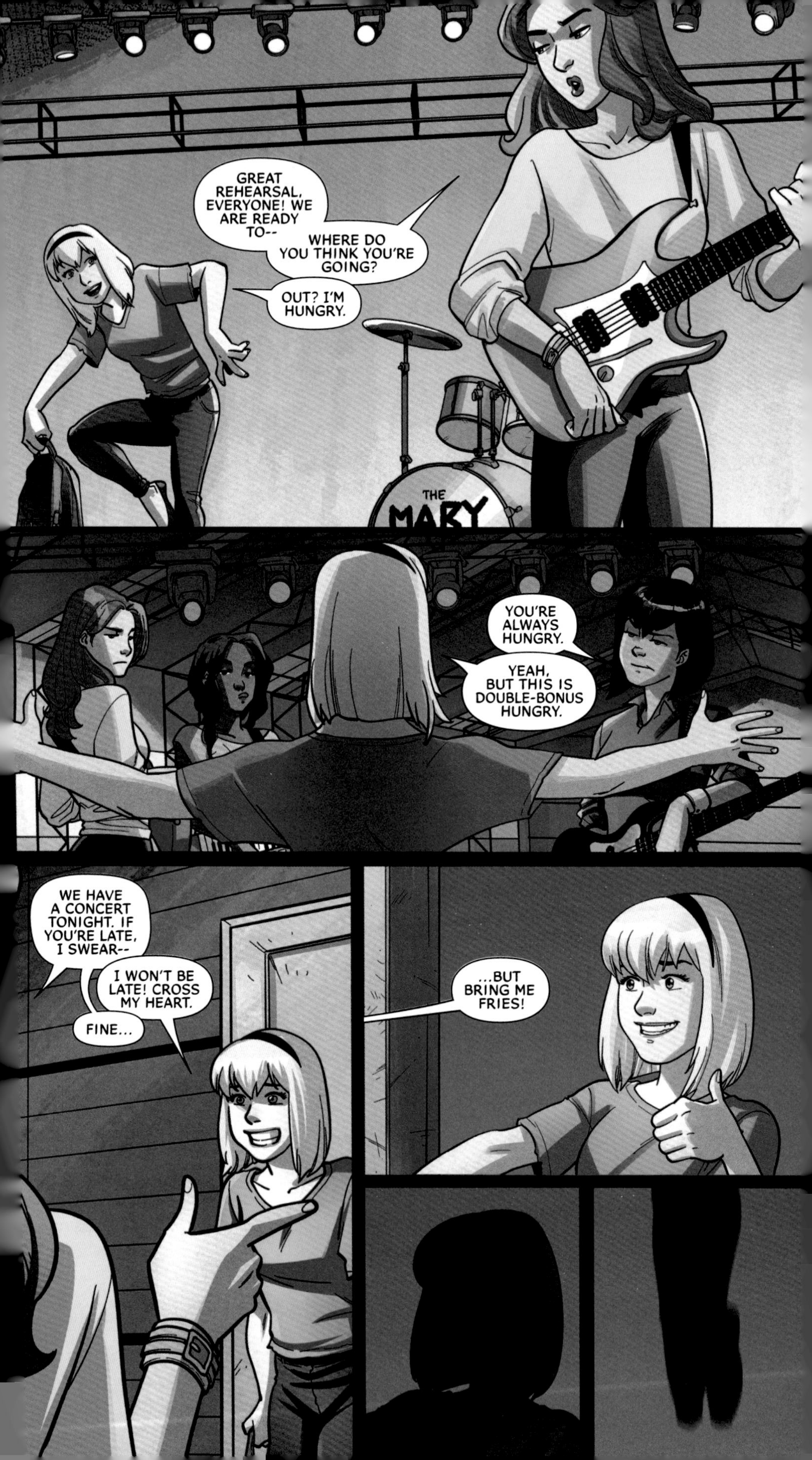
GREAT REHEARSAL, EVERYONE! WE ARE READY TO--
WHERE DO YOU THINK YOU'RE GOING?
OUT? I'M HUNGRY.
THE MARY
YOU'RE ALWAYS HUNGRY.
YEAH, BUT THIS IS DOUBLE-BONUS HUNGRY.
WE HAVE A CONCERT TONIGHT. IF YOU'RE LATE, I SWEAR--
I WON'T BE LATE! CROSS MY HEART.
FINE...
...BUT BRING ME FRIES!

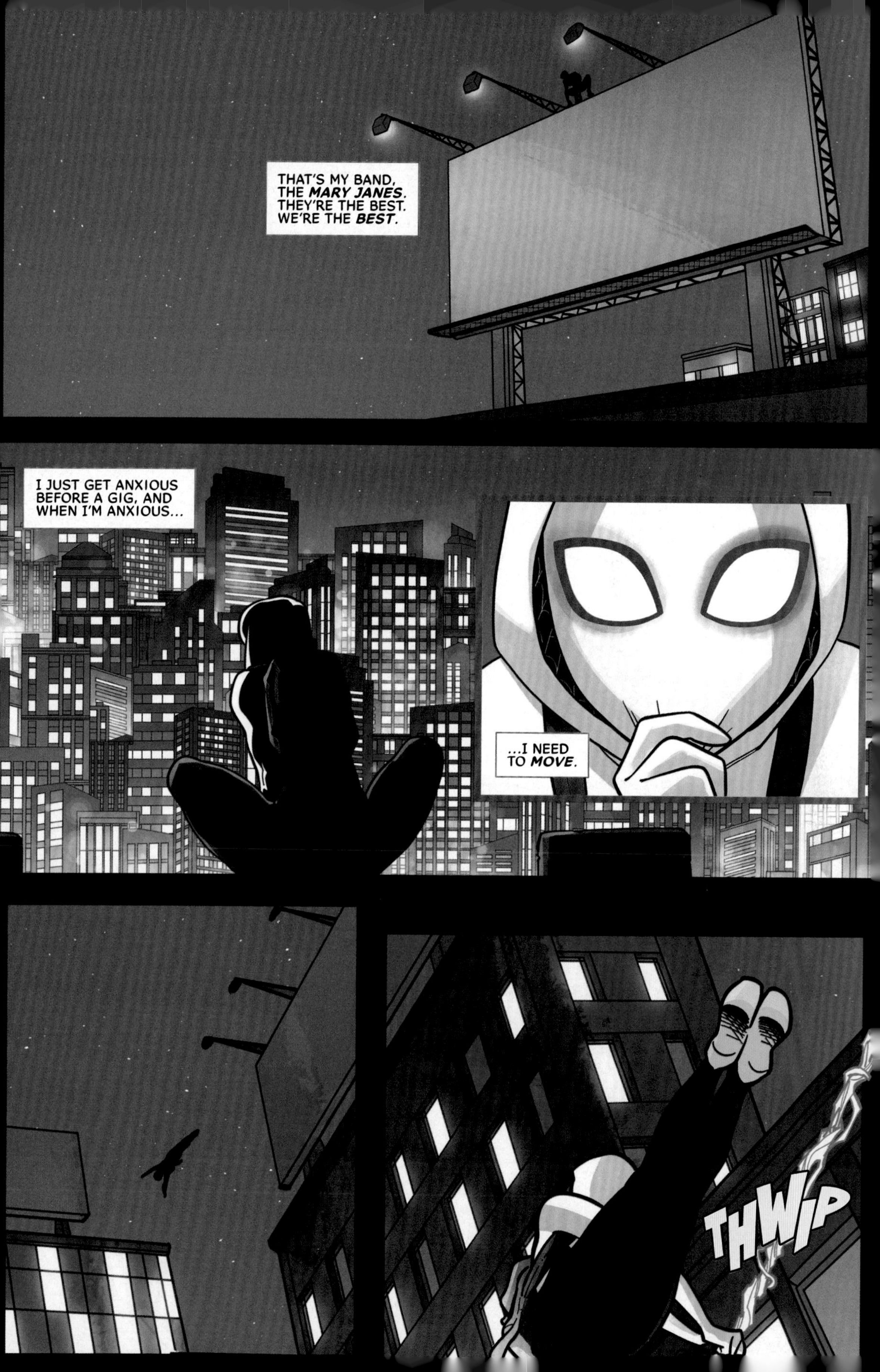

THAT'S MY BAND, THE MARY JANES. THEY'RE THE BEST. WE'RE THE BEST.
I JUST GET ANXIOUS BEFORE A GIG, AND WHEN I'M ANXIOUS...
...I NEED TO MOVE.
THWIP

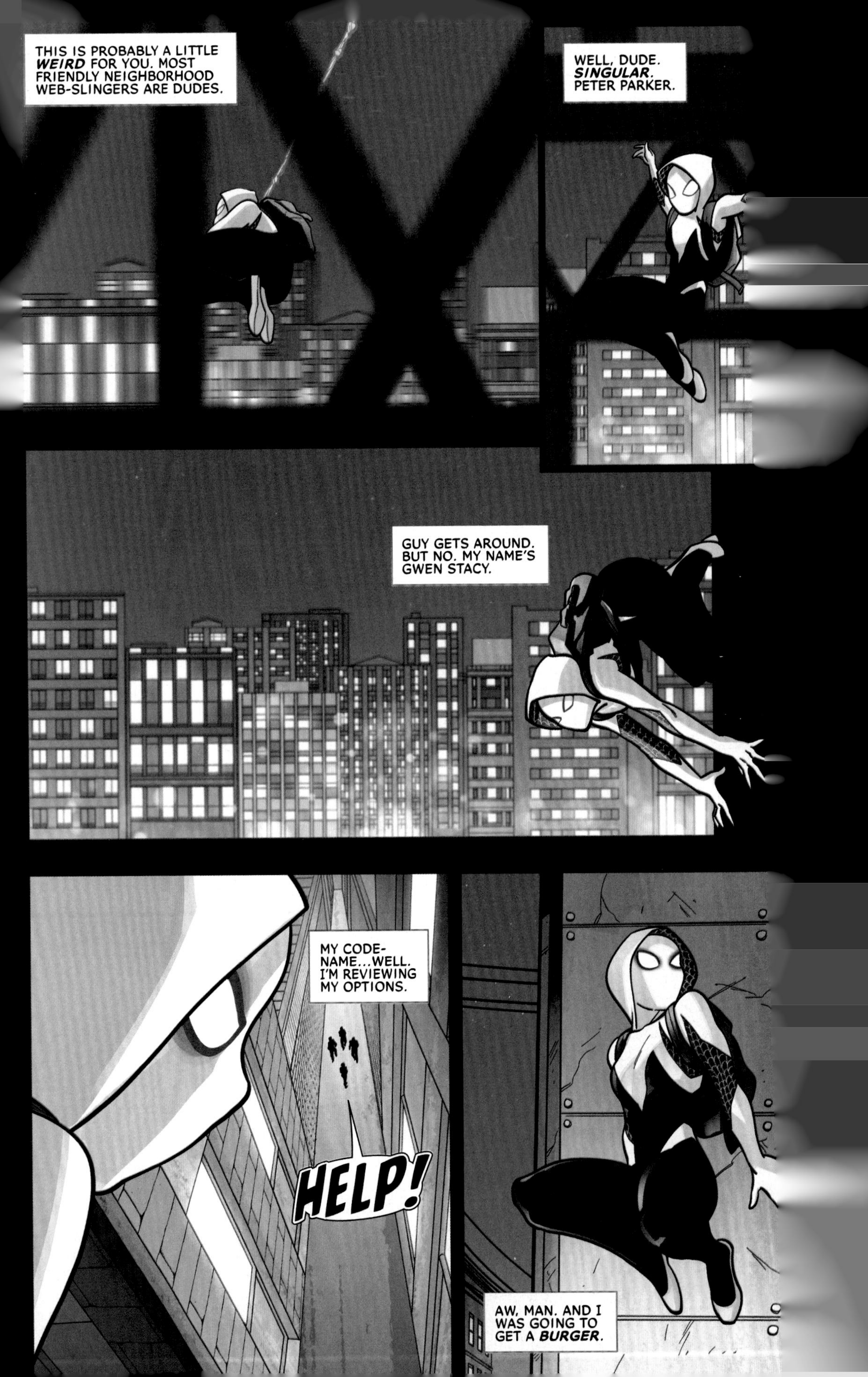
THIS IS PROBABLY A LITTLE WEIRD FOR YOU. MOST FRIENDLY NEIGHBORHOOD WEB-SLINGERS ARE DUDES.
WELL, DUDE. SINGULAR. PETER PARKER.
GUY GETS AROUND. BUT NO. MY NAME'S GWEN STACY.
MY CODE-NAME...WELL. I'M REVIEWING MY OPTIONS.
HELP!
AW, MAN. AND I WAS GOING TO GET A BURGER.

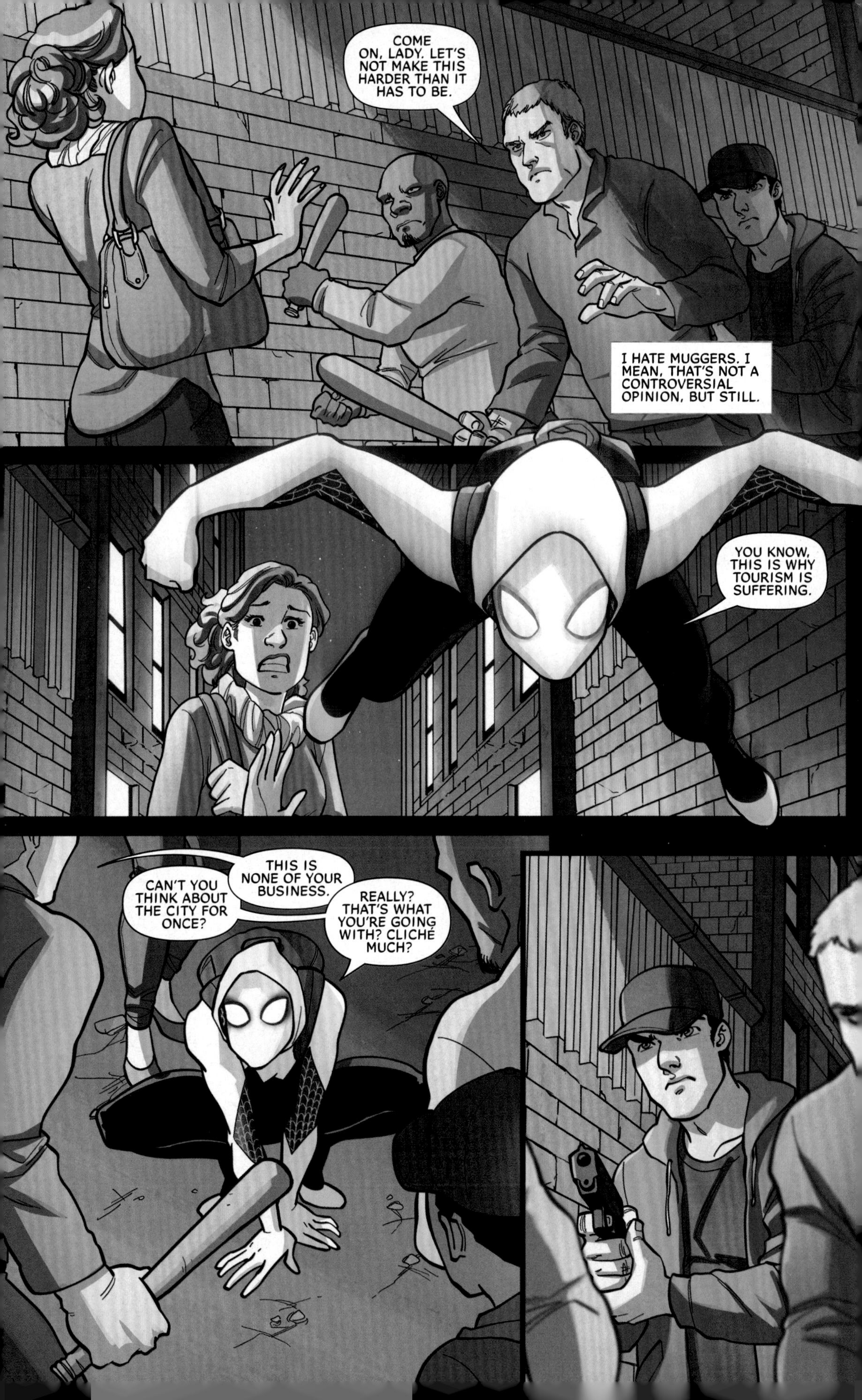
COME ON, LADY. LET'S NOT MAKE THIS HARDER THAN IT HAS TO BE.
I HATE MUGGERS. I MEAN, THAT'S NOT A CONTROVERSIAL OPINION, BUT STILL.
YOU KNOW, THIS IS WHY TOURISM IS SUFFERING.
CAN'T YOU THINK ABOUT THE CITY FOR ONCE?
THIS IS NONE OF YOUR BUSINESS.
REALLY? THAT'S WHAT YOU'RE GOING WITH? CLICHÉ MUCH?

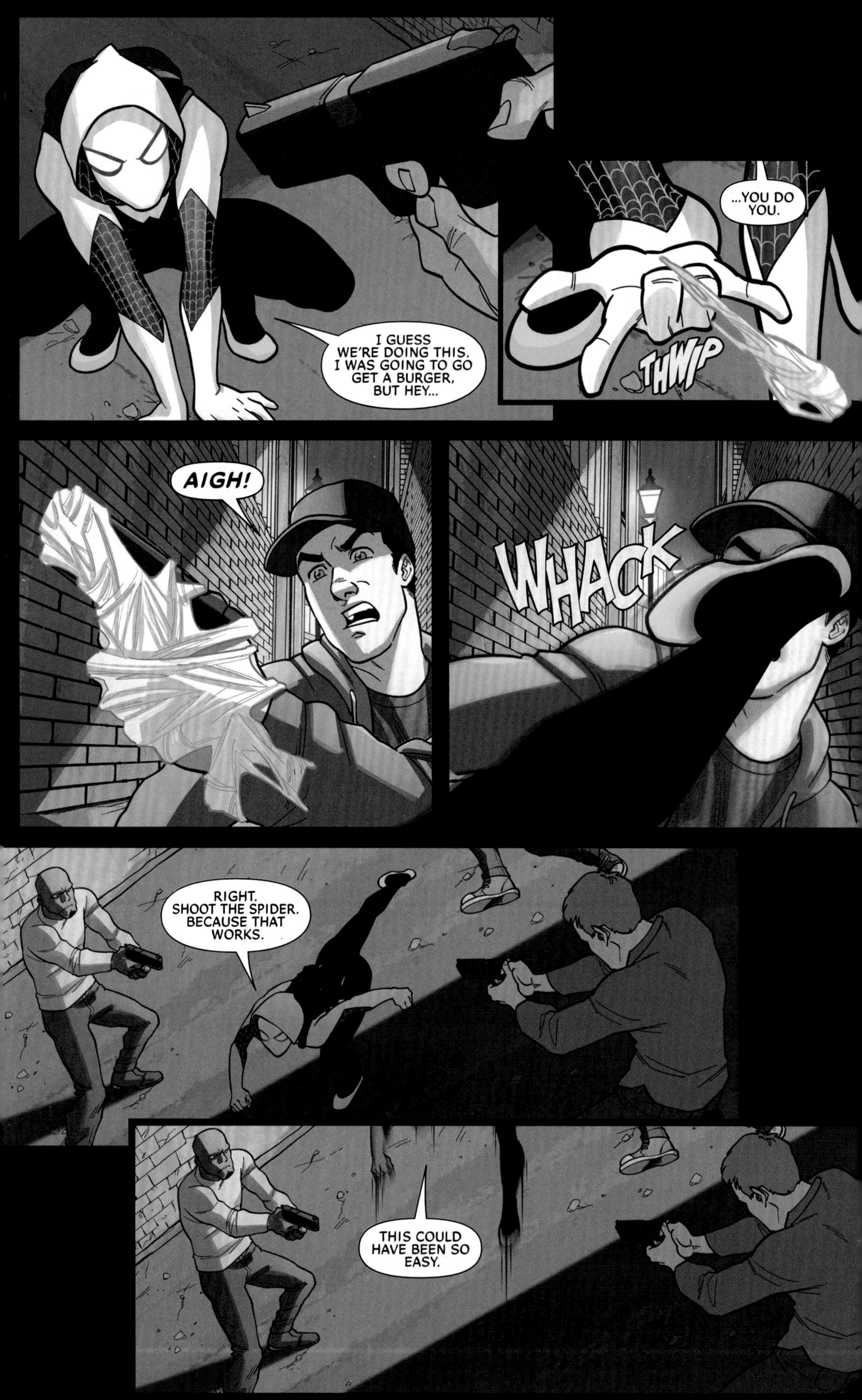
I GUESS WE'RE DOING THIS. I WAS GOING TO GO GET A BURGER, BUT HEY...
...YOU DO YOU.
THWIP
AIGH!
WHACK
RIGHT. SHOOT THE SPIDER. BECAUSE THAT WORKS.
THIS COULD HAVE BEEN SO EASY.

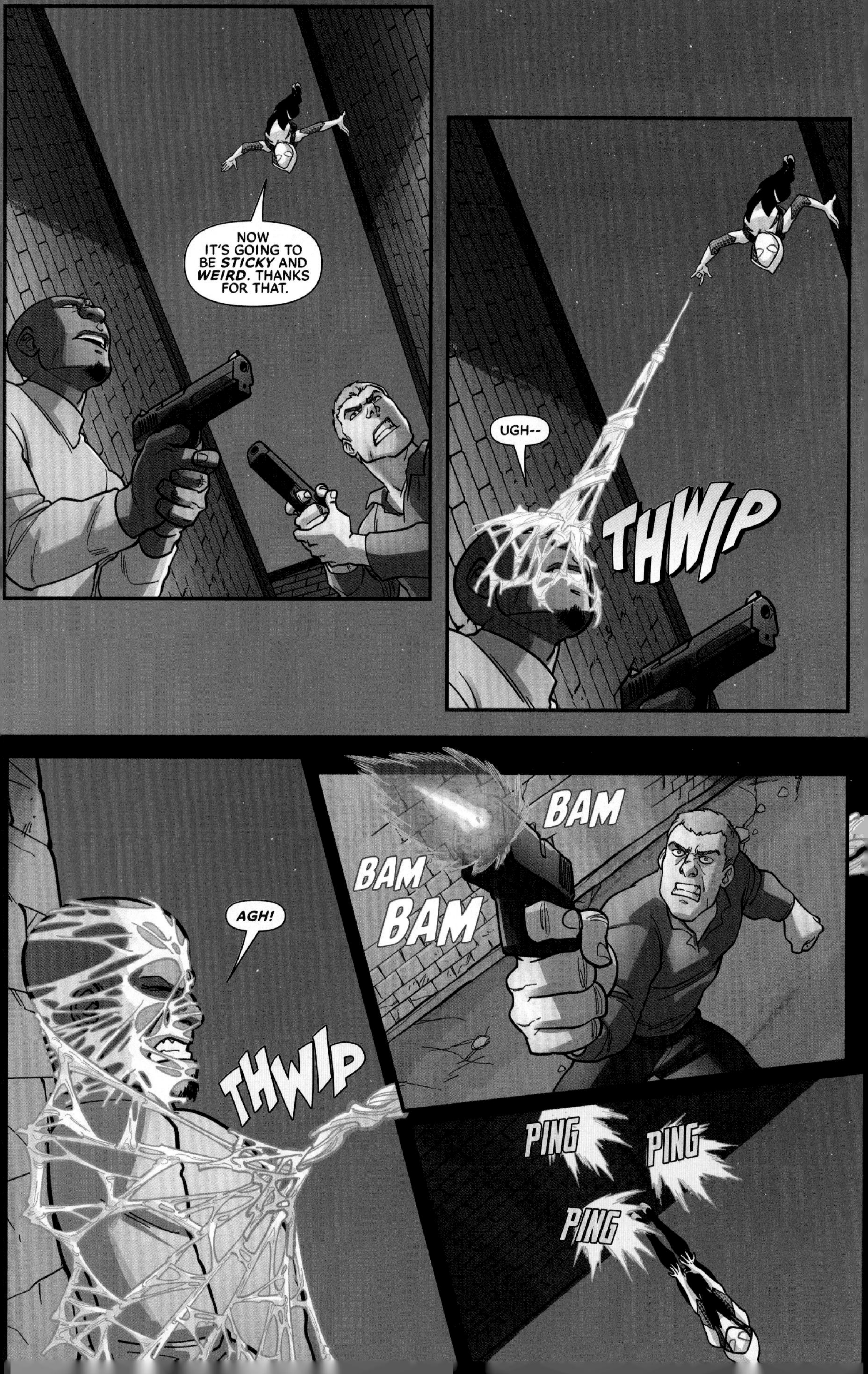
NOW IT'S GOING TO BE *STICKY* AND *WEIRD*. THANKS FOR THAT.
UGH--
THWIP
AGH!
THWIP
BAM
BAM
BAM
PING
PING
PING

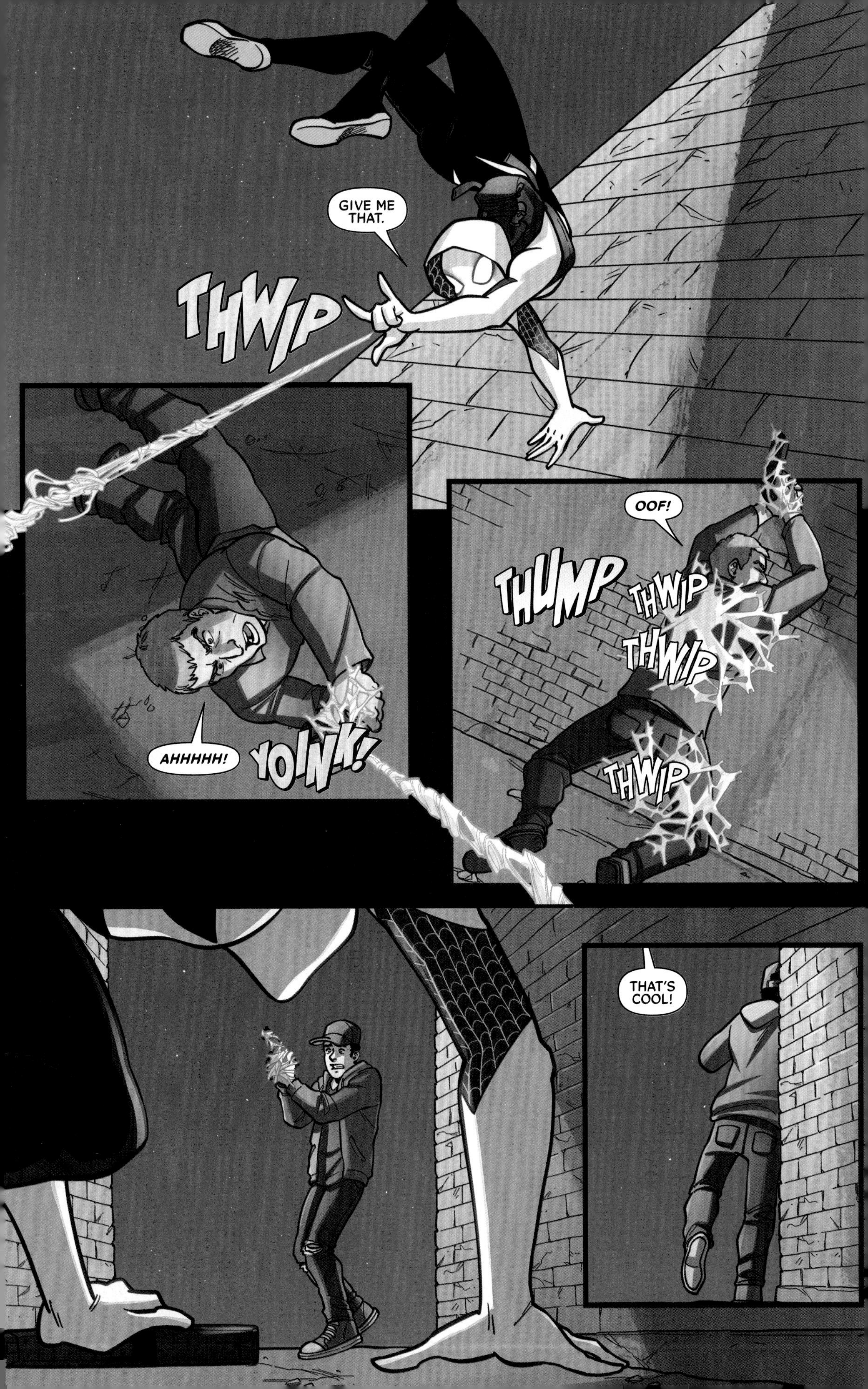
GIVE ME THAT.
THWIP
AHHHHH!
YOINK!
OOF!
THUMP
THWIP
THWIP
THWIP
THAT'S COOL!

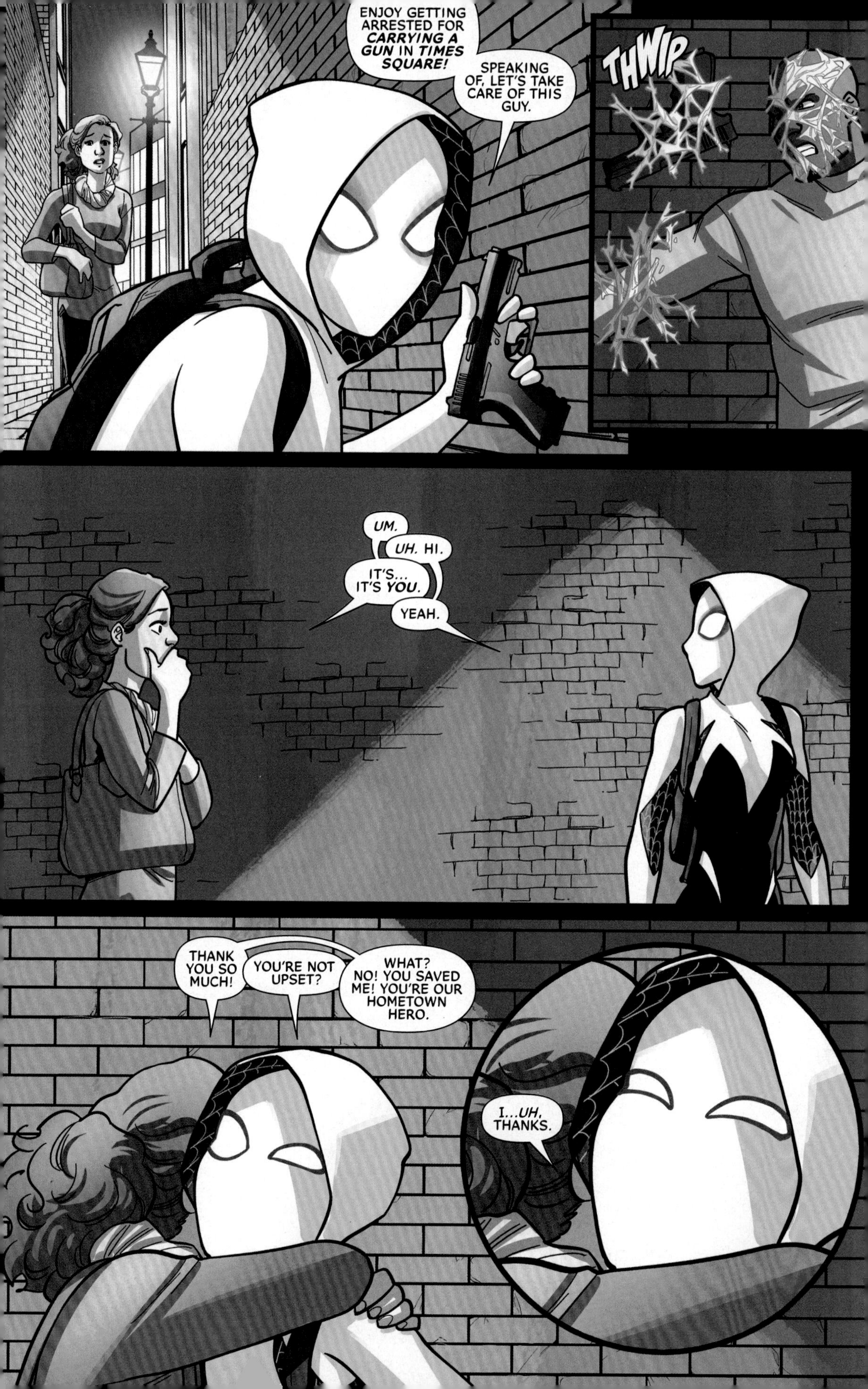

ENJOY GETTING ARRESTED FOR CARRYING A GUN IN TIMES SQUARE!
SPEAKING OF, LET'S TAKE CARE OF THIS GUY.
THWIP
UM.
UH. HI.
IT'S... IT'S YOU.
YEAH.
THANK YOU SO MUCH!
YOU'RE NOT UPSET?
WHAT? NO! YOU SAVED ME! YOU'RE OUR HOMETOWN HERO.
I...UH, THANKS.

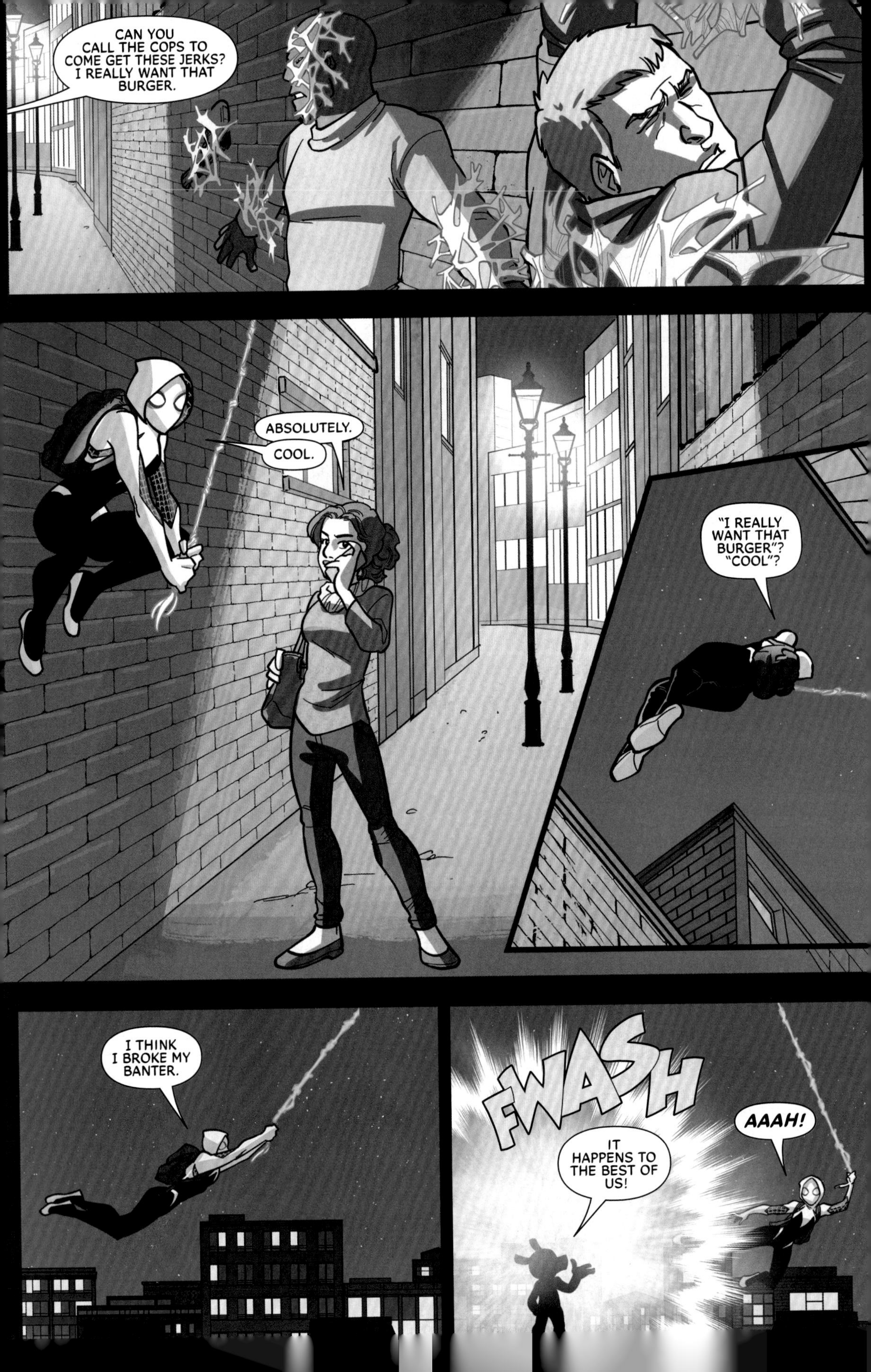
CAN YOU CALL THE COPS TO COME GET THESE JERKS? I REALLY WANT THAT BURGER.
ABSOLUTELY.
COOL.
"I REALLY WANT THAT BURGER"? "COOL"?
I THINK I BROKE MY BANTER.
FWASH
IT HAPPENS TO THE BEST OF US!
AAAH!

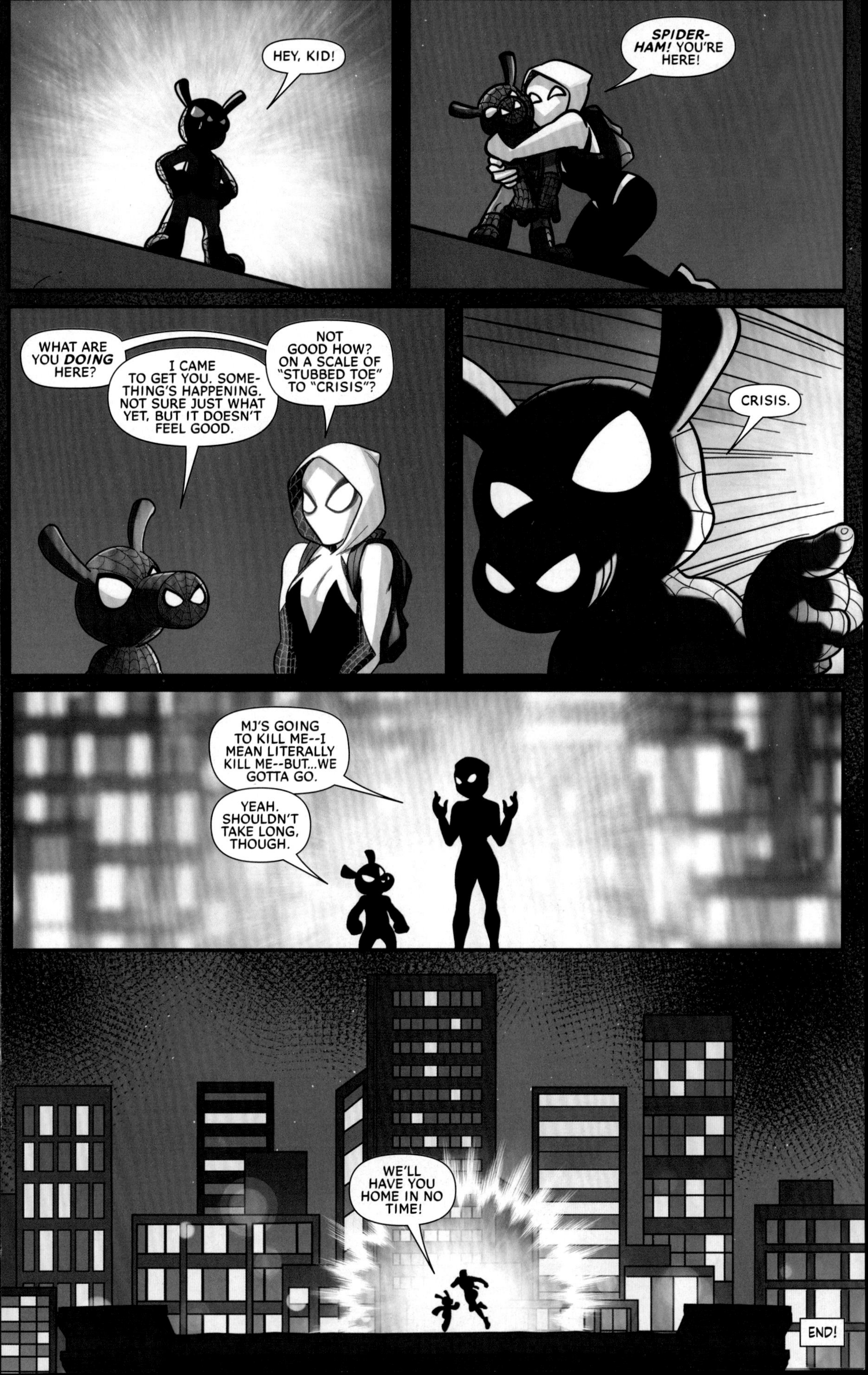
HEY, KID!
SPIDER-HAM! YOU'RE HERE!
WHAT ARE YOU DOING HERE?
I CAME TO GET YOU. SOMETHING'S HAPPENING. NOT SURE JUST WHAT YET, BUT IT DOESN'T FEEL GOOD.
NOT GOOD HOW? ON A SCALE OF "STUBBED TOE" TO "CRISIS"?
CRISIS.
MJ'S GOING TO KILL ME--I MEAN LITERALLY KILL ME--BUT...WE GOTTA GO.
YEAH. SHOULDN'T TAKE LONG, THOUGH.
WE'LL HAVE YOU HOME IN NO TIME!
END!

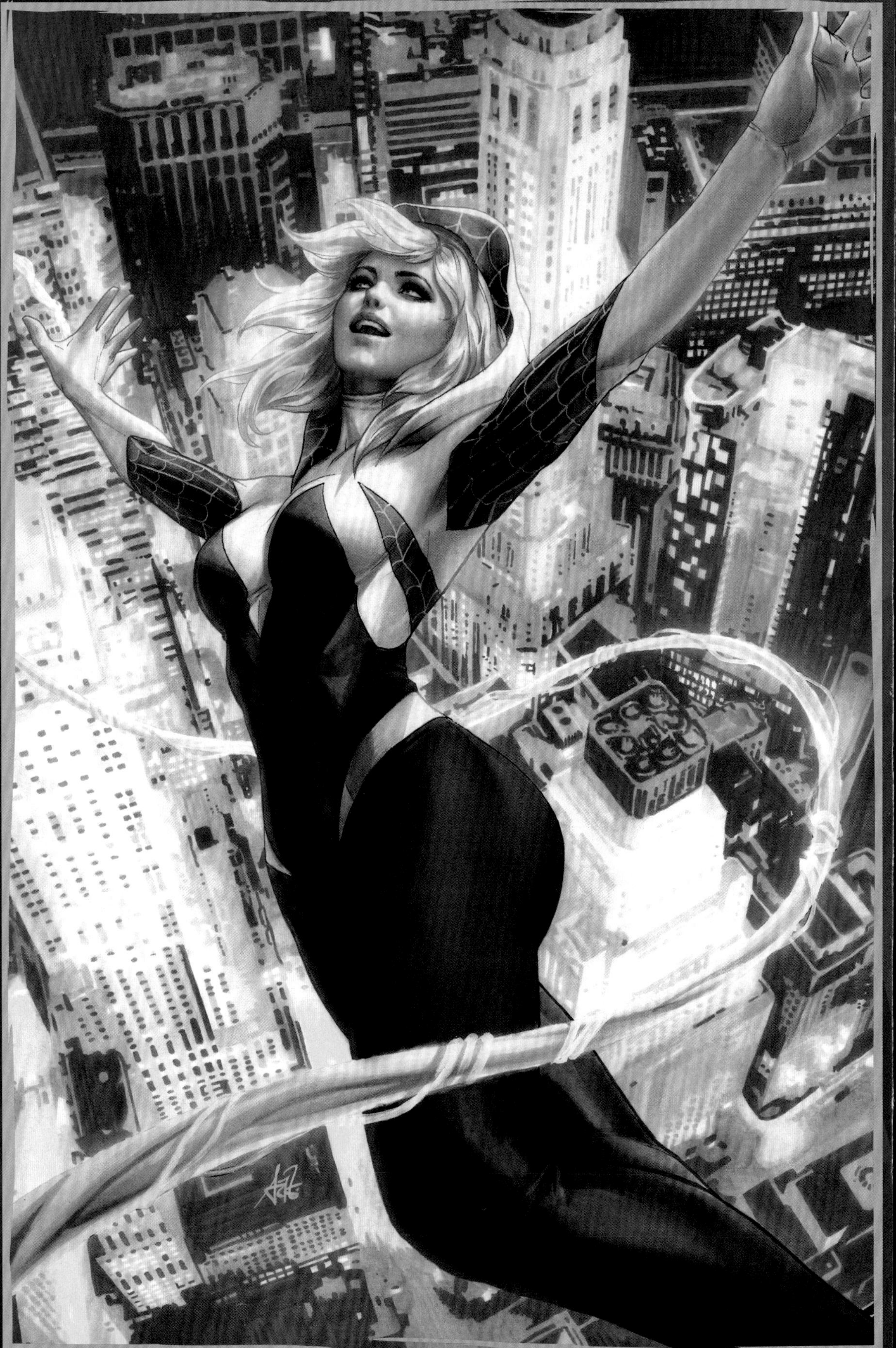

#I VARIANT BY ARTGERM

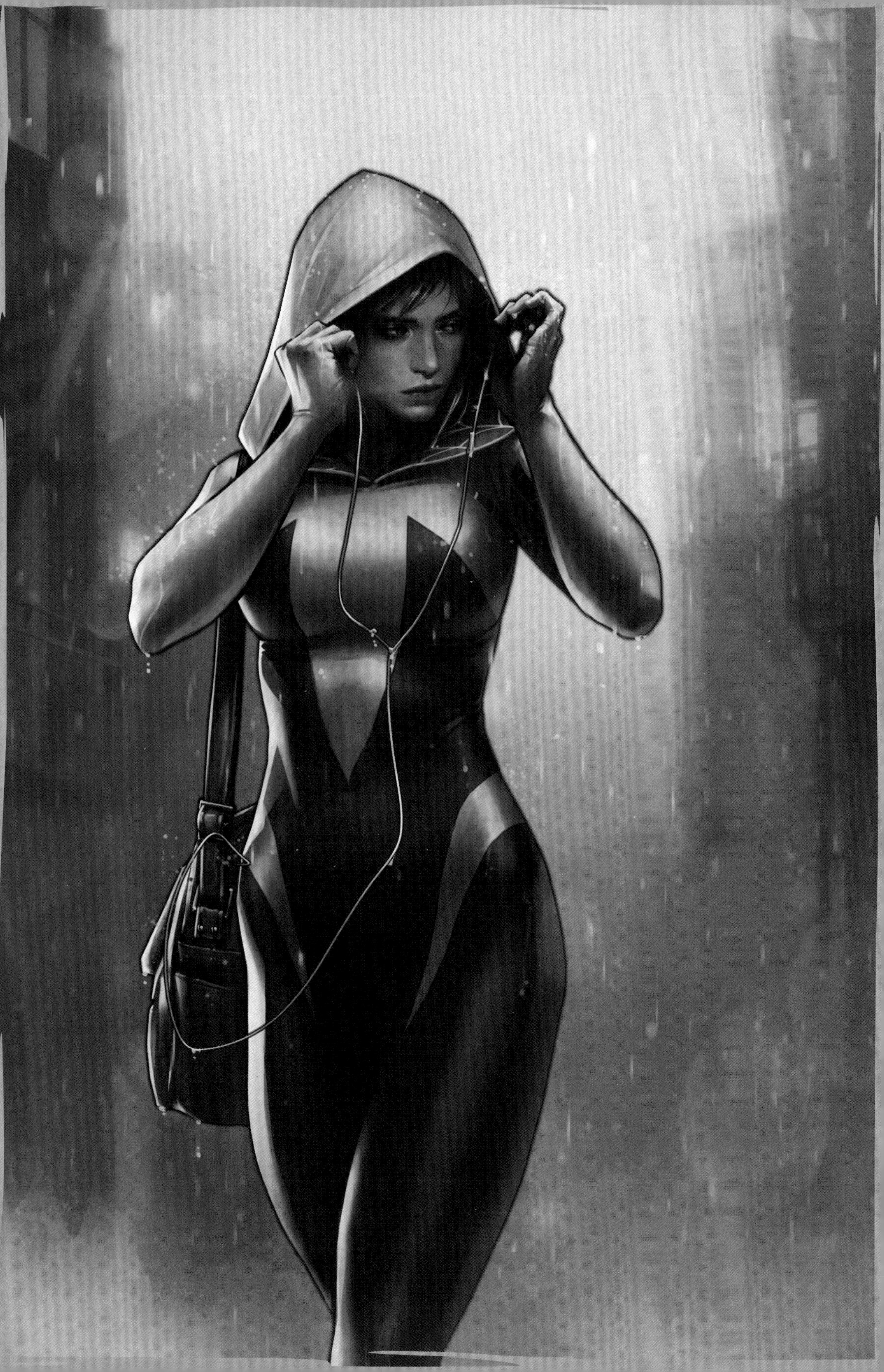

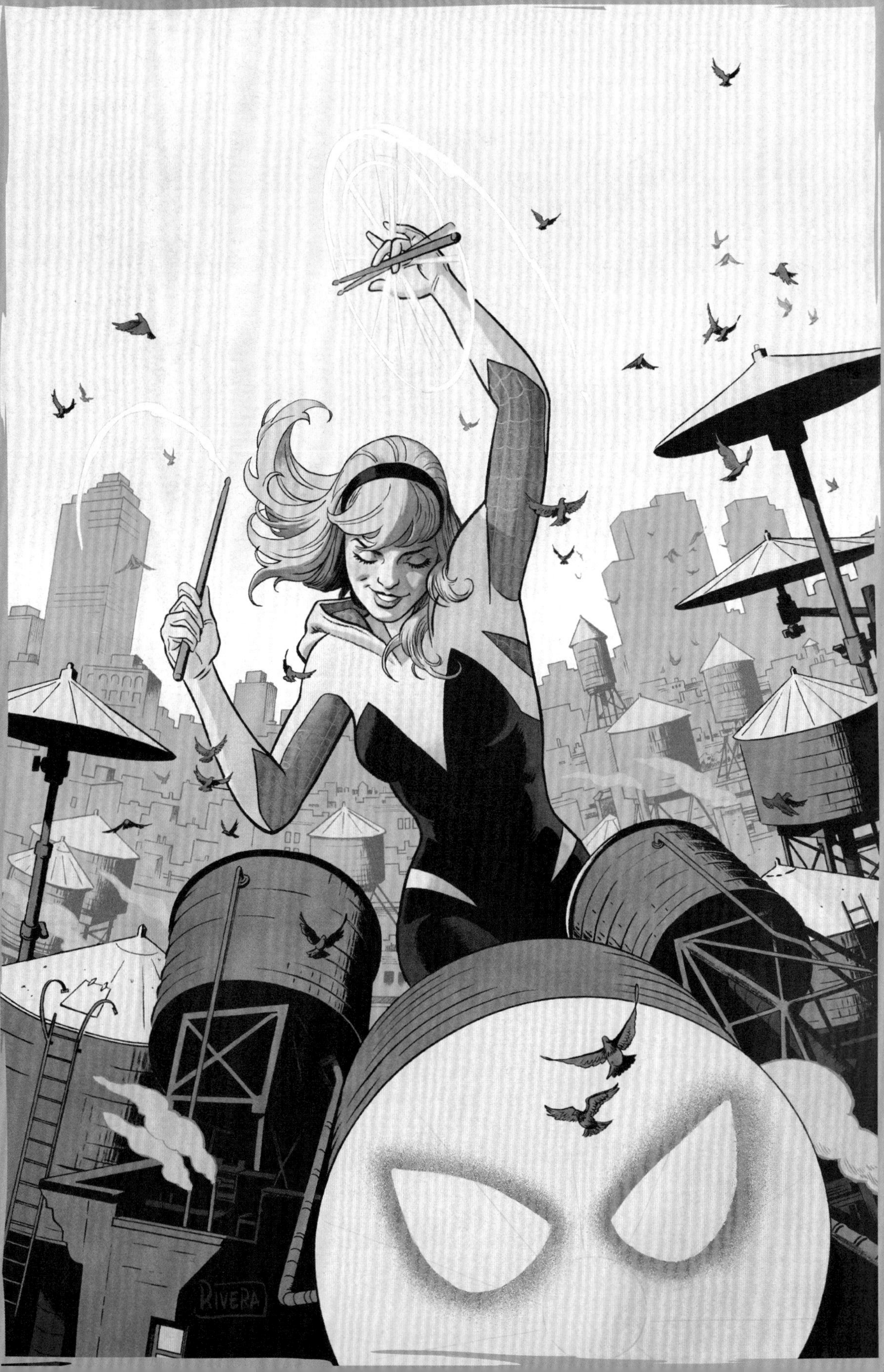
RIVERA

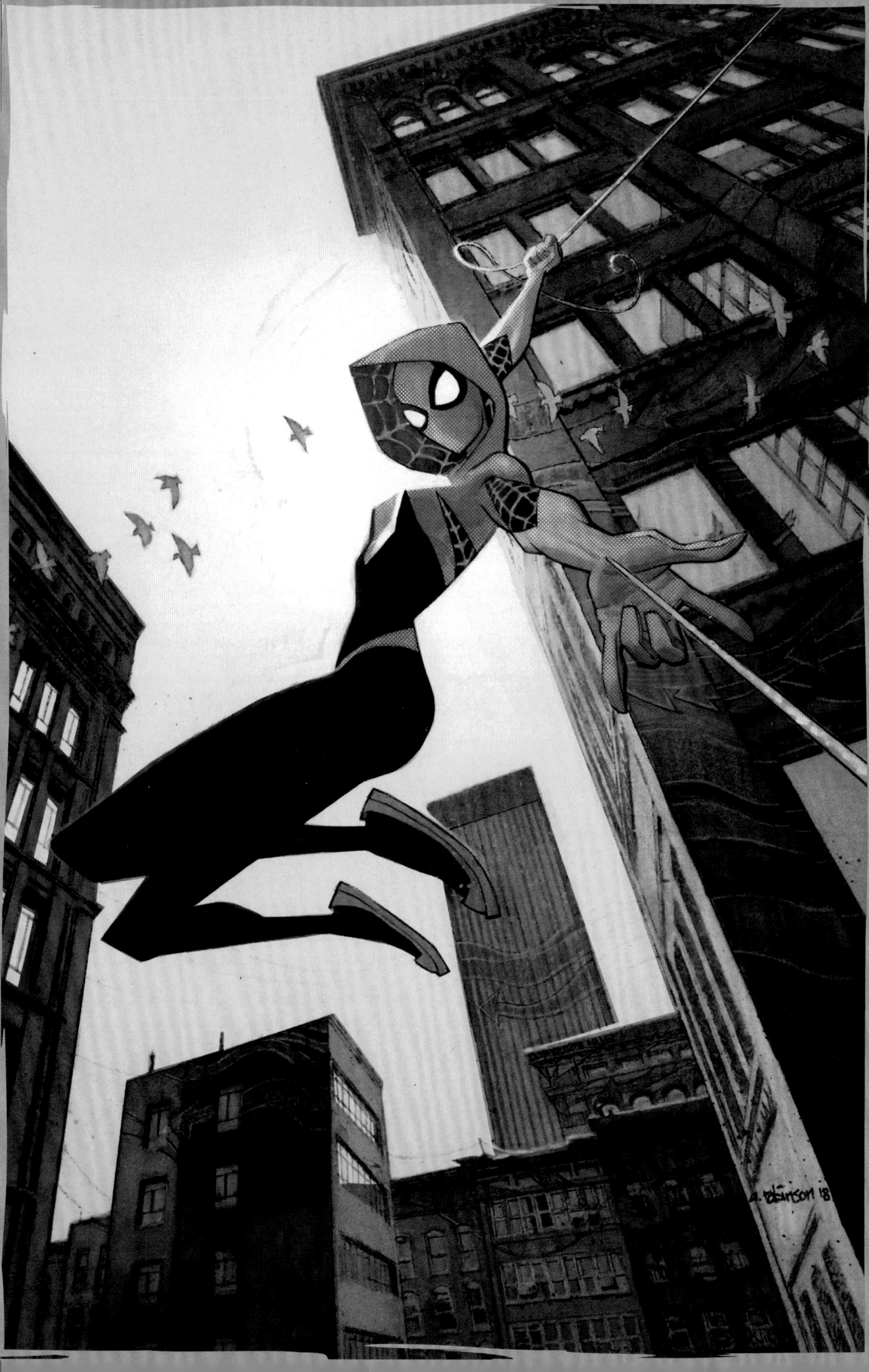

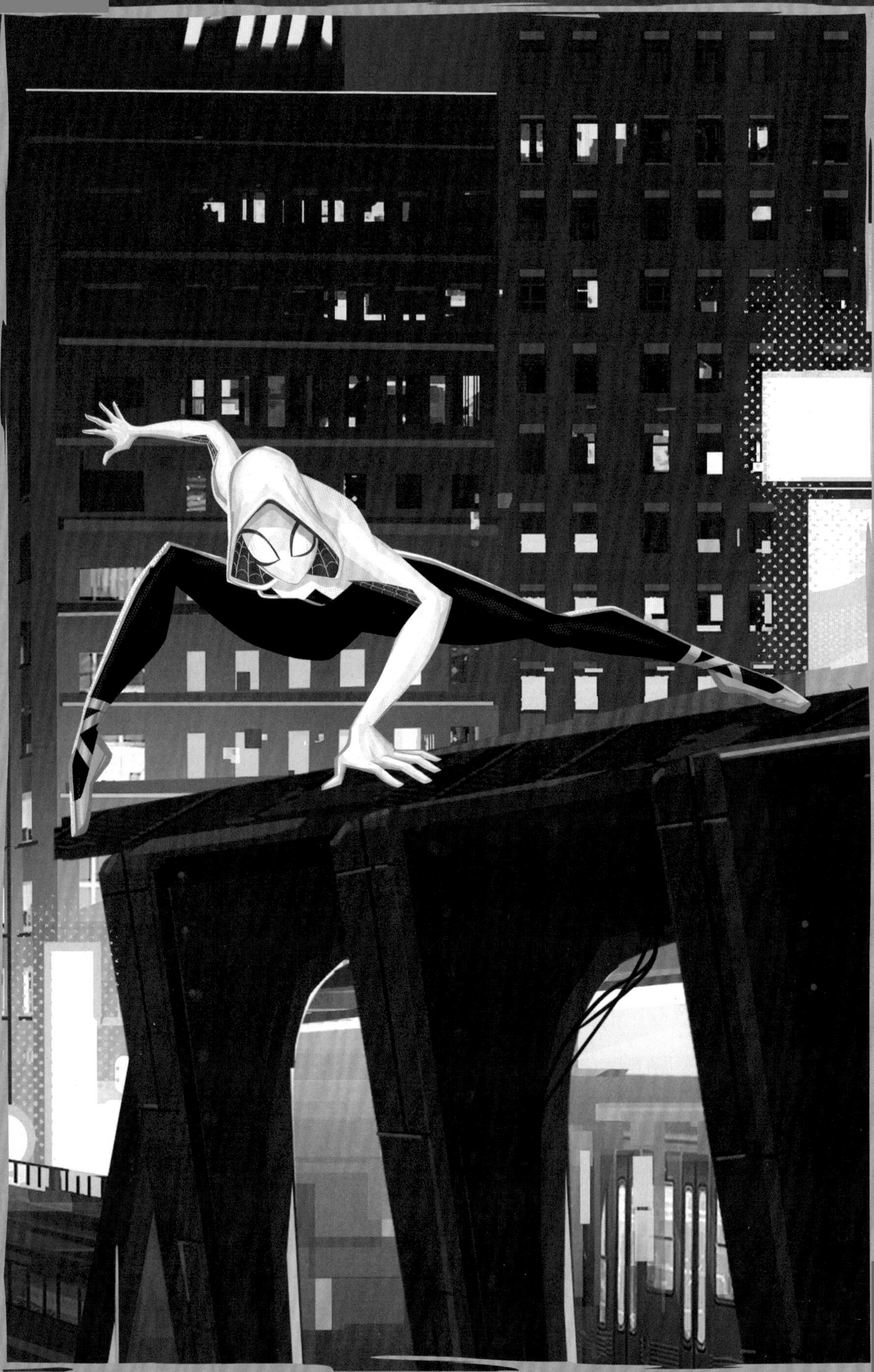

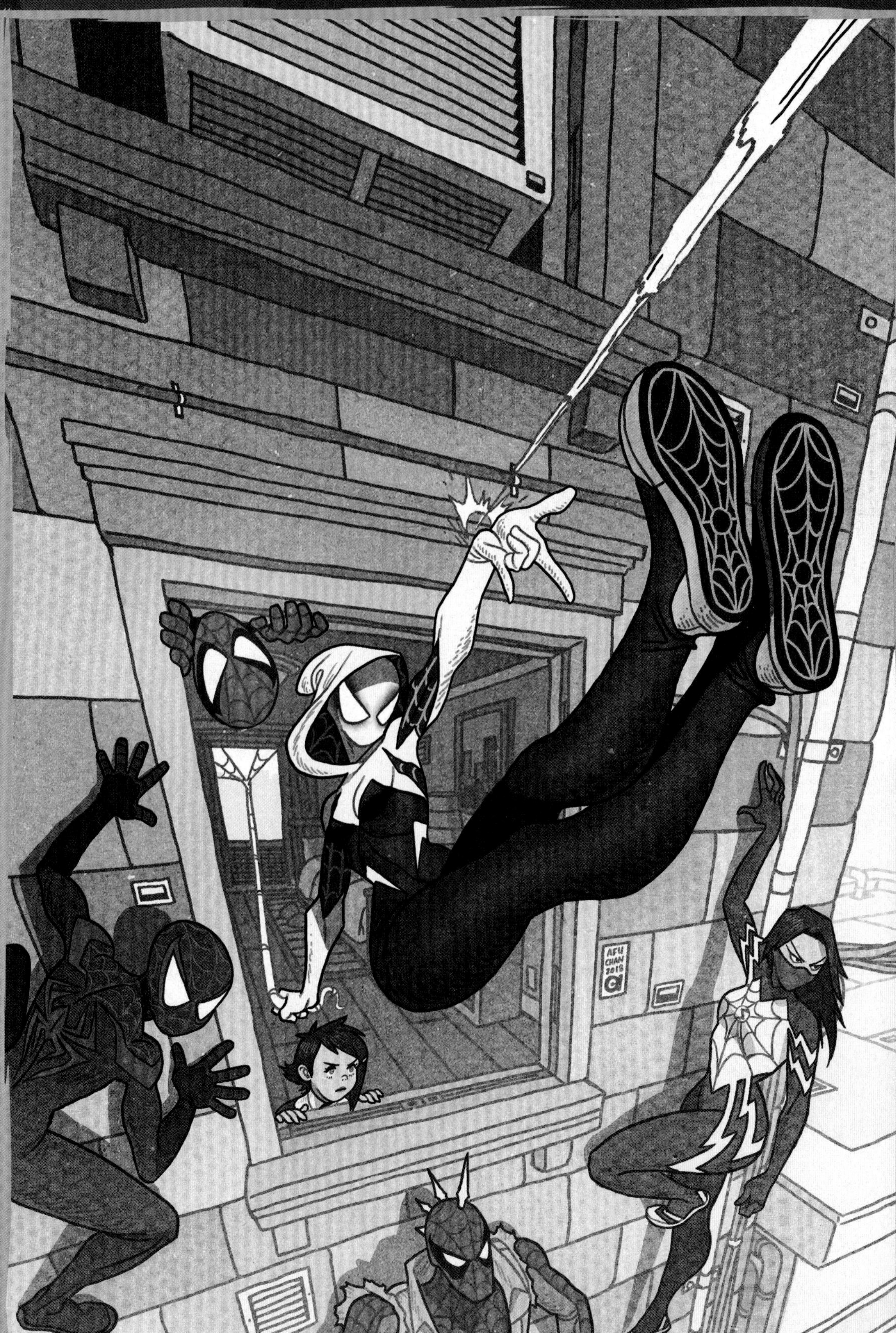
AFU
CHAN

#2 VARIANT BY AFU CHAN

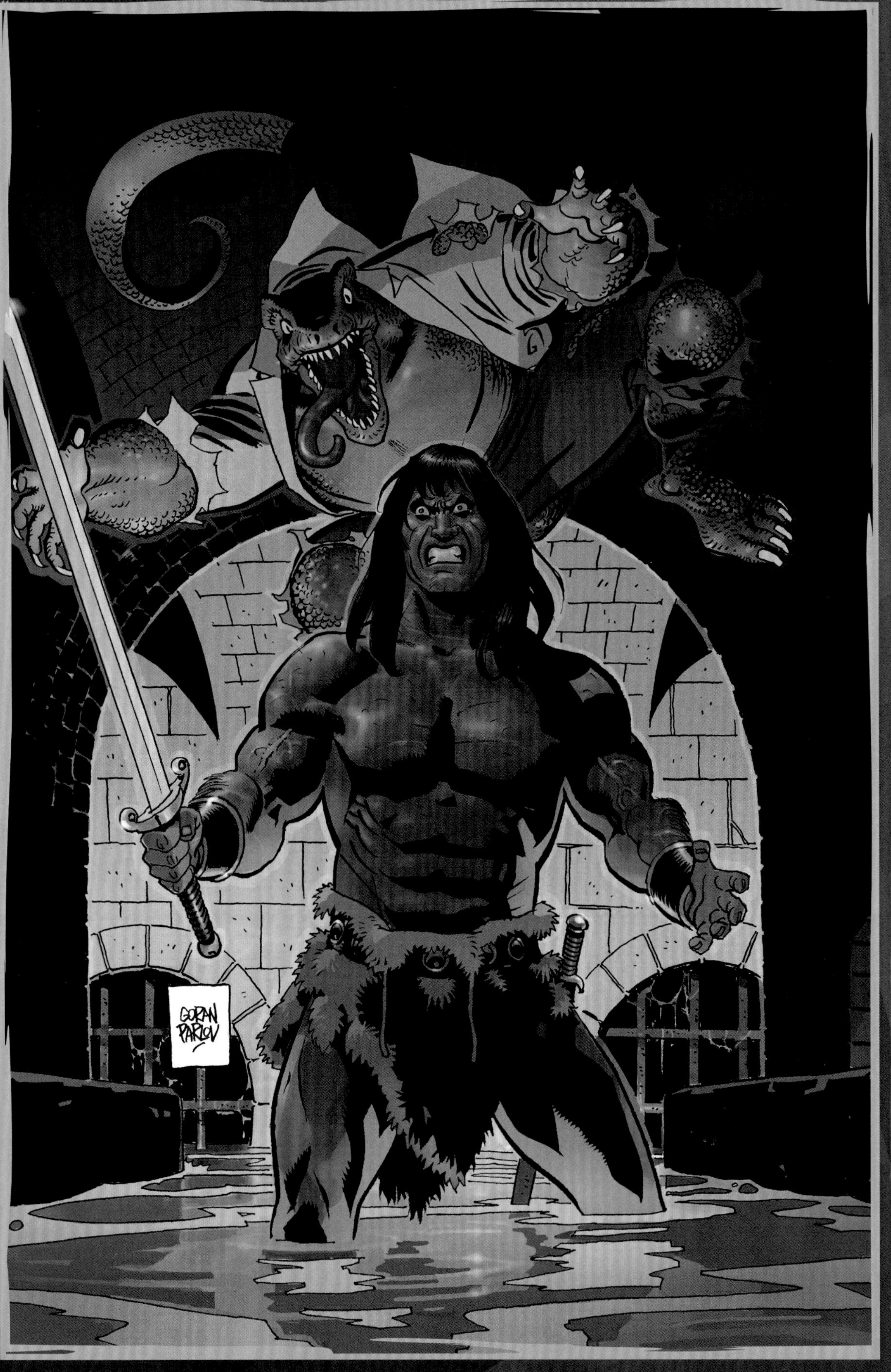
GORAN
PARLOV

#4 CONAN VS. VARIANT BY GORAN PARLOV

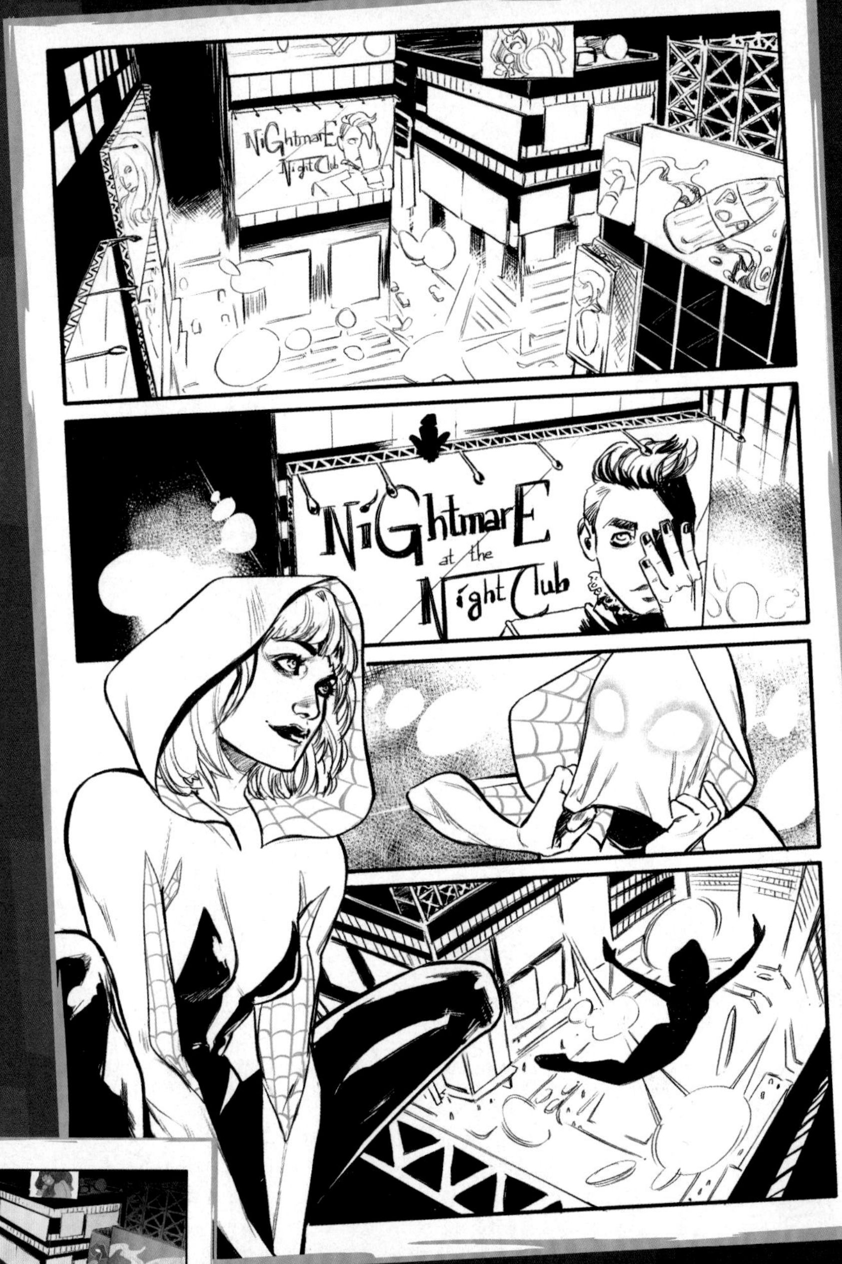
NiGhtmarE
Night Club
NiGhtmarE at the Night Club

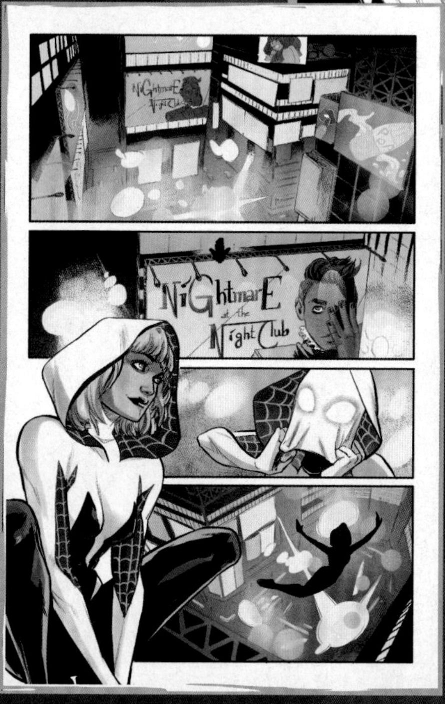
NiGhtmarE at the Night Club

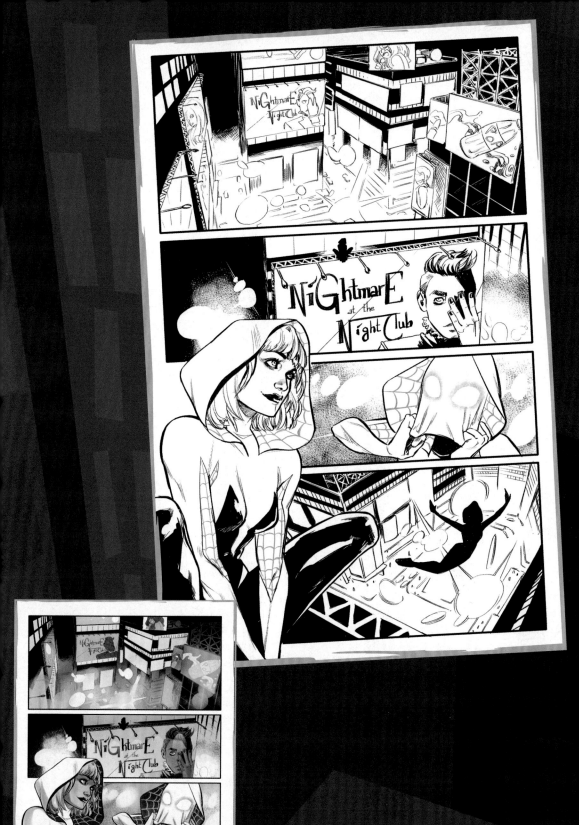

#1, PAGE 1 ART PROCESS BY
ROSI KÄMPE & IAN HERRING

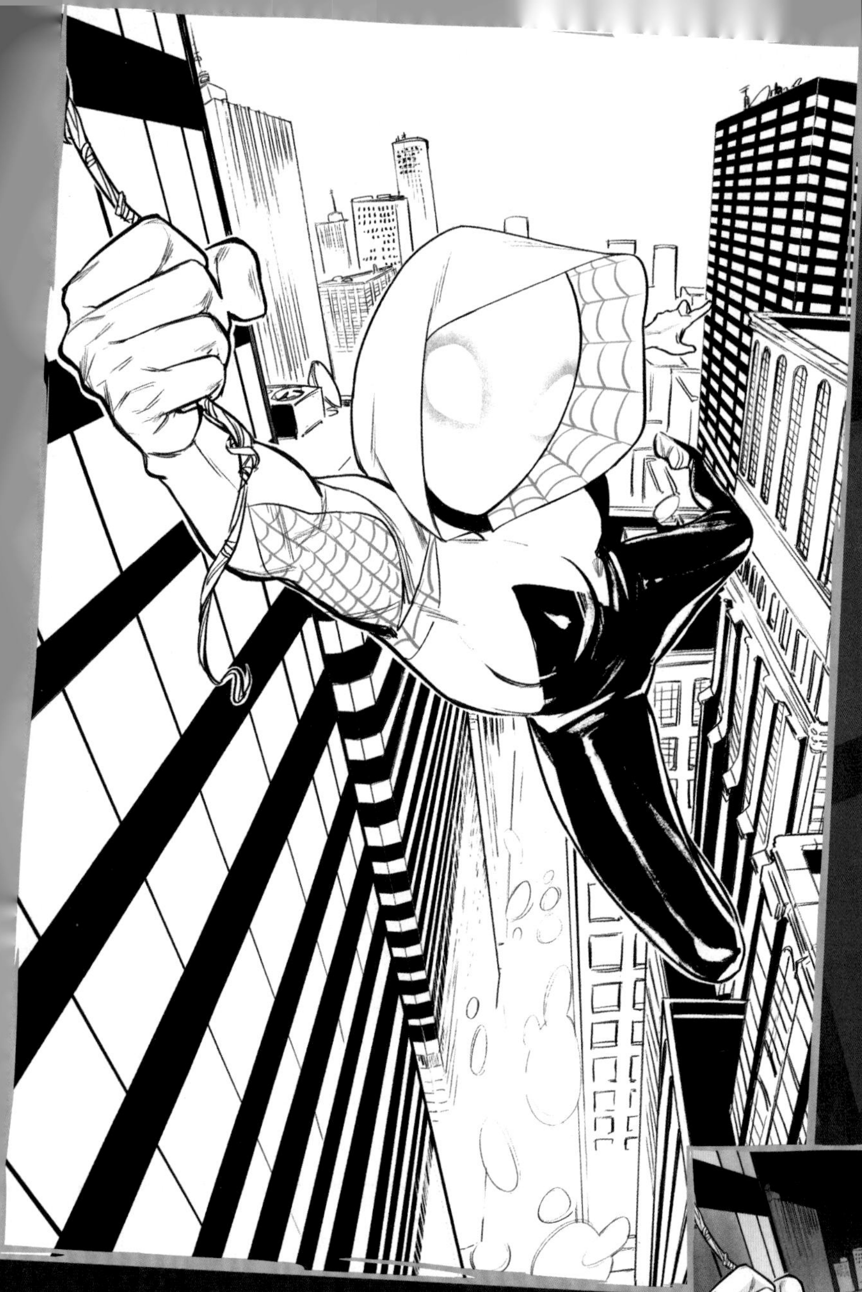

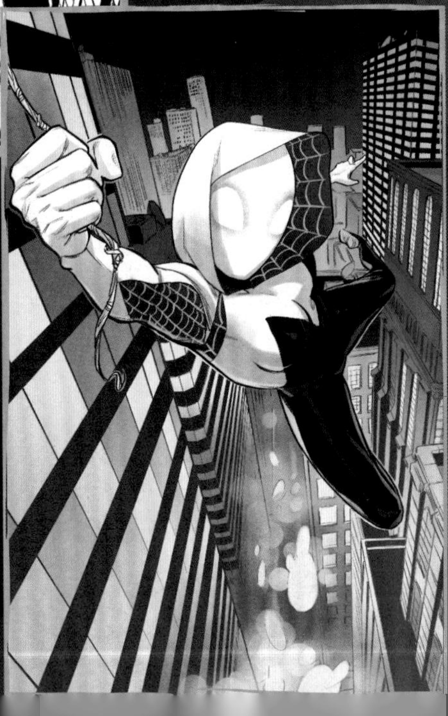

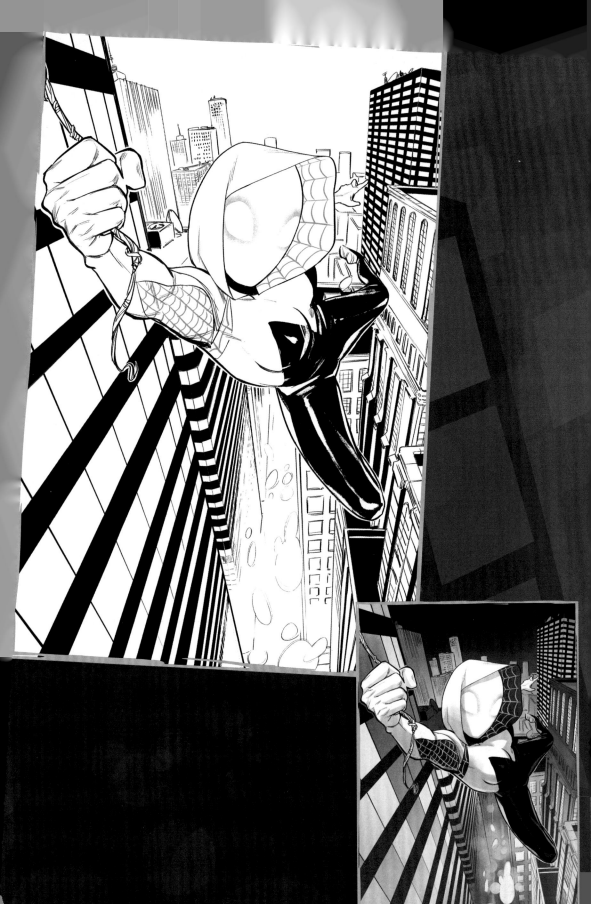

#1, PAGE 2 ART PROCESS BY
ROSI KÄMPE & IAN HERRING

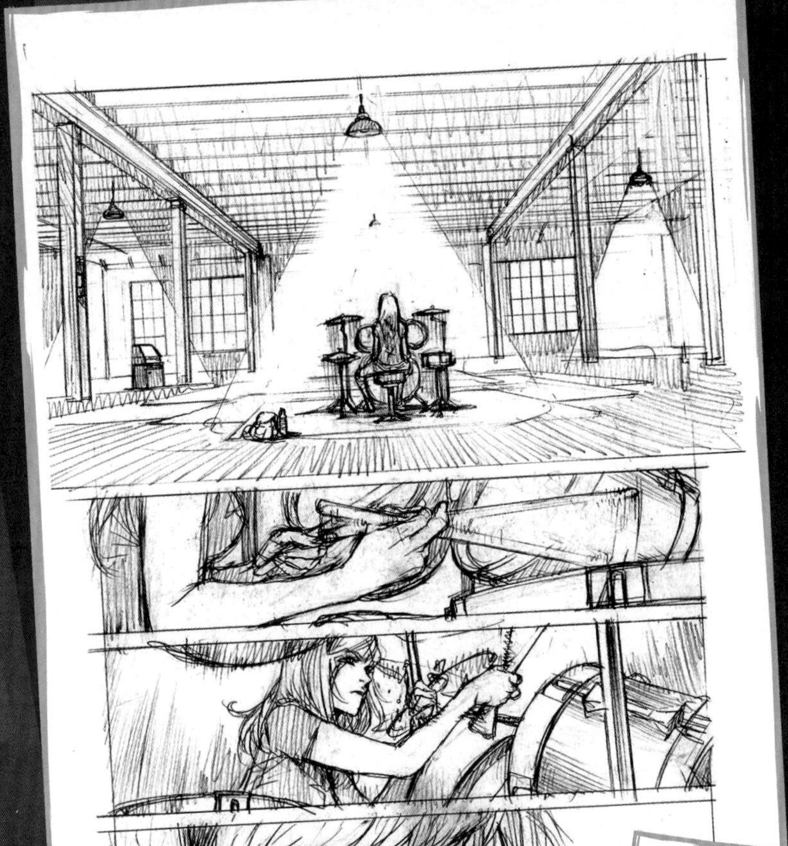

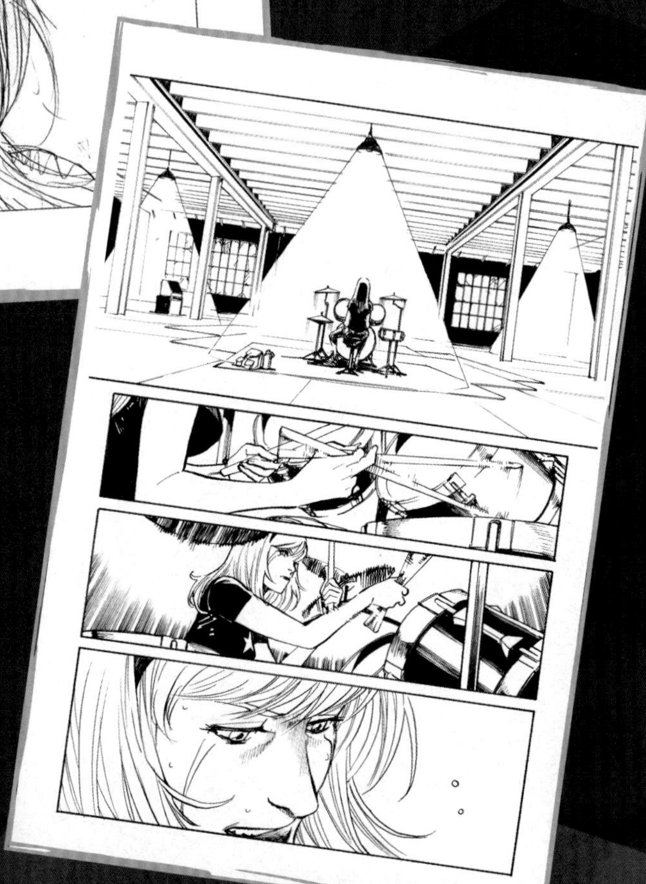

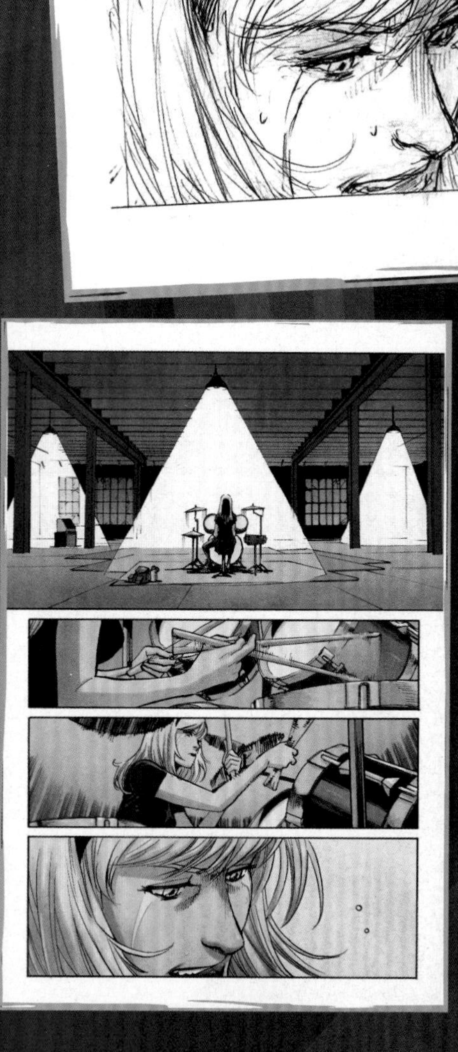

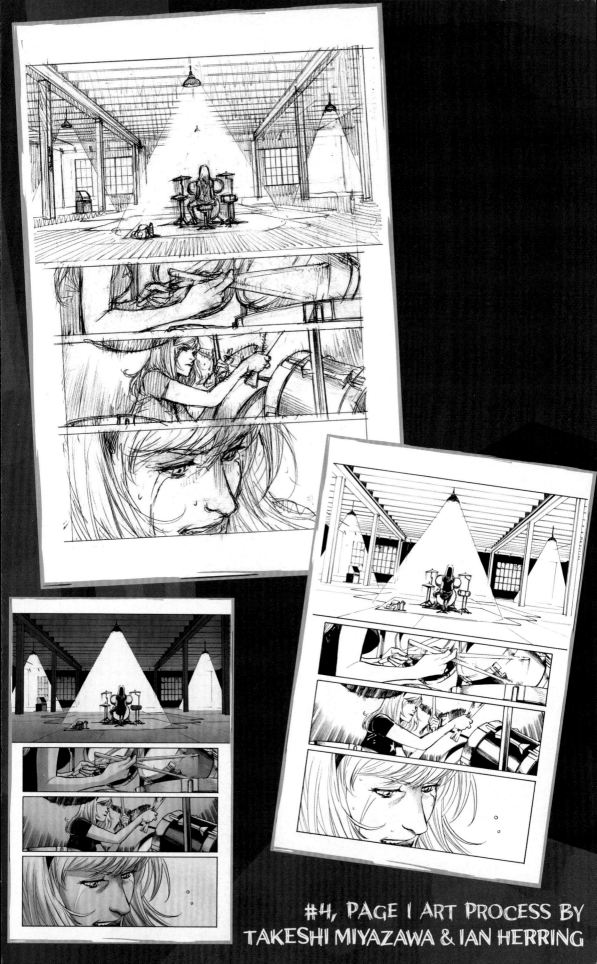

#4, PAGE 1 ART PROCESS BY
TAKESHI MIYAZAWA & IAN HERRING

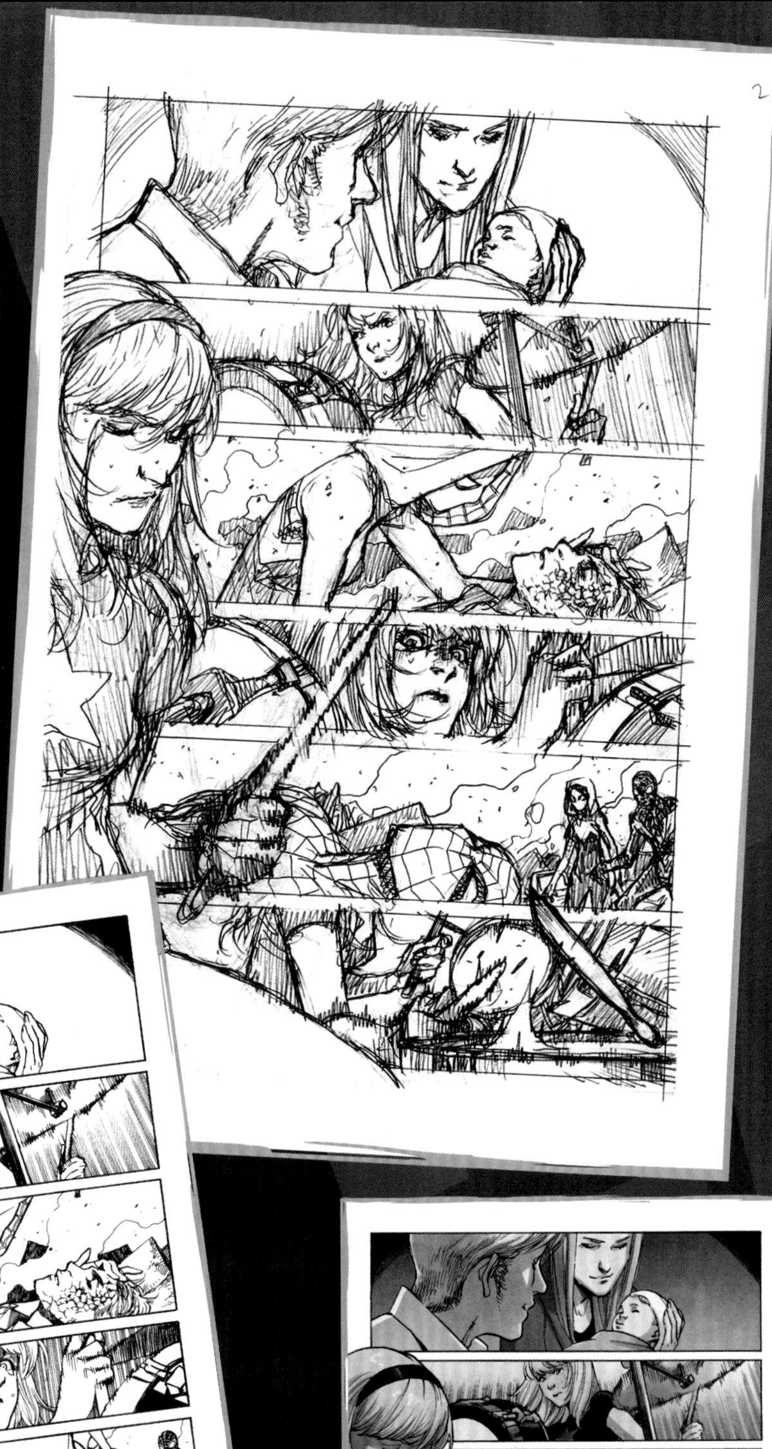

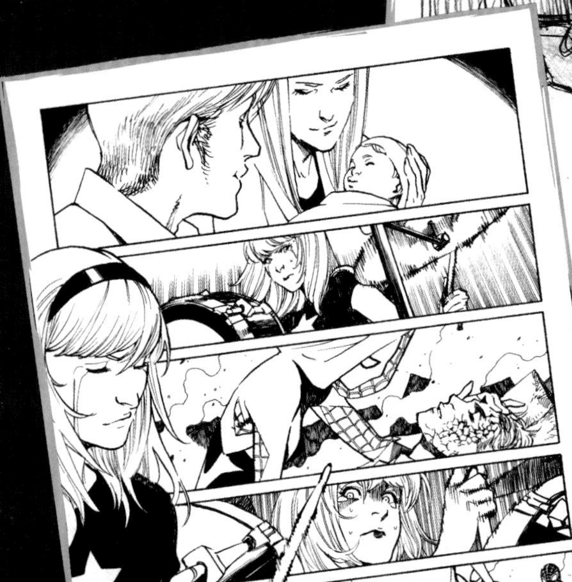

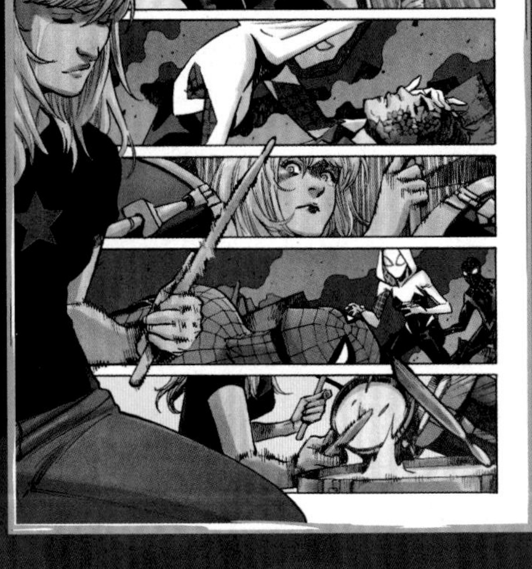

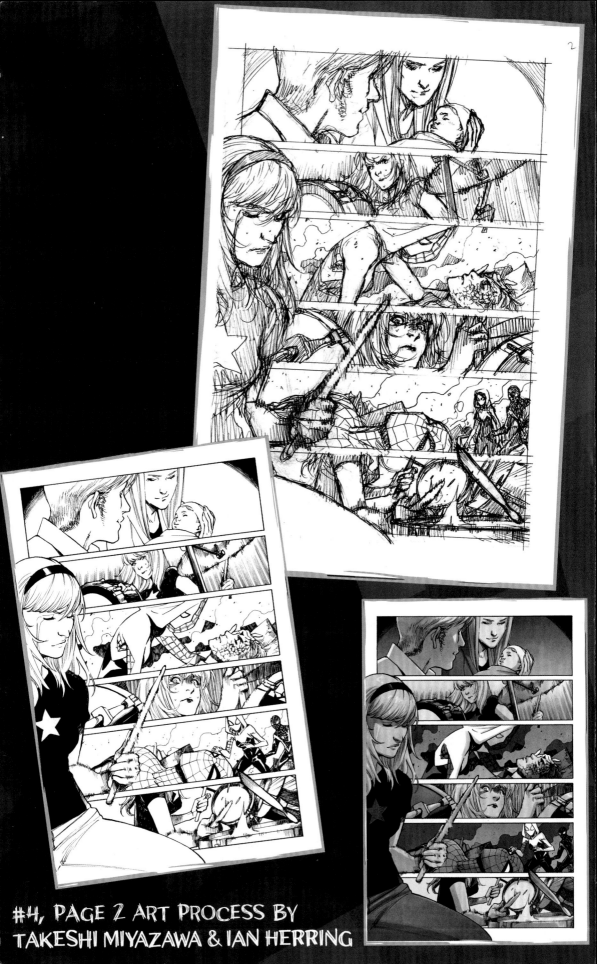

#4, PAGE 2 ART PROCESS BY
TAKESHI MIYAZAWA & IAN HERRING

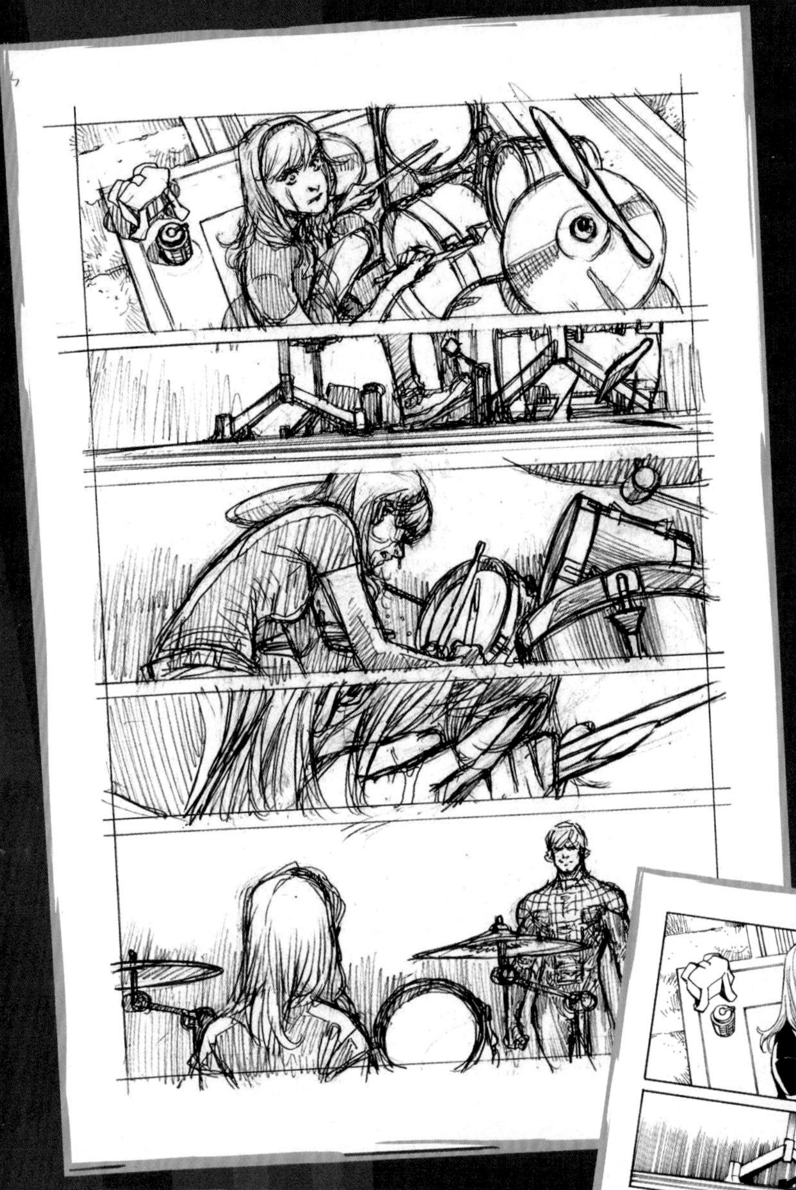

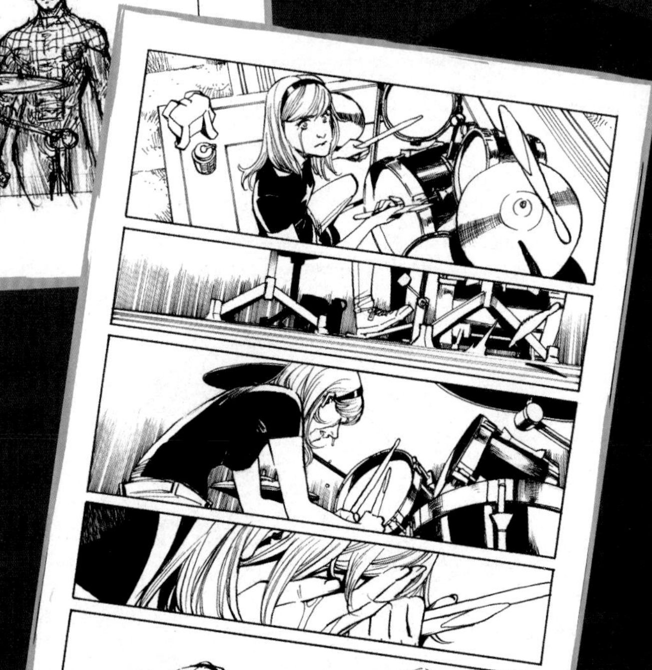

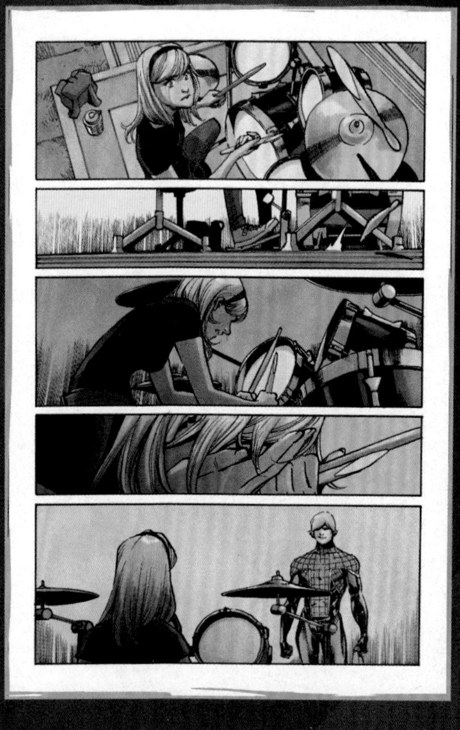

#4, PAGE 3 ART PROCESS BY
TAKESHI MIYAZAWA & IAN HERRING

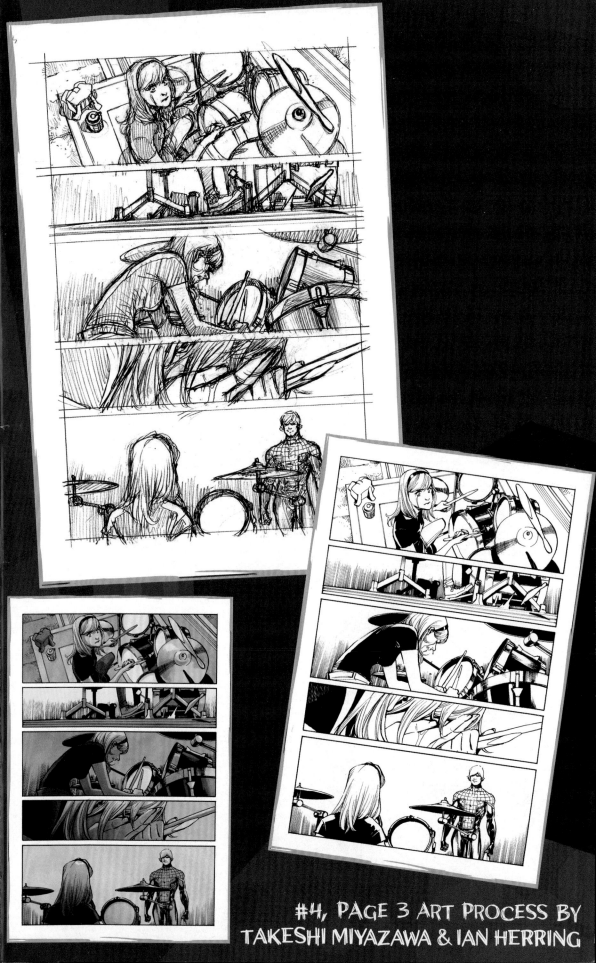

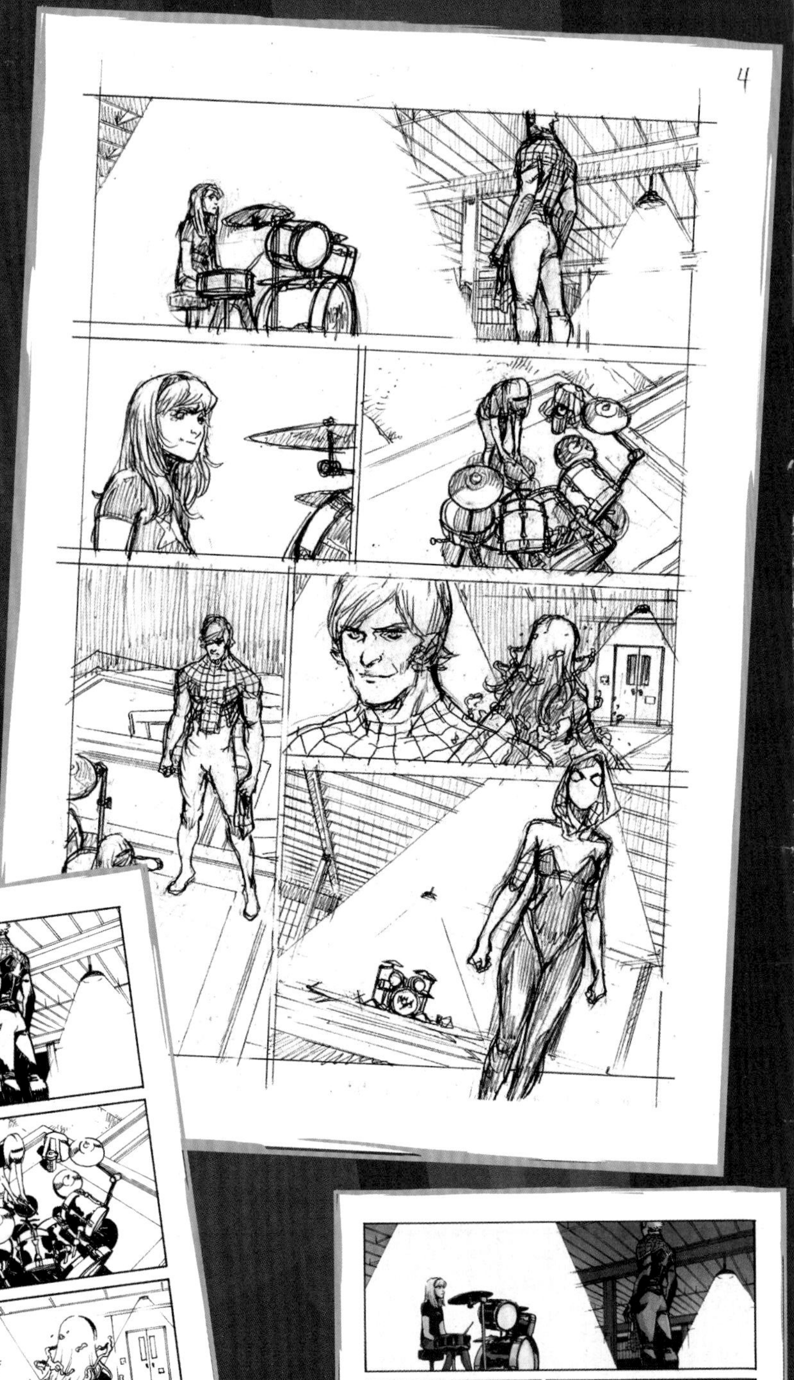

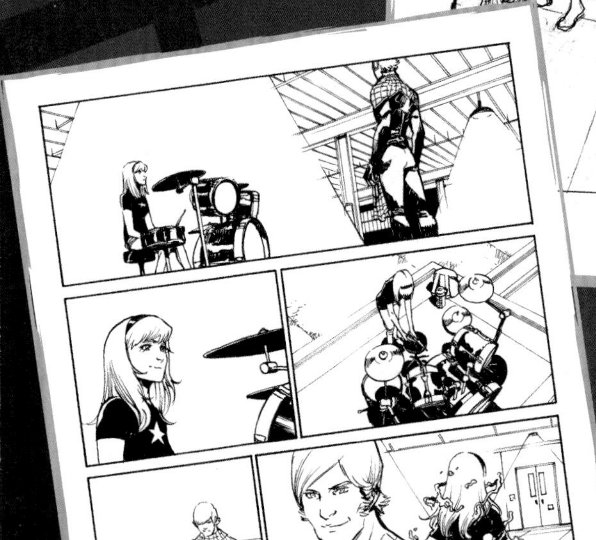

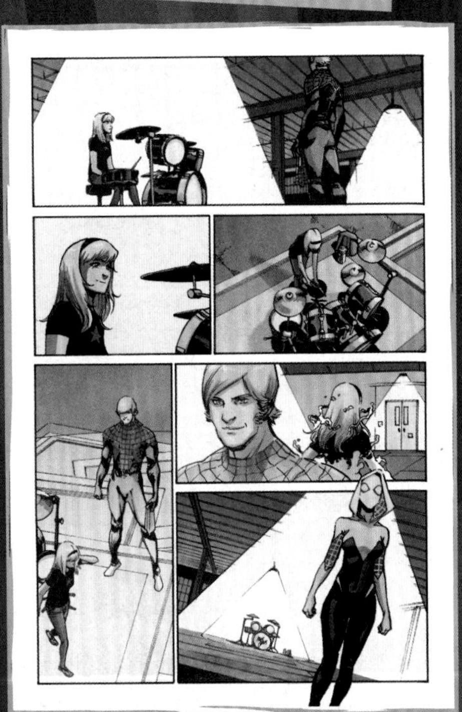

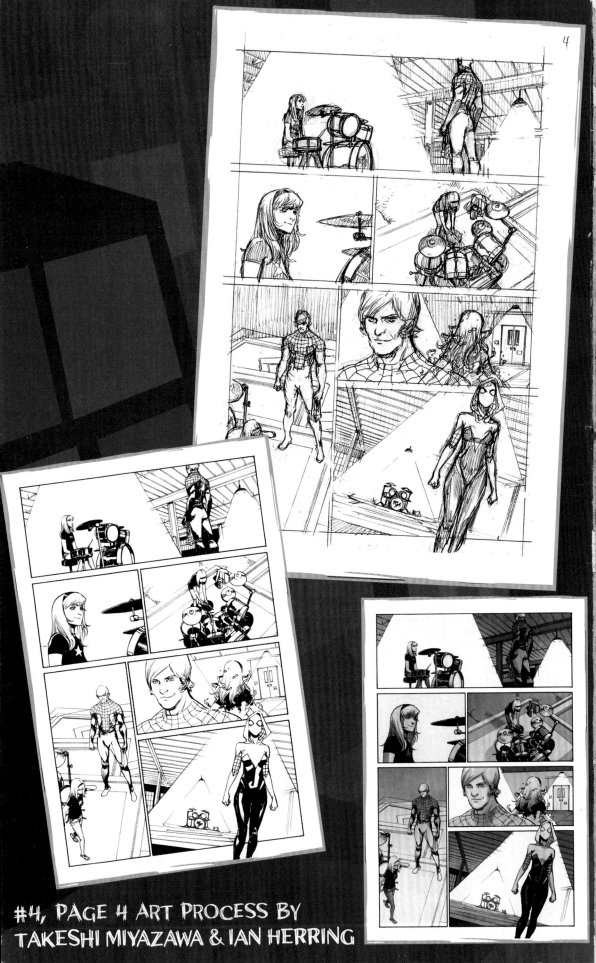

#4, PAGE 4 ART PROCESS BY
TAKESHI MIYAZAWA & IAN HERRING